The Rise of
the Paris Red Belt

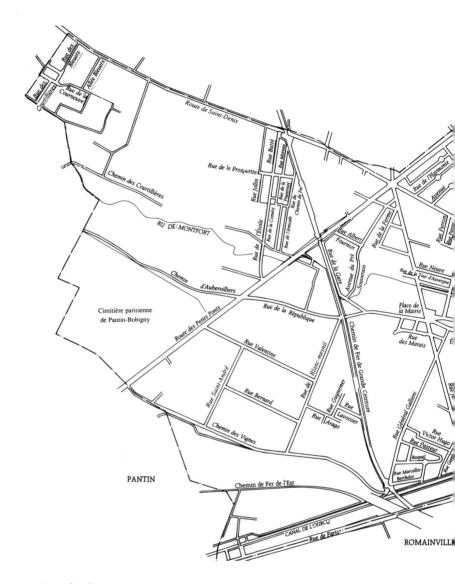

Plan of Bobigny.

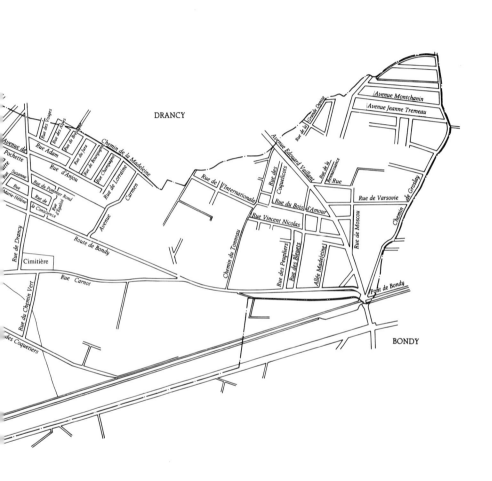

The Rise of
the Paris Red Belt

Tyler Stovall

UNIVERSITY OF CALIFORNIA PRESS
Berkeley • *Los Angeles* • *Oxford*

University of California Press
Berkeley and Los Angeles, California

University of California Press, Ltd.
Oxford, England

Library of Congress Cataloging-in-Publication Data
Stovall, Tyler Edward.
  The rise of the Paris red belt / Tyler Stovall.
    p.   cm.
  Bibliography.
  Includes index.
  ISBN 0-520-06320-1
  1. Communism—France—Bobigny—History.   2. Communism
  —France—Paris Suburban Area—History.   3. Bobigny
  (France)—Politics and government.   4. Paris Suburban Area
  (France)—Politics and government.   I. Title.
HX270.B63S76   1990
306.2'0944'361—dc20   89-35860
                                                               CIP

Printed in the United States of America
1 2 3 4 5 6 7 8 9

The paper used in this publication meets the minimum
requirements of American National Standard for Information
Sciences—Permanence of Paper for Printed Library Materials,
ANSI Z39.48-1984.   ∞™

To the memory of

HARVEY GOLDBERG

"The history of peoples' struggles is not contained within the library."

Contents

Maps

Tables

Acknowledgments

How does one begin to thank people for nearly ten years of one's life? From the moment that I began work on my historical study of the Paris suburbs as a graduate student at the University of Wisconsin, I have benefited from the aid of many friends and colleagues. Without their contributions this book would probably never have seen the light of day or would at least have been significantly inferior. Although I could not acknowledge the contributions in detail, I would like to recognize the people who most helped to make this book a success. They should feel entitled to share the credit for its merits; its defects remain the responsibility of the author alone.

Funding for this book has been generously provided by numerous sources. The Chancellor's Minority Postdoctoral Fellowship Program of the University of California at Berkeley not only gave me the rare opportunity to revise my dissertation for two years without teaching but also funded two brief research trips to Paris. Its work on behalf of minority scholars continues to be pathbreaking and important. The College of the Humanities of Ohio State University paid for the maps in this book, and the Division of the Humanities of the University of California at Santa Cruz funded the index.

Credit for valuable suggestions goes to many people in many different places. In Madison, Edward Gargan, Steve Stern, Ron Aminzade, Stanley Schultz, Robert Frost, Scott Haine, and David Wright read all or part of the original dissertation and indicated where it could be strengthened. While at Berkeley I received useful advice on revising the manuscript from Lynn Hunt, Mark Traugott, Ted Margadant, Jo B. Margadant, Herrick Chapman, Karen Offen, Dena Goodman, Margie

Beale, Suzanne Desan, Earl Lewis, Joshua Cole, Sarah Farmer, Paul Rabinow, and John Merriman.

I owe thanks to friends and colleagues on the other side of the Atlantic. Jacques Girault and Annie Fourcaut were both welcoming and willing to share with me their work on the history of Bobigny and the suburbs of Paris. I would like to acknowledge the important assistance I received from the staffs of the Bobigny Municipal Archives, above all Colette Portillon; the Archives de la Seine; the Archives of the Department of the Seine–Saint-Denis; the Archives of the Prefecture of Police; the Archives Nationales; and the Bibliothèque Nationale. My good friends Jean and Melvin McNair, Jim Cohen, Michael Liebman, Paula May, Elisabeth Altschull, and François Gaudu did all they could to make my stays in Paris both profitable and enjoyable.

Thanks for technical assistance in preparing this book are due to David Smith, Carol Seiden, and the staff of the Alcohol Research Group in Berkeley, and to Dan Wenger of the University of California, Santa Cruz. Yvonne Holsinger of Ohio State prepared the maps. Thanks also to the *Journal of Social History* and the *Journal of Contemporary History* for allowing me to include material from previously published articles.

Three people in particular deserve special mention and acknowledgment for their contributions to this book. My wife, Denise Herd, provided not only much needed emotional support but also new ways of looking at old intellectual problems. In spite of the pressing demands of her career, she has always been ready to lend a sympathetic yet critical ear. Susanna Barrows served as my mentor during my postdoctoral fellowship at Berkeley, but her real contribution exceeded that official role. Susanna read two drafts of this manuscript and gave me endless good advice, the insights and inspiration of a brilliant intellect, great food, and constant encouragement.

Finally and most important, I owe a profound intellectual debt to my mentor, friend, and graduate advisor, the late Professor Harvey Goldberg at the University of Wisconsin at Madison. Harvey suggested that I write about Bobigny and saw the dissertation through completion, but I owe him much more than that. Harvey Goldberg was a paragon who combined first-rate scholarship, an unexcelled ability to make history come alive in the classroom, and a passionate, adamant commitment to the struggle for social justice that inspired me. He helped make Madison a special place and set me an example I shall never forget. I miss Harvey, I cherish his memory, and it is to him that I dedicate this book.

Introduction

In *The Painting of Modern Life,* T. J. Clark describes the failure of artists like Manet to come to terms with the spread of Paris beyond its traditional boundaries into the surrounding countryside in the late nineteenth century. Clark notes that such artists often viewed the environs of Paris not as a new urban civilization in the making, but rather as a zone of corruption and confusion. Ultimately they chose not to view them at all.[1]

The twentieth-century suburbs of Paris have often remained beyond the boundaries of popular imagination. In few of the world's great cities is the contrast between urb and suburb so dramatic as in Paris; as soon as one crosses the *périphérique,* the outer belt that is the real boundary of the city, one abruptly leaves the elegant row houses of the capital behind to enter a world of architectural disarray. Even though the Paris suburbs have grown enormously since 1900 and are now home to one out of every nine people in France, they are nonetheless terra incognita to most. Aside from their residents, only government planners and urban sociologists pay them much attention. This ignorance is especially characteristic of foreign tourists. Few Americans, in search of the bright lights of Paris and the rich charms of small provincial towns, bother to explore this most ungainly symbol of modern France.

Why then should historians rush in where so many others have declined to tread? The Paris suburbs first interested me several years ago while I was considering the prospects for a dissertation in French labor history. Although impressed by historians' advances in the field of

1

nineteenth-century social history, I was more interested in the experience of French workers after 1900, men and women who did not go through the traumas of industrialization but were born into a mature industrial society. Specifically, I wanted to study the political ramifications of contemporary working-class life in France, to discover how the patterns and conditions of this life shaped the political choices and loyalties formed by French workers.

In scanning the sociological and political landscape of twentieth-century France, I realized that the suburbs of Paris were an excellent locale for a study interested in such issues. In the early twentieth century, the suburban ring around the capital represented the largest zone of working-class settlement in all France. Although precise statistics are not available, roughly one million workers and their families lived in the suburbs of the Department of the Seine between the wars.[2] Politically the Paris suburbs are also important for the study of French workers during the twentieth century; ever since 1920 they have been the national stronghold of the French Communist party (Parti communiste français, or PCF), one of the most important forces in modern French working-class politics. To many bourgeois French men and women ignorant of suburban life, the so-called Red Belt symbolized the dangers posed by an organized and vengeful proletariat, the barbarians waiting outside the gates of the city.[3]

The Red Belt was more than a figment of frightened middle-class imaginations; for many politicized workers the Paris suburbs represented the citadel of the working class. But above all, for most Paris-area workers in the early twentieth century the suburbs were increasingly the place where they lived and worked. The patterns of industrial development in the metropolitan area during the nineteenth century had exiled most heavy industry, especially the large modern factories, beyond the boundaries of the capital and made much of the suburbs into an industrial fortress, a socialist-realist paradise come true. But behind the looming steel plants stood the grimy apartment blocks and ramshackle houses where more and more of the area's workers lived.

Some workers were forced to move to the suburbs by the absence of affordable housing in Paris: people attracted to the area by the industrial boom during the First World War, or former residents of the eastern arrondissements (districts) of the city. Others chose to come —parents with a consumptive child in search of fresh air, or *poilus,* soldiers returning after 1918, who felt that they had earned the right to their own little house in "the country." But come they did; in the decade after the armistice, the suburbs of Paris gained over one million new residents, the majority of them working class.[4]

Florence Aumont moved to the Paris suburbs with her family during World War I, when she was a little girl. Her family came from the Nord and like many other natives of that war-torn area chose to leave rather than live under German occupation. On their arrival in the Paris area they decided to live in the suburb of Bobigny, northeast of the capital. At the time Bobigny seemed a good choice; it was close to Paris, relatively uncrowded and free of noxious factories, and it offered to the young couple the possibility of buying a small piece of land and building their own house. The family of Florence Aumont bought land in an allotment (*lotissement*) and thus became suburbanites.[5]

Like the Aumont family, I chose Bobigny—though as a subject of study, not as a place to live. In researching the history of the Paris suburbs, I decided to focus on a single community, for reasons that are now common among social historians: to permit a detailed analysis of a specific population and to approximate the global perspective of "total history." The result is not a community study in the tradition of social scientists like Lawrence Wylie and Herbert Gans; it does not for the most part rely on personal experience or oral testimony. It is rather an attempt to explore the social and political development of the Paris suburbs in the early twentieth century through the history of one *commune*.

Bobigny is well qualified to serve as a local study in the history of the Paris Red Belt in this period. Since the founding of the French Communist party in 1920 Bobigny has always voted the PCF ticket; its city government has been controlled by the Party ever since, except during the German occupation. No other suburb of Paris and few towns in France match this record. Moreover, the impact of communism in Bobigny has not been limited to election days but has shaped the life of the community in many important ways. When Florence Aumont grew up, for example, she became a Communist and married a PCF member of the Bobigny city council. The literature on French communism is voluminous, yet it has so far paid little attention to the history of communism as a force in French society. By studying the PCF in one small Paris suburb, I hope to cast light on the social history of communism in the Red Belt and in France as a whole.[6]

The primary question guiding this study has therefore been, Why did Bobigny, and to a lesser extent the Paris suburbs in general, vote so heavily and consistently for the French Communist party? To answer this question I chose to focus on the period before World War II, during which the bases of the PCF's local political hegemony were laid. Whereas in 1900 Bobigny was a semirural community supporting Republican politicians, by 1939 it was well known as a working-class Communist suburb, where even the streets were named after heroes and heroines of the French Left.

In approaching this subject, I initially chose the path laid out by social historians of French workers in the nineteenth century and focused on the workplace as the key factor in local politicization.[7] I quickly discovered the inadequacies of this approach, however; unlike Saint-Denis or other better known suburbs, Bobigny had few factories or other workplaces. On the contrary, in this period it was primarily a bedroom community for workers who commuted to their jobs elsewhere in the Paris area. Furthermore, Bobigny was not at all atypical, but rather characteristic of many Paris suburbs, especially those that grew the fastest in the early twentieth century.

Bobigny's population growth was explosive in the decades after 1900. In thirty years the number of its inhabitants grew from under two thousand to over seventeen thousand. Most of the newcomers settled in allotments, which mushroomed in the community after 1905 as residents bought small lots and built their own houses on them. Life in Bobigny's allotments was no bed of roses, however. Sidewalks, sewers, utilities, and other urban facilities were usually rare or nonexistent and health conditions correspondingly poor. By 1930 a large majority of working-class Balbynians, or residents of Bobigny, lived in such allotments.

In exploring the history of Bobigny during the early twentieth century, I saw that the issues of greatest importance to its workers centered not on the workplace but rather on the residential community; unpaved streets loomed larger than strikes in the local imagination. This focus had a direct and crucial impact on political life; a major thesis of this study is that the electoral strength of communism in Bobigny derived from the success of the PCF in organizing the *mal-lotis* (residents of defective allotments) and in using its control of Bobigny's city government to deal with their problems. The history of communism in Bobigny before 1939 thus presented two closely related paradoxes. At a time when the PCF laid heavy emphasis on the workplace as the flashpoint of class conflict and politicization, in Bobigny the Party derived its support from residential issues. In addition, Bobigny's Communist voters were largely property owners, albeit small ones. The experience of Bobigny, and many other Paris suburbs, during the early twentieth century suggests that a reevaluation of working-class politicization in contemporary France, giving greater importance to residential and other nonworkplace concerns, may be in order.

The history of Bobigny and the Paris suburbs during this period offers insights not only for historians of modern France but for students of twentieth-century history as a whole. More than any other part of France, the suburbs of Paris and other French cities are creations of the twentieth century. They were virtually the only parts of the country to register significant population gains before the 1940s, for example. The suburbs of Paris are the product and symbol of an important characteristic of twentieth-century life: the sharp and increasing separation between workplace and residence. Whereas for nineteenth-century artisans work and home were usually united or closely connected, after 1900 industrial workers were much more likely to commute to their jobs. In Bobigny and other Paris suburbs this separation created a political culture that neglected workplace issues rather than seeing workplace and residential community as parts of a whole. The history of these communities thus demonstrates the development of an important aspect of contemporary working-class politics.

Bobigny in the early twentieth century is therefore significant not so much because it typified French suburbs but rather because it indicated the path that France and much of the industrialized world would take after 1900. I have divided my history of Bobigny into two parts. Part One focuses on the social and urban history of the community. The first chapter describes the development of the Paris area in the late nineteenth and the early twentieth century to explain the rise of the suburban belt around the capital. The second chapter looks at Bobigny's rapid growth and the problems that this growth produced; the third chapter offers a demographic and sociological analysis of the population of Bobigny.

Part Two focuses on the politics of life in Bobigny and the growth of the PCF there. The fourth chapter discusses the electoral history of Bobigny with particular reference to the establishment of Communist political hegemony there. The fifth chapter looks at the achievements of the PCF municipality in dealing with the problems caused by Bobigny's rapid urbanization. Finally, the sixth chapter analyzes the political culture of communism in Bobigny. This study thus considers several aspects of life in Bobigny during the early twentieth century. It is not a complete history of the modern suburbs of Paris but rather a contribution that I hope will inspire others. Although the Paris suburbs may lack style, no account of the history of twentieth-century France can afford to ignore them.

The Growth of Working-Class Suburbia

CHAPTER 1

The Suburbanization
of the Paris Region

Bobigny at the Turn of the Century

A casual visitor to Bobigny would have noticed little that distinguished the community from any of the other villages that dotted the country-side of the Ile-de-France at the turn of the century. Our hypothetical visitor—probably a Parisian who had come to Bobigny on a Sunday to escape briefly the oppressive urbanity of the capital[1]—would have observed a small town center of a few blocks around the place Carnot, consisting of small, solid two-story houses separated by rutted, poorly paved streets. Dominating the place Carnot was the church of the parish of Bobigny, an unadorned structure barely thirty years old. Extending away from the church in all directions were little more than "vast blackish-colored fields slowly worked by a silent 'gardener,' pushing his plow yoked to a Percheron."[2] Nothing suggested the integration of the community into what is today referred to as the *agglomération parisienne*. Although Bobigny is located just ten kilometers from the towers of Notre Dame, in 1900 Paris seemed far away.

Yet by the turn of the century such a view was more than a little illusory; Paris was getting closer all the time. Adjacent communities that lay nearer to Paris, such as Aubervilliers and Pantin, had already lost much of their rural character and been transformed into working-class industrial suburbs. Bobigny could no longer realistically claim to be a small provincial village. For centuries its agriculture had been integrated into the capital's food market; the "silent gardener" described by père Lhande might well have spent that morning hawking vegetables or melons at the central marketplace of Paris, Les Halles. Abbé Jules Ferret, who as parish priest of Bobigny at the turn of the century was well placed to record the changes in his community, observed that the market gardeners of Bobigny had little desire for increased contacts with Paris or Parisians. Unfortunately for Balbynians who held this attitude, the Parisians were not so standoffish: more and more of them were coming to the small community to spend time in "the country."[3] By 1900 Bobigny was firmly established as a recreational exurb. And soon weekending Parisians would be followed by many others who saw in Bobigny not merely a pleasant pastoral refuge but a place to live as well.

Thus Bobigny in 1900, on the eve of a rapid process of urbanization, was a society whose integration into the fast-expanding metropolitan area of Paris was already well established. In taking a more detailed look at turn-of-the-century Bobigny, we do well to keep in mind that the community was in transition.

Even though many Parisians visited Bobigny on weekends, it was by no means a spot of great natural beauty. Its dominant physical characteristic was homogeneity. Lying in the middle of the Aubervilliers plain, Bobigny was almost perfectly flat and regular; not a single hill rose within the town's boundaries. In fact, it had no distinguishing physical hallmarks other than the small stream in the western part of the community known as the rû de Montfort. No physical boundaries separated Bobigny from its neighbors to the north, east, and west; it was bordered on the south by the unsightly canal de l'Ourcq. Nothing remained of the almost legendary forest of Bondy that, at the eastern edge of the city, had provided a haunt for brigands in earlier centuries.[4]

Then as now the legal territory of Bobigny consisted of 671 hectares; yet in 1900 most of this area was uninhabited. The local open-field farmers (*cultivateurs*) lived in the center of town, which included no more than thirty-five hectares of the total with only five paved streets. The rest of Bobigny consisted of their farms. The town's public institutions—the church, the city hall, the post office, and a boys' and a girls' primary school—were located in the city center. Here too clustered most of the few cafés, bakeries, and other small shops that served the needs of the local populace.[5]

One indication of the beginnings of the urbanization of Bobigny comes when we examine the outlying areas of the community in greater detail (Map 1). The sharp division between housing and agricultural

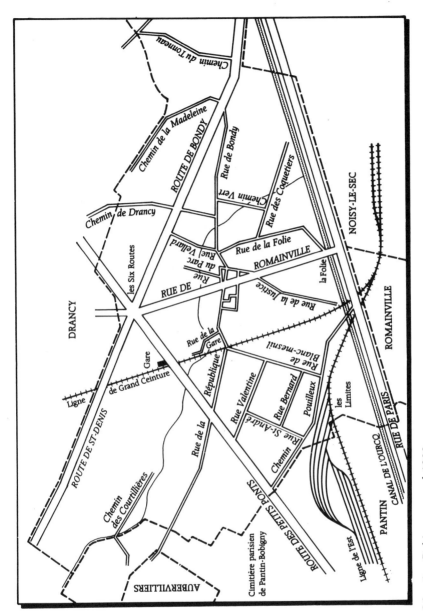

Map 1.   Bobigny around 1900.

land of a half century earlier had begun to blur, as in the southwestern part of the town, the Blanc-mesnil quarter. This area was inhabited mostly by market gardeners (*maraîchers*), who specialized in growing fruits and vegetables for the Paris produce markets. Unlike the open-field farmers, their more established neighbors, the market gardeners usually built their houses next to their plots of land and away from one another. The Blanc-mesnil quarter was thus neatly divided into small fields surrounded by low walls. Next to each plot stood the residence of the market gardener who owned it: generally a modest one- or two-story structure isolated from its neighbors.[6]

To the north of the Blanc-mesnil quarter, in northwestern Bobigny, lay La Courneuve, one of the most traditional areas of town in 1900, composed mostly of farmers' fields with few houses. Yet even here the presence of Paris could be felt, for in the southwestern corner of La Courneuve lay the greater part of the Parisian cemetery of Pantin-Bobigny. For decades the city of Paris had resorted to the practice of locating various unhealthy, noxious, and land-intensive municipal establishments outside the city's borders, in the suburbs of the Department of the Seine. The opening of the cemetery in 1884 (over the strident protests of the Bobigny city council) marked Bobigny's first experience of this practice, and thus a new stage in the suburbanization of the community. Paris was already sending its dead to Bobigny; the living would soon follow.[7]

To the south of the town's center, between it and the adjoining suburbs of Romainville and Noisy-le-Sec, extended the Limites area. Sliced up by railway lines and hemmed in by the canal de l'Ourcq, Limites was one of the more isolated neighborhoods of Bobigny. Yet the canal and the adjoining National Route no. 3 made it the section most integrated into the Paris area. Most important, it was the only section of Bobigny that had any industry. The canal de l'Ourcq, beginning in the industrialized nineteenth arrondissement of Paris and passing through Pantin before reaching Bobigny, was one of the great commercial highways of the Parisian basin. Largely because of its influence, the Limites neighborhood had a lubricants factory, a glue factory, a woodworking shop, and a harnessmaker. Resembling sub-urbs like Saint-Denis or Aubervilliers more than the rest of Bobigny, Limites exemplified the crucial role of transportation in industrializing the suburbs of Paris.[8]

Throughout our period, the Limites area remained the most indus-trialized section of Bobigny. Industrialization had little impact on other sections of the town until after the Second World War, although some important industrial development occurred in the late 1920s and early 1930s. Therefore the area that best symbolized the new, suburban, Bobigny of the interwar years was not the Limites neighborhood but the Pont de Bondy, which lay on the town's eastern fringes. It was not a neighborhood in 1900, since nobody lived there; like La Courneuve, the Pont de Bondy consisted of farmers' fields. Located farthest from Paris, the Pont de Bondy seemed so remote and unimportant that most city maps of the period did not even show it. And yet it was this area, untouched by the first stage of Bobigny's integration into the Paris area, that was transformed by the second stage of change, which made Bobigny into a working-class suburb.[9]

Turning from geographical to sociological description, we find the best indication of Bobigny's changing nature in the composition of its population. The census records of 1896 listed 1,678 inhabitants for the town; by 1902 this figure climbed to 1,946, representing a population increase of 536 percent from the population of 363 in 1856. The two major population groups were open-field farmers and market gardeners; with their dependents they made up two-thirds of the town's inhabitants. The remainder consisted of artisans, shopkeepers, railroad clerks, workers, and rentiers (pensioners).[10] Since the farmers and market gardeners dominated the town's economic and political life in the late nineteenth century, I limit analysis of Bobigny's population in this period to them, for the contrasting ways of life of these two groups, and the relations between them, bring into sharpest relief the changes associated with the initial stages of suburbanization in Bobigny.

Open-Field Farmers and Market Gardeners

After the middle of the nineteenth century the open-field farmers of Bobigny abandoned their exclusive concentration on the production of cereals and began to grow vegetables as well. The farmers had been the most important group in Bobigny; at the turn of the century they still cultivated three-fourths of the land. Yet this dominance was called into question after the 1860s, when many market gardeners began to settle in Bobigny. Henceforth Bobigny's farmers had to compete with gardeners for both land and access to the Paris vegetable market. Vegetables were more profitable than wheat, yet the competition from market gardeners led many Bobigny farmers to return a larger part of their efforts to the wheat crop in the late nineteenth century.[11]

Many market gardeners who moved into Bobigny after 1860 came from Paris, where the urban renovation unleashed by Baron Haussmann forced many Parisian market gardeners from neighborhoods like the Bastille and Vaugirard, where they had traditionally lived and worked. A larger number, however, came from the provinces, especially from the regions of Bourgogne and Morvan. These provincials were usually peasants who left their villages as a greater percentage of the agricultural land there was shifted to pasturage; the dynamism of the Paris vegetable market in the late nineteenth century attracted many to the metropolitan area.[12] The high quality of Bobigny's wet, marshy soil, the flatness of the terrain, and the large amounts of open space all attracted market gardeners. The major impetus to invade Bobigny, however, was provided by the count of Blancmesnil, the town's largest (and absentee) landowner; after 1860 he began dividing up much of his land into small market-gardening plots (*marais*) and renting them out. By 1900, when this wave of immigration was nearing its end, Bobigny had become a major center of market gardening in the Paris region, and the market gardeners composed more than half the population of the town.[13]

In the words of two later chroniclers of local life, the period from 1860 to 1900 was a golden age for Bobigny's market gardeners.[14] Parisians' desire for fresh vegetables kept the gardeners prosperous, and they were able to build a strong sense of community among themselves. Unfortunately for the social cohesion of the town as a whole, this sense of community did not extend to the farmers, whom they now outnumbered by about three to one. Farmers and market gardeners were rarely neighbors; the former usually lived in the center whereas the latter lived next to their plots south and west of the place Carnot. The two groups seldom socialized. The farmers limited their communal social life to a few religious festivals each year, which they held in Bobigny itself; the market gardeners usually went to Paris to celebrate.

Relations between the two groups were tense in this period. Maurice Agulhon notes that at the turn of the century less than 3 percent of the marriages recorded were between farming and market-gardening families. Even in politics the two groups were divided. The farmers generally voted for the Party of Order, whereas the market gardeners tended to vote for the Radical or the Radical Socialist party. The new Bobigny of the late nineteenth-century market gardeners was simply superimposed onto the traditional farming community, not integrated into it.[15]

Certainly any community that experiences the massive population shifts Bobigny underwent in the late nineteenth century is bound to experience tension between different social groups; established groups rarely react with equanimity to large-scale invasions of their territory by outsiders. Yet the problem centered on the dislocations that integrating Bobigny into the Paris area's economy caused, and on the different roles that farmers and market gardeners played. By 1900 traditional open-field grain farming was declining in the Department of the Seine, and the market gardeners' superior organization and techniques stymied the farmers' attempts to switch to vegetable production.[16]

Yet if the transition from a rural to an exurban community sharply divided Bobigny's two primary social groups, neither welcomed the prospect of Bobigny developing into a full-fledged Parisian suburb along the lines of neighboring Pantin or Aubervilliers. Paris had little to offer that the farmers wanted; as for the market gardeners, the capital was a place to sell their produce and to go to for occasional celebrations, little more. Both groups were largely self-sufficient in basic necessities and felt little need for the urban goods and services that close ties to Paris would bring.

A detailed description of the urban structure of Bobigny demonstrates what this attitude involved. The government was dominated by market gardeners, who had devoted little effort or attention to upgrading it. In spite of the growing economic links between the town and Paris, Bobigny's institutions in 1900 consequently suggested those of a small rural village rather than those of a metropolitan area. The transportation system, for example, was simple. Five large highways passed through Bobigny, which itself maintained twenty thoroughfares, nine of them unpaved rural roads. The total length of the eleven remaining streets, which composed Bobigny's urban grid, was less than seven kilometers. Public transport was minimal, a fact that is not surprising since farmers rarely went to Paris and most market gardeners drove there in their produce wagons.

The sole means of public transportation to Paris available to Balbynians was a stop on the Grand Ceinture railroad line, which ran through the community. Established in 1882, this stop enabled local residents to ride the train from Bobigny to Noisy-le-Sec, where they changed trains for Paris. The requirement of changing trains, plus the relative isolation of the stop from the center of Bobigny and its service by only five trains a day, made the Grande Ceinture railroad an inconvenient way to reach the capital; few people used it. So although the connections were not bad for what was still a small town, only in 1902 did the extension of tramway service to the community make working in Paris and living in Bobigny practical.[17]

Bobigny lacked many other services that urbanites take for granted. The town had no hospital or health care facility, and no physicians, pharmacists, or midwives resided in the community; the municipal government sent ill residents for treatment to hospitals in Paris. Bobigny had only one post office (built in 1893) and no municipal marketplace. There was a volunteer fire department but no police department; police service was provided by the first Noisy-le-Sec gendarme brigade located in Pantin. The commercial life of the community closely resembled that of a rural village. The retail stores in Bobigny numbered fewer than twenty at the turn of the century, most of them small establishments catering to the basic needs of the population. Located in the center of the community, these establishments hardly added up to anything approaching a downtown shopping district.

In 1900 Bobigny had a fairly extensive cultural life for a small town but did not offer the amenities of an urban area; the most significant cultural institutions were the cafés. The community did possess a municipal library with about two thousand books, mostly novels. The municipality also sponsored an annual festival, usually held for three days during Pentecost in the place Carnot. The major event and symbol of the well-attended festival was the launching of a giant hot-air balloon. Rounding out the panorama of Bobigny's cultural establishment was a music society, the Réveil balbinien, with twenty members. The town had no theaters, music halls, or other places of mass entertainment.[18]

Bobigny had nothing approaching a modern system of utilities. The town had no supply of running water, which the majority of the population saw as unnecessary. The community also lacked a sewer system; given the flat and swampy local terrain, this deficit would create serious health problems as the population grew. Bobigny did have gas service, but only for street lighting. Electrical power and telephone service were as yet unheard-of luxuries in the town.[19]

In general, the rudimentary sociocultural institutions and city services of Bobigny were characteristic of a small, rural community where social life was above all family life and where people were used to depending on their own resources. Not all Balbynians liked this state of affairs; some advocated developing and modernizing local services. Yet by 1900 these people had been able to do little against the more traditionalist farmers and market gardeners, who had no wish to pay for services they did not need. Bobigny's urban structure was significantly modernized only when the agricultural sector dwindled to a minority of the town's population and lost control of the municipal government.

Janus-like, Bobigny presented two faces to the world at the turn of the century. One was that of a peaceful, stable provincial hamlet. Although it was already changing, a sizable percentage of the local population nevertheless believed in this image of their community and hoped to preserve it. The town's other aspect showed important changes Bobigny had already experienced in the previous half century, and even more drastic ones it was to witness in the next thirty years. The conflicts between farmers and market gardeners produced by Bobigny's transition from rural village to exurb had been important; but old conflicts were overshadowed by new tensions between the two dominant groups and a newly arrived working-class population. The bucolic image of Bobigny in 1900, dear to farmers and market gardeners alike, was to vanish in a short time.

The Growth of Paris
in the Late Nineteenth Century

The transformation of Bobigny was part of the general development of a suburban belt around Paris after 1860. Paris had suburbs well before the late nineteenth century (the Latin Quarter was originally one); but in this period its suburban area increased to cover most of the Department of the Seine. In the process the city of Paris itself was transformed (Map 2). Suburbanization was merely the most visible redivision of urban functions that population growth and economic change produced, in their increasing capitalist imprint on the metropolitan area. The patterns of production and consumption, of work and leisure that developed in the suburbs differed in many ways from those of Paris; in effect the suburbs were a new urban form.

In the first half of the nineteenth century Paris grew at an impressive rate, from a population of 546,856 in 1801 to one of 1,174,346 by 1846. The population's increase in the second half of the century was even more spectacular. By 1901 the population had increased to nearly two and one-quarter times that in 1851 (Table 1).[20] In the most dramatic period of population increase, from 1851 to 1856, Paris grew by over 20 percent, adding a quarter of a million inhabitants.

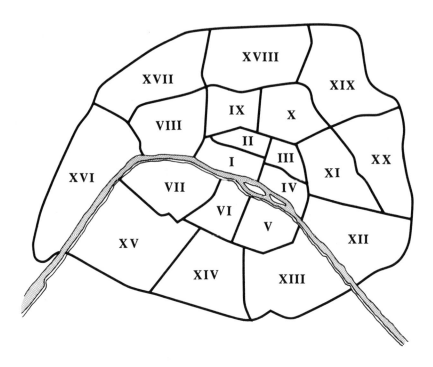

Map 2.   Paris after 1860. From Norma Evenson, *Paris: A Century of Change,*
1878–1978 (New Haven, 1979), p. 363.

TABLE I

POPULATION OF THE CITY OF PARIS
(1860 boundaries)

Year	Population	Percentage
1851	1,227,064	100
1861	1,696,141	138
1872	1,851,792	151
1881	2,269,023	185
1891	2,477,957	202
1901	2,714,068	221

SOURCE: Louis Chevalier, *Laboring Classes and Dangerous Classes* (Princeton, 1973),
p. 182.
NOTE: The 1860 boundaries resulted from the annexation of the inner suburbs, which
became the 11th–20th districts.

As was the case from 1800 to 1850, the growth of Paris in the late nineteenth century derived from immigration, not natural increase. The excess of births over deaths in Paris was even lower than in the first part of the century; at no point did it exceed 1 percent from 1860 to 1900. More than ever before in its history, the population of Paris was failing to reproduce itself and turned to the provinces to renew its ranks.[21]

Although immigration dominated in peopling the city throughout the nineteenth century, immigrants who came after 1850 differed in many ways from those who had preceded them. They no longer came mostly from northeastern France but came increasingly from all over the country. The number of immigrants from Lorraine (incorporated into Germany in 1871) declined, whereas from Brittany and the massif Central the number rose. Thus a much larger percentage of the new Parisians came from poor, less developed areas. The Great Depression of the 1870s to the 1890s brought hardship to many French peasants and forced those living a marginal existence off the land altogether; the development and expansion of the national railways ensured that many of the dispossessed eventually made their way to Paris.[22]

The greater percentage of immigrants from impoverished regions may explain why the new immigrants were more homogeneously working class than the old; no longer could it be said that migration to Paris was "a conquest and not a defeat."[23] In addition, more of these workers were unskilled, in contrast to the skilled workers and artisans that the city had traditionally attracted. The annexation of the inner suburbs in 1860 had already added a working-class population of 350,000 to Paris; the new immigration further increased the proletarian character of the city's population.[24]

This proletarian shift arose from changes in the Parisian economy of the late nineteenth century. The wave of immigrants in the early 1800s had been prompted by an expansion of the traditional artisanal industries of Paris. The growth of the city itself increased the need for workers, especially in the construction industry. The high point of this expansion came in the 1850s and 1860s, when the renovations of Paris directed by Baron Haussmann produced an unparalleled boom in both construction and immigration.

Yet after 1860 modern large-scale industries began to assume a larger role in the economy of the Paris area. More traditional sectors like textiles declined, whereas newer sectors like the metallurgical industries employed an increasing share of Parisian workers. By the turn of the century the metropolitan area was home to a large and prospering heavy industrial sector organized along more modern lines of production. Even though most industries were located in the suburbs of Paris, by 1896 the city itself had well over two thousand factories employing more than twenty workers, of which over two hundred utilized a work force greater than one hundred. By 1900 Paris had definitely entered the industrial age.[25]

The rise of a modern industrial sector in Paris depended not on any natural resources or advantages the region possessed, but rather on the city's position as the national capital and largest urban area in France. Of crucial importance was its place as the national center of railroad freight traffic. Major merchandise railway stations created at La Chapelle, Saint-Ouen, and elsewhere in Paris and its adjacent suburbs in this period facilitated the shipment of raw industrial materials to the city's factories. Developing freight railways and a system of ports gave Parisian manufacturers increased access to national and international markets, so that the rise of Paris as an industrial center in the late nineteenth century was linked to the development of an integrated national market.[26]

This period's increasingly complex industrial organization and more sophisticated investment banking made access to credit markets a factor in the success or failure of a given firm. Since Paris was the country's financial center, it gave an advantage to French industrialists who located their operations there. And in this cyclical process, the presence of a large and diverse working-class labor force in Paris, attracted by the capital's broad range of employment opportunities, provided a further incentive for businessmen to establish factories in the area. The high quality of this labor force, no longer dominated by trained and highly specialized artisans but still skilled, was an additional attraction. After 1860, through its economic power and geographic distribution, industrial capitalism had a large part in shaping the landscape of the Paris area and contributed significantly to the rise of suburbia.[27]

In analyzing the rise of a suburban belt around Paris in the late nineteenth and the early twentieth century, we must examine the changing living conditions that faced workers in Paris. The city's increasing inaccessibility to the working class in the late nineteenth century was a key factor in developing the suburbs of the Department of the Seine.

We have touched on Baron Haussmann's renovation of Paris after 1860 and the changes it caused in the social fabric of the city.[28] The impact on the Parisian popular classes was twofold. First, by demolishing many ancient slums in the Ile de la Cité and the central Right Bank, Haussmann's reforms drove many workers out of central Paris into the outer districts (especially the nineteenth, twentieth, and thirteenth arrondissements) annexed to the city in 1860. (The new social configuration emerged in the failure of the communards to hold the city center during the last bloody days of the Paris Commune of 1871, when they retreated to make a final stand on the city's eastern periphery.) By depopulating the center, Haussmann's reforms sharply increased Parisians' residential segregation, for as the working class moved to the northern and eastern edges of the city, middle-class and wealthy inhabitants moved into newer quarters in the western part of Paris, especially the sixteenth arrondissement. The Parisian working class was more spatially marginalized and isolated from its neighbors; before long the majority of this class would be forced out of the city altogether.[29]

Concomitant with the greater concentration of Parisian workers in the outer districts of the north and east was their intensified overcrowding. The Parisian population increased most in the outer districts. From 1861 to 1896 the population from the eleventh arrondissement through the twentieth grew by 103 percent, whereas that of the first arrondissement through the tenth grew by only 7.1 percent. These areas had been sparsely populated suburbs fifty years earlier and were thus poorly equipped to house large numbers of newcomers. In many cases people moved into former single-family houses, subdividing them into small individual housing units. Attics, basements, and even stables were converted into apartments. Many working people, both individuals and families, lived in furnished single rooms known as *garnis,* notorious at the time for their unsanitary condition. Some of the poorest Parisians even resorted to building their own shacks on open land at the edges of the city; these squatters' settlements were merely the most dramatic example of the dire shortage of moderately priced housing in Paris during the late nineteenth century. The 1896 census revealed that 14.9 percent of the city's population lived in overcrowded housing; the percentages for the thirteenth, nineteenth, and twentieth arrondissements were 64.2, 65.5, and 66.0 percent respectively.[30]

Haussmann's renovations of Paris helped create this overcrowding, but they cannot explain it. Of greater immediate importance were the patterns of housing construction in Paris during this period. The housing industry was active in the late nineteenth century, with the construction of new dwellings reaching a peak in the years 1875 through 1884; most houses were built in the outer districts, which had the greatest vacant space. Yet it was the wealthier arrondissements of the western end of Paris that benefited, not the more proletarian ones to the east. From 1878 to 1889 the amount of available housing in the sixteenth district rose by 62.7 percent, while its population increased by 47.2 percent; by contrast, the thirteenth district experienced a 41.6 percent increase in population but only a 29 percent rise in available housing stock. Moreover, much of the housing in the poorer arrondissements was built for middle-class residents. While new buildings in more prosperous neighborhoods stood vacant for lack of tenants (at least of tenants able to pay the high rents), those Parisians who most desperately needed good housing were least able to find it.[31]

There were several reasons for the failure of the Parisian construction industry to build sufficient low-cost housing in this period. To a much greater extent than before, housing in Paris was built by large companies that purchased extensive tracts of land for speculation rather than immediate construction. Speculation made it imperative to realize the greatest possible profits, and such profits did not come from building for working-class occupants. Much more lucrative was renting to members of the large new middle class, employed in branches of the tertiary sector like banking and commerce, whose incomes were both higher and more stable.

Government policies also discouraged the construction of low-cost housing. Municipal charges on owners of buildings adjoining public thoroughfares were steep and increased with each road improvement: these costs were passed on to tenants, and those with little to spend on rent could not afford them. Also, taxes on inexpensive buildings were proportionately heavier than on costly ones. Yet the essential problem lay elsewhere: the Paris construction industry in the late nineteenth century was composed of private entrepreneurs who built housing for monetary reward, not to fulfill a social need. Since there were plenty of middle- and upper-income people to build housing for, it is easy to see why the construction industry neglected the housing needs of the Parisian working class.[32]

Only major government intervention into the housing industry could have made a difference in this period. Yet neither city nor national government took significant action to deal with this crucial problem. Throughout the period many public officials expressed concern over the poor condition of working-class housing, seeing it as conducive to the spread of disease, moral degeneracy, and political instability.[33] Yet these officials, holding fast to the tenets of economic liberalism, rejected state intervention in the housing market as illegitimate and as a first step on the road to collectivism.[34]

The sharp increase in population of the 1880s and the decrease in construction after 1884 did lead the Paris city council to consider a number of proposals to deal with the housing crisis, such as municipal guarantees for bank loans on low-cost housing and tax exemptions to builders of inexpensive rental units. The prevalent belief in the efficiency of the free market, however, prevented all such ideas from winning approval; a proposal by socialist city councillor Jules Joffrin for the construction of municipal housing was voted down in 1884 by a margin of four to one. Advocates of housing reform limited themselves to encouraging the efforts of private charitable societies. Yet these organizations contributed little to resolve the problem, either because construction was too unprofitable to attract outside investment or because the rental units that were built were too expensive for most working-class tenants.[35] The same logic that ruled the private construction industry effectively circumscribed philanthropic efforts for working-class housing.

The major example of government intervention to deal with the housing crisis came in 1894. Widespread public concern over the problem had led to the foundation of the Société française des habitations à bon marché (HBM) in 1889. A private organization, the society viewed its role as advisory, to encourage the construction of low-cost housing by private individuals, companies, and charitable organizations. Five years later the national government voted to subsidize the work of the society by offering fiscal exemptions and low-interest loans to builders of inexpensive housing units that met certain government specifications. Yet because local and departmental governments, charged by the national government with implementing the law, took few steps to do so, the society accomplished little in this period. Between 1895 and 1902 it built only 1,360 HBM dwellings in all of France.[36] Clearly, Parisian workers in the late nineteenth century frantically searching for affordable housing of decent quality could expect assistance from neither the Paris city council nor the national government.

One consequence of the insufficient low-priced housing in Paris was a rise in rents. Most workers in this period could not afford to pay rents of more than 300 to 350 francs a year. Yet because of the patterns in housing construction, the percentage of rental units available at such prices was in decline. In 1880, 67.6 percent of housing units in the city rented for less than 300 francs; this percentage dropped to 47.6 percent by 1900. The absolute number of such units fell by 69,093 from 1880 to 1889, whereas the total number of rental units rose by 104,836. Parisian workers were forced to spend more of their meager earnings on housing: the proportion of an average working-class budget devoted to rent rose from 13.5 percent in 1862 to 18 percent in 1900. The shortage of low-cost housing and the resultant overcrowding of the working class in Paris also had serious implications for public health. The inadequate sunlight and air that characterized many modest dwellings undermined the health of their occupants, as did the rudimentary sewage and trash collection in poor neighborhoods; the crowded living conditions of the poor and working class facilitated the spread of contagious diseases. Consequently, in poor neighborhoods more than in wealthy ones mortality rates were high, especially for infants: from 1893 to 1897 the rate was 25 percent in the thirteenth arrondissement, 11 percent in the eighth.[37]

It is true that this gap cannot be attributed to housing alone; the poor quality and quantity of food consumed, among other factors, also had their effect. Yet if we look at death rates from tuberculosis, a disease closely related to housing conditions, we see an even more drastic gap. From 1896 to 1900 the rate of death from tuberculosis was close to five times as high in the poor twentieth district as in the wealthy eighth. The housing crisis was thus a factor in the inequality before death that separated Parisians in this period.[38]

It must not be thought that Parisian workers accepted their situation with equanimity. Hatred of the landlord was a common theme of the period, as reflected in popular songs referring to the landlord as "M. Vautour" (Mr. Vulture) and suggesting that he be hanged from the nearest lamppost:

> If you want to be happy
> In the name of God,
> Hang your landlord![39]

Political groupings that appealed to a working-class clientele played up the poor living conditions of the Parisian working class. Yet the political dominance of capitalism and the government's determination to preserve housing as a free-market activity forestalled any solution to the crisis of working-class housing conditions. In spite of a slight easing of these conditions after the 1880s, any real solution seemed to be as far away as ever.[40] Bertillon and DuMesnil studied the housing problem in the poorer areas of Paris near the end of the century, noting the persistence of overcrowding and poor sanitary conditions.[41] By 1900 the basic question—Where is one to live?—still had no answer for the workers of Paris.

Within the context of this question we must now shift our focus from the city of Paris to the Paris suburbs in the late nineteenth century. In the rise of the suburbs we will find a partial answer to this question.

Suburban Development
in the Late Nineteenth Century

The growth of population throughout the Department of the Seine was every bit as dramatic as that of Paris alone. The great waves of immigration that brought hundreds of thousands of people from the provinces to the capital in the late nineteenth century affected both the city and its suburbs (Table 2). Yet impressive as these figures are, the growth rates recorded by the Paris suburbs (that is, the department excluding Paris) are even more spectacular (Table 3). From 1861 to 1866, for example, the rate of population increase in the Paris suburbs was over three times as great as that in the capital.[42] In 1861 the suburbs composed only 13 percent of the population of the Department of the Seine; by 1901 they had doubled their share to 26 percent. With the stabilization of the city's population and the even more explosive growth of the suburbs in the early twentieth century, by the 1940s the Paris area contained as many suburbanites as Parisians.[43]

The industrial sector of the capital's suburban belt, the most important initial cause of suburbanization, began to grow before the middle of the nineteenth century. Although it established itself as a suburban industrial economy part of and yet distinct from that of Paris only after Paris expanded to its present boundaries by annexing the inner suburbs in 1860, development had already begun in the 1840s. This period created a crucial element of industrial suburbia, a modern commercial transportation network.[44]

It has become a truism to point to the role of transportation in the history of urban expansion.[45] Nonetheless, industrial transport, especially by rail, supplied growing industrial suburbs just as, around the turn of the century, mass transit swelled the population. In the north, the opening of the Saint-Denis canal in 1821 and the canal de l'Ourcq the following year linked the northern suburbs with the river transportation network of the Seine as a whole. In the southern suburbs, the river

TABLE 2

POPULATION OF THE DEPARTMENT OF THE SEINE

Year	Population	Percentage
1851	1,422,065	100
1861	1,953,660	137
1872	2,220,060	156
1881	2,799,329	197
1891	3,141,595	221
1901	3,669,930	260

SOURCE: Louis Chevalier, *Laboring Classes and Dangerous Classes* (Princeton, 1973), p. 182.

TABLE 3

POPULATION OF THE DEPARTMENT
OF THE SEINE EXCLUDING PARIS

Year	Population	Percentage
1861	257,519	100
1866	325,642	126
1872	368,268	143
1876	422,043	164
1881	530,306	206
1886	626,539	243
1891	693,638	269
1896	803,680	312
1901	955,862	371

SOURCE: Louis Chevalier, *Laboring Classes and Dangerous Classes* (Princeton, 1973), p. 182.

traffic on the Seine had allowed the earlier industrial development of Ivry and Charenton; the opening of the Paris–Orléans railway in 1843 further spurred the expansion of the industrial sector in this area of the suburbs.

Perhaps the key development in industrializing the Paris suburbs was the opening of large freight railway stations outside the city in the 1870s. Suburban industrialists had depended on the freight stations at La Chapelle, in northern Paris, to import raw materials and export their manufactures by rail. In 1872–1873 the La Chapelle–annex freight station was built to transport heavy industrial materials like iron and stone. Later in the same decade other major freight stations were created in the northern suburbs, at Saint-Ouen and in the Plaine Saint-Denis, followed by one at Le Bourget in 1884, and one at Pantin in 1890. By the last decade of the century a separate industrial railroad had been created to serve Aubervilliers, Gennevilliers, and the Plaine Saint-Denis. Partly because of this freight railway network, the 1870s marked the turning point in the rise of heavy industry in the northern suburbs of the Department of the Seine.

The southern suburbs did not keep pace with their northern counterparts in industrial development in these years. There was no freight station of any consequence in this area; the Seine therefore remained the major means of industrial transport.[46] The southern suburbs of Paris industrialized later and to a lesser extent than those to the north, where heavy industry had established itself by the late 1870s. Except for Ivry and Charenton, the southern suburbs began to develop a heavy industrial sector only in the 1890s.[47]

The first industries to develop in the Paris suburbs were chemicals and textiles, which dominated the economies of certain suburbs, like Clichy, Saint-Denis, and Gentilly, in the first half of the nineteenth century. Clichy had 137 bleaching establishments (*blanchisseries*) in 1848, with a work force of fifteen hundred, and by 1855 Saint-Denis had over three thousand textile workers employed in manufacturing printed fabrics. After the midcentury, however, the textile industry in the Paris region declined, as more and more plants relocated to the provinces. Employing 11 percent of Parisian laborers in 1847, the textile industry accounted for only 3.4 percent by 1860.

Well before their eclipse, textiles contributed to the rise of the chemical industry, prominent in the Paris suburbs in the middle third of the nineteenth century. A large number of the suburban textile firms produced printed colored fabrics, for which they needed a constant, ample supply of dyes and other colorants from the chemical industry. Because it was close to Paris, the suburban chemical industry had a steady source for raw materials: bones, hides, animal fats, and other by-products came from Parisian slaughterhouses. The slaughterhouse of La Villette, for example, led to the creation of the Floquet tannery in Saint-Denis during the 1860s.[48]

The first chemical factories, producing white lead, were established in the Paris suburbs in 1809, and similar factories followed in the next decades. It was in the period from 1840 to 1870, however, that the chemical industry carved out a dominant position in suburban manu-facturing. In 1847 the Combes tannery was founded in Saint-Denis, followed by the Guibal rubber factory in 1851 in Ivry, the Saulnier bone treatment plant in Aubervilliers in 1860, and the Saint-Denis branch of the Central Pharmacy of France in 1867. By 1870, nine thousand of the twelve thousand industrial workers employed in Saint-Denis worked in the chemical industry.

After 1870 the chemical industry continued to expand in the Paris suburbs, but it was increasingly overshadowed by another branch of manufacturing, whose rise completed the nineteenth-century suburban industrialization and gave these communities much of their character- istic twentieth-century appearance. This was the metallurgical industry, and it was built on both the chemical industry and the railroad network. The expansion of the railways led to a greater need for metal parts and thus to the establishment of a new industrial sector composed of foundries, rolling mills, mechanical construction firms (*carrosseries*), and repair shops. Before 1870 such firms had existed; the Letrange foundry, for example, was founded in Saint-Denis in 1855. Only in the 1870s and 1880s, however, did they begin to assume real importance. Their need for certain chemical products, such as varnishes, led them to locate in the suburbs with the chemical firms, whose market they enlarged. The development of these two industries was mutually reinforcing.

Their development involved the railways as well: the expansion of heavy industry increased imports of raw materials, which intensified the traffic on the network of railways, thus necessitating its expansion, and so on. After 1880 a new branch of the metallurgical industry, automo- bile manufacturing, began in the Paris suburbs; the first such factory was founded in Puteaux in 1883, followed by three others in 1888, 1897, and 1900. By the turn of the century half of the ten thousand workers employed in Saint-Denis worked in the metallurgical industry, with another quarter employed in chemical plants.[49]

Before concluding this outline of the rise of a heavy industrial sector in the Paris suburbs during the last half of the nineteenth century, we must look at the ways suburban industries differed from those that started at the same time in the city of Paris. Louis Chevalier defines the early stages of industrial suburbia:

> The entreprise, factory, workshop, or entrepot is no longer at the immediate service of the clientele, but at the service of one or several entreprises that maintain with the public, or only with commerce, direct exchange relations. The fashioning of primary materials that will be enabled by a further technique, the utilization of by-products and waste materials, marginal and preliminary tasks, such is the domain of this industrial zone.[50]

Chevalier accurately describes the economic structure of the Paris suburbs by the end of the nineteenth century. Much of the Parisian economy was specialized, oriented toward satisfying the needs of the consumer market. Thus industries such as food and clothing, which catered most directly to this market, were most likely to locate within the capital. Conversely, industries such as metallurgy, whose products served other industries, would derive little advantage from a Parisian location. Since their markets were national and international, access to modern transportation facilities was important in determining their location; the northern suburbs supplied these facilities.[51]

Two other related differences between Parisian and suburban industries in this period were the size of factories and the nature of production. In both city and suburbs the size of the average factory grew from 1850 to 1900; by the closing decades of the century a trend toward establishing the largest plants outside Paris was apparent. In 1896 the percentage of factories employing more than one hundred workers was almost twice as high in the suburbs of the Department of the Seine as in Paris; in 1906 the percentage of factories employing over five hundred workers was over three times as high in the Paris suburbs as in the city. The suburbs had more room (and cheaper land) than Paris had, so plants needing more space would be inclined to locate in the suburbs. It is also true that suburban industries, whatever their reasons for locating there, tended to produce on a larger scale. Thus, by the opening of the twentieth century a combination of factors had produced the classic division of the manufacturing sector into a city of small and medium workshops and a suburban constellation of large plants.[52]

Suburban industries tended to be more "modern" not only in their larger size and production, but also in their greater mechanization and simplified production procedures, which decreased the need for a skilled labor force. Again, the character of the industries that chose to locate in the suburbs explains much of this modernity: industries requiring the least skill situated themselves in suburbia. This geographical division of functions operated in the metallurgical industry, which located more skilled assembly work (*travail de montage*) in the city of Paris and less sophisticated operations like foundry work and sheet metal production in the suburbs.[53]

In general, the late nineteenth-century growth of modern, large-scale heavy industry was not distributed evenly throughout the Paris area. It was concentrated instead in the suburbs of the Department of the Seine, especially those north of the capital. The expansion of employment in the tertiary sector of banking and commerce in Paris, which did not occur in the suburbs, accentuated the economic differences between the two areas after the turn of the century. We must emphasize, however, that Paris and its suburbs were not two separate economies but rather geographically specialized functions within one economy. Their distinct development showed in spatial terms the growing specialization of consumption- and production-oriented sectors, the latter located more and more outside Paris.

Turning from industrial development to immigration patterns and population structures, we discover similar differences. To a large extent the history of the peopling of the Paris suburbs is the history of the forming of a modern industrial proletariat. In both a physical and a social sense, it developed on the margins of the preexisting order, in an isolation that heightened the impact of its novelty.

Looking at the social composition of the Parisian suburbs around midcentury, before the development of a heavy industrial sector, we find that the local populations generally consisted of small landowners, artisans, shopkeepers, and rentiers; only Saint-Denis had an industrial bourgeoisie during this period. Although the government of Louis Philippe built new fortifications around Paris in the 1840s, bringing workers and soldiers into suburban communities like Aubervilliers, the basic social structure of the Paris suburbs remained constant. There were no significant long-term increases in population until the 1860s and 1870s.[54]

In the suburbs as in Paris itself, the population increased in the late nineteenth century almost entirely by immigration, the excess of births over deaths being low as well. Immigrants into suburbia in this period came from poorer, less developed areas of France. Of those who settled in the southern suburbs, a large percentage came from relatively backward departments of southern France. This pattern held also in the northern suburbs, which were situated in the path of immigrants arriving from the more advanced northern and eastern parts of the country. In 1869, only 45 percent of the immigrants into Saint-Denis came from these areas (which included the Paris region); the rest came from the massif Central, the west, and the mountainous areas of the country.[55] This pattern that Saint-Denis somewhat precociously experienced was soon duplicated in much of the remaining suburban area.

A second distinguishing characteristic of suburban immigration was its occupational composition. To a greater extent than the capital, the suburbs received unskilled workers. In 1871, for example, they composed 61 percent of the working population of Gentilly. It is not surprising that immigrants coming from economically backward, rural France should possess few skills. Even more advanced areas of the country, however, such as the Nord and the Moselle, which continued to export large contingents of migrants to the Paris region, sent a disproportionate number of their unskilled workers to the suburbs; the more highly trained were able to find jobs in Paris.

As heavy industry developed in the Paris suburbs, it attracted more unskilled workers, especially to the northern suburbs. The rise of heavy industry and the influx of this unskilled working-class population paralleled and reinforced each other. In the pattern that emerged, unskilled immigrants from rural France came to Paris, found jobs (and housing) more easily in the suburbs than in the city itself, and moved into the suburb where they worked. Many immigrants went directly to the suburbs from the provinces without passing through Paris. Just as Paris rejected the least attractive urban installations and assigned them to suburbia, so it did with the least desirable workers.[56]

The differences in economic structure and immigration patterns between Paris and its suburbs meant different experiences of industrialization for the two communities. For Paris, rich in small workshops and a large population of skilled workers and independent artisans with their own proud traditions, the transition to an industrial economy was gradual and complicated. For the suburbs, by contrast, this process was much simpler. Most employers did not face the delicate task of subduing independent artisans and turning skilled workers into machine operatives, since much of their work force was unskilled and of rural origin. It was in the suburbs, therefore, that the industrial proletariat was to be found.[57]

The Rise of Mass Transit in the Paris Area

So far this chapter has focused on communities in the Department of the Seine closest to Paris, and their integration into the economy of the Paris metropolitan area. Towns like Montrouge, Ivry, Pantin, and above all Saint-Denis became the French symbols of industrial suburbia by 1900. Yet the Department of the Seine contained many other communities, such as Bobigny, which lay at a greater distance from the capital and were untouched by the earlier transformation (Map 3). Moreover, the suburbs discussed so far generally lacked that attribute

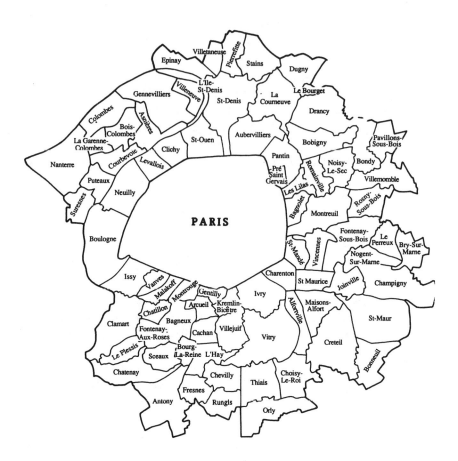

Map 3.   Paris and the Department of the Seine in 1920.

which has come to be seen as a hallmark of suburbia, a large commuting population. Not until the twentieth century did the Paris area develop a major residential suburban sector in Bobigny and other exterior communities of the Department of the Seine. The Parisian housing crisis and the development and restructuring of the metropolitan economy contributed to this phenomenon. But before moving on to analyze its manifestation in Bobigny, we must consider one specific change in late nineteenth-century Paris that had great significance: the construction of mass transit. It was the mass transit system, especially the tramways, that helped solve the Paris housing crisis and restructure the metropolitan area by creating what were, in effect, new working-class ghettos outside the city.

The growth of Paris during the Second Empire made some form of mass transit almost inevitable. Annexing the outer districts in 1860, moving the population toward the periphery, and restructuring central Paris into a nonresidential central business district—these changes made commuting a fact of life. Moreover, experiments in American cities suggested that tramways were the best available urban mass transit.[58]

The first extensive tramway network in Paris was created in 1873. In that year the French government granted the General Omnibus Company a concession to operate a tram network of eleven lines within Paris. Two other companies, Tramways North and Tramways South, also received concessions to operate ten tramlines from Paris into the suburbs. Thus right from the outset commuting was part of modern mass transit in Paris. By 1884 Tramways North had built extended lines as far as Saint-Denis, Gennevilliers, Suresnes, and Pantin, and Tramways South had instituted service between Paris and Charenton, Vitry, and Clamart. While the Paris tramway network prospered in the 1870s and 1880s, both suburban companies soon encountered major financial problems and by 1884 had gone out of business. But suburban mass transit went on: in 1890 the bankrupt lines were taken over by two new companies, the Tramway Company of Paris and the Department of the Seine (Compagnie des tramways de Paris et du département de la Seine, or TPDS), and the Parisian General Tramways Company (Compagnie générale parisienne de tramways, or CGPT).[59]

The takeover by TPDS and CGPT showed that, despite the financial vicissitudes of individual companies, suburban mass transit was an idea whose time had come. As the city grew and an important economic sector arose in the suburbs, commuting became necessary for much of the working population of the Department of the Seine. Also, given the entrepreneurial nature of the construction industry and the high price of land in the capital, public and private planners in the late 1880s saw little likelihood for decent and inexpensive housing in the capital. Therefore a solution to the lack of working-class housing would have to involve the suburbs.

A key component of suburban working-class housing was the "worker-landowner" (*ouvrier-propriétaire*) concept. Developed by Frédéric Le Play and his followers in the journal *La Réforme sociale*, this idea held that the poor quality and collective conditions of working-class lodgings in Paris weakened family life and thus caused moral degeneracy among the working class.[60] This decay led to political instability: "If family life does not exist among the working classes, it is linked to the smallness and filth of the dwellings. The cabaret thus becomes a place of meeting and relaxation: one becomes there at the same time envious, greedy, revolutionary, skeptical, and finally a Communist."[61]

The solution was to move workers from crowded urban slums to their own homes in the countryside. Such a program would improve the physical health of workers and reinforce their family life by giving it a more fitting center. Moreover, home ownership would teach workers the virtues of thrift and sobriety, and strengthen the political system by removing the housing question as a source of workers' discontent and by instilling in them respect for property rights.

Since it was obviously impossible to resettle Parisian workers en masse in the countryside, individual working-class housing would have to be constructed in the suburbs. The problem was to make these suburbs accessible to those who worked in Paris. An inexpensive mass-transit system linking city and suburbs was the only feasible way to accomplish this goal; many planners who proposed resettling workers in the suburbs both as a practical solution to the Paris housing crisis and as a means of fighting socialism were strong proponents of it. Together, private mass transit and private individual housing would solve the "social question."[62]

The decades from 1890 through 1910 represented the high point of tramway development in Paris. In 1890 there were twenty-five tram-lines, each of which carried over four million passengers annually; this figure had almost doubled to forty-six lines by 1909. After 1900 the tramways faced formidable competition from a new source, the Paris métro, or subway. Yet although subway patronage went from sixteen million rides in 1900 to three hundred twelve million in 1909, figures for tramway patronage remained stable during this period. Since the métro served only the city of Paris, this seeming stability in fact represented a tremendous growth in traffic between Paris and its suburbs.[63]

A substantial reason for the popularity of the tramways was their low fares. A ride in a second-class tramcar anywhere within Paris cost a flat ten centimes (roughly the price of two pounds of potatoes); rides beyond the city limits cost an extra ten to fifteen centimes. One company, Left Bank Tramways, charged no supplement at all for suburban trips, so that anyone could travel from southern suburbs like Vanves or Montrouge into the heart of Paris for only ten centimes. Contributing to the trams' popularity was the practice of running "working-class trams." After 1891 government concessions for electric tramlines required that during commuter hours (generally before 7 A.M. and from 6 to 8 P.M.) admittance to certain tramcars would cost only half the normal second-class fare. This fare, open to all, made it possible for workers to commute between suburbs and city for only five centimes each way.[64]

The competitive Paris tramway lines and their low fares, added to the expense of electrical equipment, produced a crisis in the industry at the turn of the century. Overspeculation and an unstable stock market throughout Europe in 1900 were also contributing factors. By 1900 several large tramway lines were operating at a loss; Left Bank Tramways' expenses were almost twice as high as its revenues, to take the worst case.[65] In spite of an impressive performance in the 1890s, in the first few years of the new century the Paris tramway network was in danger of collapse.

At this point the national government stepped in. Previously the government had opposed any public involvement in tramway development other than regulating it and granting concessions, both of which were handled by municipal and departmental authorities.[66] Yet the service furnished by the Paris tramways was so important that if the private tramway companies were allowed to go bankrupt, the government would be forced to take a more direct role of maintaining mass transit in Paris.

National officials therefore dealt with the crisis through a two-pronged strategy of temporary expedients. They allowed the tramway companies to raise fares for both Paris and the suburbs by about five centimes, which wiped out the operating deficits of several Parisian tram companies. In addition the national government overruled the Paris city council to let tramway companies place electrical lines overhead within the capital. The change freed the companies from the greater expense of equipping their Paris lines with surface conduit conductors. These measures provided short-term relief for the Paris tramway companies, which soon experienced further difficulties; the great floods of 1910 threw the system into chaos, necessitating additional government intervention. Private mass transit in Paris came to an end in 1921, when the national government took over the tramway companies. It united them into the Société des transports en commun de la région parisienne (STCRP), under the control of the Department of the Seine.[67]

There is a certain contrast between the French government's reluctant intervention to maintain mass transit in the Paris area and its inability to resolve the crisis in working-class housing within the city. It did not deliberately and consciously promote mass transit in order to resettle working-class Parisians in the suburbs. The law on low-cost housing proposed a level of governmental involvement that went beyond anything done for the tramways. Within the dominant economic liberalism of the period, it was possible to ensure mass transit, whereas to solve the housing problem would have required an unacceptable level of public investment. Opening up the outer suburbs to working-class settlement through mass transport was one way to ease the Paris housing crisis. Although we cannot argue that the government consciously chose this expedient as a policy, its position on public intervention meant the de facto adoption of this solution.[68]

In any case, by 1914 mass transit had a permanent place in Parisian life. In 1909 the system carried over three hundred thirty million passengers; the largest line, linking Montrouge with the capital's Gare de l'Est, carried over seventeen million alone that year.[69] By this time the system served most communities in the Department of the Seine and even more distant areas, such as Versailles and Saint-Germain. The development of mass transit in the Paris area created a subculture: life in the suburbs and work in Paris. The shape of the Paris housing market and low tram rates meant that many commuters would be working class. By World War I, therefore, the transportation system necessary to create and maintain a vast ring of working-class suburbs around Paris was in place.

Suburbanization in the Interwar Years

Unprecedented growth took place in the suburbs in the 1920s and the 1930s: it involved more than one million new residents. The early 1920s saw a flood of immigrants invade this area, surpassing all earlier migration and causing for many immigrants miserable living conditions that in turn became a major social issue in the region during the interwar years.[70] At the source of this phenomenon lay the increase in the working-class population of the Paris area caused by World War I. The occupation by German troops of the most advanced industrial areas of France—where, for example, 53 percent of the country's prewar metallurgical capacity had been located—necessitated a geographical shift in French industry. Because the Paris area had a large industrial labor force and was the seat of government (and was thus the place where wartime contracts were handed out), many of the new factories opened up there. This wartime activity greatly stimulated the chemical and metallurgical industries, which were already well established in the Paris region. Much of the industrial expansion, following patterns already described, took place in the suburbs. Fed by the reconstruction of the war-devastated regions and the takeoff of the new automobile and aviation industries, the area's industrial boom continued well after the armistice of 1918.[71]

Not surprisingly, one consequence of this industrial activity was to increase the number of Paris-area workers. After the first year of the war, in which the army's massive mobilization produced dislocations and severe unemployment in Paris, the needs of the wartime economy caused a labor shortage in the region. Employment figures in the metallurgical industry, for example, were 125 percent of prewar levels. The expansion of the central administration to direct the wartime economy also required more clerks and other lower level white-collar workers. Wartime refugees from occupied areas also flooded into Paris. Many of these new Parisian workers stayed on after the war as both employment and wage levels remained high. As a result, from 1911 to 1921 the population of the Paris agglomeration as a whole increased by 350,000 people.[72]

This sharp population increase would have created a housing shortage in any case, since before the war Paris already lacked inexpensive dwellings. But the housing crisis in Paris during and after World War I owed its severity to additional factors. The reorientation of the French economy to meet the needs of war brought housing construction to a halt after August 1914; many buildings in Paris that had been partially completed when hostilities broke out remained exactly as they were until the war's end. The lack of available labor, the high cost of construction materials, and the laws preventing rent increases and evictions for nonpayment all discouraged the building of new housing.[73] As always, it was the moderately priced dwellings, ones low-income families could afford, that were the hardest to find.

The immediate postwar years brought no easing of the Paris housing crisis. Priority in housing construction was given to the formerly occupied areas of northern and eastern France; even there, the building of new housing proceeded slowly. More important, the government's decision to maintain rent control in the Paris area and to increase regulation of the whole French housing market made capitalists reluctant to invest in residential construction. The general shortage of capital in France and the relatively high wages prevalent in the construction industry further exacerbated the problem. Moreover, property owners not only refused to build more housing but declined to invest money in maintenance, allowing existing housing stock to fall into disrepair. Finally, some residential buildings were converted into office buildings, movie theaters, and the like, which offered greater possibilities for profit.[74]

The combined result of these factors was a housing crisis of unparalleled proportions in Paris by the early 1920s. Parisians, especially those with limited resources, crowded into smaller living spaces; the number of people in the Department of the Seine living in *garnis*—furnished rooms—rose from 295,000 in 1914 to 390,000 in 1921. Unlike the housing shortage during the late nineteenth century, the one after 1914 affected not only the city of Paris itself but also the built-up areas of the inner ring of suburbs. It was only natural that many Parisians, hard pressed to find living space, therefore began to consider moving out into "the country," to those areas of the Seine that were still underdeveloped.[75]

Settling in the outer reaches of the Department of the Seine was a more attractive option for those of low incomes than it had previously been. The tramways existed, as we have noted. High wages and low unemployment during World War I and the 1920s meant that more workers were willing to consider the long-term financial commitment of buying suburban housing. Also of great importance was the enactment of legislation in 1919 granting French workers an eight-hour day. The additional time workers gained allowed commuting from the suburbs and greater choice of suburban location. Of course, many workers were forced to sacrifice part or all of their new leisure time to dealing with the housing crisis, whether they wanted to become suburban commuters or not.[76]

While some deliberated, many low- and moderate-income people indeed wanted to move out of the slums of Paris to give their children space to grow in and fresh air to breathe. The war intensified this desire in many Parisians. During the war the government had encouraged working-class families to set up gardens in the "zone" immediately surrounding the capital; many became accustomed to the joys of a garden and began planning to live where they could have one permanently. The fact that many soldiers sent their wives and children to live in the country with relatives also certainly had an impact; the old rooms in the city slums must have seemed drearier than ever when they returned. Finally, many *poilus* undoubtedly felt at war's end that, having sacrificed for their country, they and their families deserved something better out of life; now was the time to think seriously about acquiring that long-desired dream house in the country.[77]

> After the war of 1914–1918 the ambition of almost all workers was to own their own homes. The rise in wages, which outstripped increases in the cost of living, made this possible. The abundance of work for nearly a decade seemed to have exorcised the phantom of unemployment. . . . The allotments, multiplying in the Paris suburbs and on the fringes of large cities, allowed the realization of this ardent desire. In all the factories where I worked between 1920 and 1930, this was a frequent theme of conversation between workers. The Communists were every bit as attracted to the right of property as others were.[78]

The phenomenon that grew from these dreams of suburbanization in the interwar years is known as the allotments (*lotissements*), in which nearly seven hundred thousand people, the majority of those who moved into the suburbs in the 1920s and the 1930s, were lodged in the Paris region.[79] Allotments were unimproved housing subdivisions, created by developers (*lotisseurs*) from farmland. Sold most often to lower-class families escaping the vicissitudes of the Paris housing market, they usually included no provision for utilities, sanitary facilities, or even sidewalks. Consequently, the allotments quickly degenerated into suburban slums in the fields. As the case of Bobigny demonstrates, living conditions in such areas were usually not better, and sometimes worse, than the poorer Parisian neighborhoods they replaced.

The suburban region, both industrial and residential, that sprang up around Paris in the late nineteenth and the early twentieth century was merely the most extreme manifestation of the economic specialization and physical segregation reshaping the Paris metropolitan area. This tendency ultimately demonstrated in urban space the growing importance of capitalist values in France, and their ability to transform physical landscapes. The functional specialization of land use was the urban equivalent in space of the division of labor; both were important components of capitalist efficiency. Rising land prices in central Paris prompted industrial capital to transform the inner suburbs into a vast urban workshop and accentuated the physical separation of heavy from light industry in the metropolitan area. These same prices also restricted the supply of low-cost housing in the capital, thus increasing social segregation and pushing workers toward the periphery of the city.

The same process affected both city and suburbs but to a different degree. Paris was reshaped by capitalist urbanization; but its dense precapitalist urban structure resisted major change. The suburbs, by contrast, were created by industrial capital; their past was not so much reshaped as simply submerged. Far more than Paris, therefore, the suburbs embodied the capitalist vision of the city in the late nineteenth and the early twentieth century.

Two aspects of specialization were particularly important in the rise of the Paris suburbs in this period: residential segregation by class, and division between production and consumption. The former transformed the suburbs into great working-class ghettos, representations in urban space of the political weakness and marginal status of their inhabitants. The latter allocated to the suburbs those economic activities, like metals and freight activities, most separated from consumer markets. It was the convergence of these two aspects in the early twentieth century that transformed Bobigny and other villages on the fringes of the Department of the Seine into suburbs. These suburbs represented a greater specialization than their more developed neighbors; whereas the older suburbs contained both workplaces and homes, the new suburbs were residential. By dividing working-class life more sharply between workplace and residence—between production and consumption—capitalist urbanization produced a situation in Bobigny and similar suburbs in which community issues could emerge as a predominant and separate form of politics. At the same time, residential segregation by class in the metropolitan area meant that working-class attitudes had a consequential role in shaping the political life of these suburbs. The changes that overtook Bobigny in the early twentieth century were part of the evolution of the Paris area from the 1860s to the 1930s. The rise of residential working-class suburbia had great consequences for the small community.

CHAPTER 2

The Urbanization of Bobigny

As the twentieth century began, the suburban development along the outer edges of the Department of the Seine offered a happy solution for the problems of working-class housing in Paris. It would give workers not just a place to live but also a way to enjoy more healthy surroundings and to own property and a house of their own. It would bring new opportunities to the housing industry, enabling it to provide low-cost housing within the free market. Finally, for social reformers suburbanization held out the hope of creating a new working class, tying it firmly by property ownership to middle-class morals and politics. Like the American West, the Paris suburbs offered the tantalizing prospect of a physical resolution for social conflict.

Yet as Bobigny demonstrated, the Paris suburbs became a symbol not of class conciliation but of sharpened class warfare. The workers who moved out to the suburbs after 1900 wanted cheap housing and a decent place to live as well. Their disappointed hopes were a crucial factor in the birth of the Paris Red Belt. The failure to develop urban facilities quickly enough for the rapidly growing population caused miserable living conditions in these new suburbs. Above all, the proliferation of defective allotments in the suburbs turned large areas into instant slums and deeply embittered their new residents, showing them clearly that low-cost housing built by the free market was low-quality housing. As the workers of Bobigny learned, class differences did not end at the city limits.

The Growth of Bobigny

In all the Department of the Seine, the problem of defective allotments was most severe in the northeastern suburbs of Paris, especially in the fastest growing canton of Noisy-le-Sec. Whereas the suburbs of the Seine as a whole increased in population by 253 percent between 1896 and 1931, the rate for the communities of the Noisy canton over the same period was 671 percent. The rapid growth of the area was reflected in the pace of housing construction. From 1896 to 1926 the number of buildings in the Seine suburbs increased 244 percent; the corresponding increase in the Noisy canton was 579 percent, and Drancy, the community growing fastest, achieved an astounding 4,820 percent. The canton's greatest increase was in the number of two-story buildings, the most common type of construction in the allotments.[1]

Suburbanization proceeded so rapidly in the northeastern suburbs because they offered more open land, thanks to the success of early twentieth-century market gardening, which preserved this area's agricultural landholding patterns. In addition, the proximity of the Noisy canton to the most proletarian and industrial areas of Paris made it a favored location for the working-class families who were a large percentage of the migrants to the suburbs in these years. Finally, mass transit facilities between this area and Paris underwent a major expansion; the number of tramway lines serving the area rose from three in 1901 to thirteen in 1930. The combined effect of these factors made the canton of Noisy-le-Sec an especially attractive and accessible choice for working-class families trying to move to the Paris suburbs.[2]

Among the communities in the interwar period, Bobigny illustrates the region's unplanned urbanization and the plight of the *mal-lotis*, or residents of defective allotments. Not its most extreme case, Bobigny was nonetheless severely affected by the process; moreover its political reaction to urbanization was especially sharp. Therefore the experience of Bobigny in the early twentieth century offers valuable information on the impacts of rapid urbanization.[3]

Although the nearby communities of Bondy and Drancy outstripped it, Bobigny grew dramatically in this period.[4] The population of Bobigny began growing markedly at the beginning of the century (Table 4); the peak years of its expansion were from 1916 to 1931, when the city's size increased by 357 percent. During these years the

TABLE 4

GROWTH OF THE POPULATION OF BOBIGNY

Year	Population	Percentage
1896	1,678	100
1901	1,946	116
1906	2,438	145
1911	3,660	218
1916	4,860	290
1921	6,757	403
1926	11,412	680
1931	17,370	1035
1936	17,676	1053

SOURCE: Listes nominatives du recensement, Bobigny: 1896–1936.

phenomenon of allotments reached its apogee in the Paris area, and characterized the settlement of Bobigny.

One important index of urbanization is the pace of construction. From 1896 to 1926 the number of buildings in Bobigny multiplied by more than eight times. In 1900 Bobigny had approximately 250 houses; by 1911 this figure had climbed to over 650 and to nearly 3,500 by 1936. Between 1911 and 1926 more than 2,500 houses were built, at an approximate rate of 170 new houses each year. A city council report from 1923 notes that 600 new houses were erected in Bobigny in the first half of 1922. This number (perhaps extravagant) indicates the frenetic pace of housing construction that characterized Bobigny in the first three decades of the twentieth century. In 1926, for example, 280 new houses were built; most had two stories and were located in the eastern part of the community, especially in the Pont de Bondy, the main neighborhood of allotments.[5]

The changing ratio between improved and unimproved property provides another indication of Bobigny's rapid growth. In 1900, according to municipal tax rolls, unimproved property produced slightly more in tax revenues than did improved property: 4,571 francs to 4,421 francs. By 1915, however, the tax revenue produced by improved property was 225 percent of that produced by unimproved property. Since most of the latter was agricultural land, this statistic demonstrates Bobigny's progressive urbanization.[6] Population growth in Bobigny brought about a higher population density. In 1901 there were fewer than three people per hectare in Bobigny, whereas there were ten by 1921 and twenty-six by 1931. Thus by the 1920s the town attained a population density that at the turn of the century had characterized only its center. This population density became uniform across Bobigny; the average number of households per building, for example, remained between 1.5 and 2 from 1896 to 1936.[7]

Urbanization thus converted former fields or gardens into housing developments, usually in allotments. Rather than crowd more people into areas that were already inhabited and expand services, it had to develop their rudimentary components from scratch in the areas of new settlement. Both increased population density and its concentration in certain areas, especially the eastern end, contributed to the problems Bobigny faced in trying to absorb new immigrants.[8]

Although proximity to working-class Paris and the availability of cheap land explain the suburbanization of Bobigny in the early twentieth century, the factor of greatest immediate significance in unleashing this process was the establishment in September 1902 of tramway service between Bobigny and Paris. Because of the tramway's role in integrating Bobigny into the Paris metropolitan region and promoting settlement in the community, Sam Bass Warner's term, "streetcar suburb," applies here. Tramway service was not simply a factor promoting urbanization; it also helped determine the quality of life in Bobigny. The innovations and deficiencies of public transportation conditioned Bobigny's problematic urban development.[9]

The formation of allotments and the influx of newcomers into Bobigny slightly antedated the first tramway line. It was already possible, although difficult, to reach Paris via public transportation; the first allotment was opened in 1901. However, the interest in Bobigny that real estate developers showed before 1902 was essentially speculative, based on the evolution of the land market in the northeastern suburban area. As abbé Ferret noted, the arrival of the tramway in 1902 quickened the hopes of these prospective developers and made the suburbanization of Bobigny inevitable:

> The peasants of Bobigny contemplated these ravages, thinking dolorously that their land would be spoiled; but upon reflection they said to themselves: "These . . . speculators, these land salesmen are making a false step. Who would want to move to our city, where the only work is agriculture, where there is no means of transport to get to Paris?"
>
> They were wrong. One day an unforeseen, extraordinary piece of news circulated among them: a tramway! A tramway was going to be established in Bobigny![10]

In spite of Ferret's account, its arrival in Bobigny was not unforeseen. A tramway was not only anticipated but loudly demanded by certain residents. The Bobigny correspondents of the regional newspaper *Paris-Est*, representing the community's Radical forces, took an especially lively interest in establishing tramway service and called on the city council to set it up. Petitions to be sent to the East Parisian Tramway Company demanding the opening of tramway service in Bobigny also circulated among the local population. In general Balbynians strongly favored such a move; the tramway was a representative of progress and modernity, and of the growth of their community. *Paris-Est* argued that, in addition to its convenience, a tramway would bring more taxpayers to Bobigny and thus make it easier to pay for improvements like new schools.[11]

On this issue the market gardeners were divided. On the one hand, they seemed to accept the prevailing idea that a tramway equaled progress and to favor the convenience that it would bring. On the other, many feared that a tramway linking Bobigny to Paris would provoke a rise in land prices as the speculators moved in and thus in rents they paid for their own plots. Since Bobigny's Radicals—largely supported by and identified with the market gardeners—were firm advocates of the tramway, this group's general identification with the well-being and development of Bobigny probably overrode their fears of the consequences of this change.[12]

In July 1902, after much public debate in Bobigny, Mayor Antoine Boyer went to the director of the East Parisian Tramway Company to lobby for tram service to Bobigny. Insisting on the impossibility of a direct tramway line between Bobigny and Paris, the director proposed an alternative: a line would go from the place de l'Opéra in Paris to the Limites area on the border of Pantin and Bobigny; travelers would be able to continue to downtown Bobigny by shuttle service. Ultimately this form of service was decided on, and the Bobigny–Opéra line opened for business in September 1902. Tramcars were scheduled to run every forty minutes from the Limites area, from 5:40 A.M. to 9:40 A.M.[13]

The tram company's decision to grant only partial service, a shuttle from Pantin instead of a direct line from Paris, was coolly received by Balbynians. In addition to the inconvenience it involved, this route seemed to suggest that Bobigny was worthy only of second-class service; it grated on local pride. So although the people of Bobigny were glad to have tram service, they felt that the particular form did not suit the needs of their community. Discontent with the tram in its first few years of operation was intensified by its failure to run on time; people complained of waiting in vain forty minutes for the tram. Not until the summer of 1904 was the shuttle system replaced by a direct Bobigny–Opéra tramline.

Tram service expanded in 1911 when a second line came into operation. This line, Bobigny–Les Halles, went from the Six Routes area in north central Bobigny to Les Halles in the middle of Paris. Passing through the capital's industrial nineteenth district, the new tramline eased the commute for many of Bobigny's workers. These two lines provided their public transportation until 1921 when a third line, from Six Routes to the place de la République in Paris, was added to the community's tram network.[14]

Although public transportation expanded from one tramline in 1902 to three in 1921, Balbynians continued to argue that it failed to meet their needs. Not until the 1930s, when the tram network in the city was further expanded and supplemented by bus lines, did the amount of service available seem adequate to local inhabitants. The deficiencies of public transportation involved, however, not just the quantity of its service but also its quality and organization. Since complaints about tram service in the first three decades of the century focused on a few central grievances, I will look at public transportation in Bobigny in this period as a whole, rather than chronologically.

Perhaps the greatest source of discontent over Bobigny's tram network was the system of working-class trams. These were simply the third-class cars on the trams; third-class tickets had to be purchased in advance, in book form. However, trams carried third-class cars only during the week, and then only during prime commuting hours. Most important, local commuters complained, was the shortage of working-class trams. In Bobigny the typical rush-hour tram consisted of one or two third-class cars, each with a capacity of forty to fifty passengers. Since most commuters took the tram, these cars were seriously overcrowded. In 1911 a city council report noted that the morning's first tram regularly carried over one hundred fifty people in its two third-class cars; normally maximum capacity was forty-seven people per car. Until 1915 there was only one third-class car on the Bobigny–Opéra line in the morning. In the evening, for working-class commuters the situation was worse. Since the morning's tram originated in Bobigny, finding a place in the morning was easier than during the evening's rush hour. Moreover, the number of third-class cars was sometimes reduced from two to one in the evenings. Therefore those holders of third-class tickets who could find no place in the working-class car would be forced either to pay more to ride in a first- or second-class car or to walk home. On more than one occasion, the overcrowding led workers to heated arguments and even fistfights.[15]

The trams' morning schedules also caused difficulties, especially in the winter, since the first trams did not leave until 6:30 A.M., instead of 5:30 A.M. as in the summer. Many workers commuting to jobs in Paris would fail to arrive on time at their workplace. As a result, some walked to work in the winter, often starting out at 5 A.M. The lack of working-class tram service on weekends not only hindered Balbynians' freedom of movement but also prevented Parisians of modest means from traveling to Bobigny on Sundays.[16]

Another inadequacy of Bobigny's public transportation strongly concerned workers, although it was not linked to working-class trams: the absence of any tramlines serving the Pont de Bondy or eastern Bobigny. This problem was partially corrected in the early 1920s, when a branch of the Bobigny–Opéra line was extended to Pavillons-sous-Bois, east of Bobigny. As residents of the Pont de Bondy complained, however, these trams were often full in the morning by the time they got to Bobigny. Since eastern Bobigny contained the largest concentration of working-class commuters, many of these workers had to walk two to three kilometers from the tram stop in Six Routes to their homes.[17]

Finally, the cost of public transportation presented a problem to some Balbynians. As we noted earlier, in the Paris area a tram fare was inexpensive; the round-trip fare between Bobigny and Paris on a working-class tram was seventy or eighty centimes. Still, it did represent an important sum (roughly an hour's wages) for Bobigny residents of modest means; a city council report noted in 1908 that many women and apprentice workers walked to their jobs in Paris rather than pay the tram fare. Moreover, the cost went up for travel out of commuter rush hours, or for those occasions when workers rode in first- or second-class cars because the third-class ones were full.[18]

In 1927 two new tramlines significantly improved the amount of public transportation available to Bobigny's residents. In that same year Bobigny's first bus line, the EN, began running from Le Bourget to Noisy-le-Sec; this line enabled factory workers to reach their jobs in other northeastern suburbs without first going through Paris. A total of six public transportation lines served the community, which kept this level of public transportation until World War II. By 1937 the tram lines had been replaced by six bus lines.[19]

As we can see, for Balbynians in the early twentieth century the problem of public transportation was commuting to work. They used trams and buses to get to their jobs during the week. Because of Bobigny's low level of industrial development before the late 1920s, the majority of its residents worked elsewhere. Of the 599 Bobigny workers whose places of employment I traced from the 1931 census, over 70 percent worked in other cities (Table 5).[20]

Commuting to work, which gave workers greater choice of where to work and how to deal with the housing shortage in Paris, nevertheless had disadvantages. The most obvious was the time it consumed. To get from Six Routes in Bobigny to the place de la République in Paris by tram took nearly one hour. Therefore, a resident of the Pont de Bondy who worked in Paris would probably need well over two hours for the commute, which swallowed up any gains in leisure time created in 1919 by the eight-hour day. Those who worked in adjacent communities like Pantin were fortunate in avoiding such long commutes. By contrast, because direct connections between suburbs were few, Balbynians who worked in more distant communities like Saint-Denis usually had to transfer in Paris first, making their daily commutes even more arduous.[21]

For suburban workers, the expense of commuting did not stop at transportation. In addition they had to pay for meals at local restaurants since they could not go home for lunch.[22] Moreover, if workers lost their jobs, those living in the industrial areas of Paris could turn to other workplaces in the immediate area for a new job. Living in a commuter suburb made it more difficult to find another. Without an

TABLE 5

BOBIGNY WORKERS' PLACES OF EMPLOYMENT

Place	Number	Percentage
Paris	217	37
Bobigny	176	29
Noisy-le-Sec	67	11
Pantin	61	10
Romainville	20	3
Other	58	10

SOURCE: Listes nominatives du recensement, Bobigny: 1931.

income, workers found the costs of searching for a job farther away more imposing.[23]

In sum, public transportation made Bobigny's metamorphosis into a working-class commuter suburb possible. Yet until the late 1920s it did not adequately serve the community. Whereas the suburb's population grew sixfold from 1902 to 1926, the carrying capacity of the trams only tripled. Moreover, in eastern Bobigny, where population growth was greatest and new working-class and lower-middle-class commuters were most dependent on public transportation, the transit system was poorest. Thus in public transportation, as in other aspects of Bobigny's urbanization, there was a serious lag between population growth and the development of corresponding adequate urban services. The gap did not close until the late 1920s and 1930s.[24]

The Crisis of Allotments

This gap between size of population and urban development most troubled Bobigny's residents in the matter of allotments. Until the national government's efforts to clean up the defective allotments began to bear fruit in the early 1930s, the allotments would symbolize the difficulties of over-rapid and unplanned urbanization.[25] By the 1930s roughly sixty allotments had been established in Bobigny. The first one opened in 1901, and by 1911 Bobigny had eleven allotments; seven more started up before the First World War. The high point in the development of allotments in Bobigny came in the 1920s: nineteen allotments were established from 1922 to 1928. No more occurred between 1928 and the end of the 1930s; the Sarraut Law of 1928 set binding conditions on developers that made the opening of allotments like those in Bobigny either illegal or unprofitable. The development of allotments thus followed the pace that prevailed in the Paris region.[26]

Few of Bobigny's allotments were created by the original landowners themselves. Instead, real estate developers bought the land and divided it into individual lots. Abbé Ferret describes this process:

> There were certain well-advised people who understood the need of the Parisian population to spread out beyond the city walls; this need could be exploited and become a gold mine, a good business.
>
> Forty, sixty, eighty thousand [square] meters of agricultural land was bought up at low prices, 1 franc, 1.25, 1.50, 1.75 the meter, a price that was nevertheless a good deal for the peasant seller, who had earlier bought the same lands at 25 or 50 centimes a meter at most.[27]

Although several small developers in Bobigny owned a single allotment, large entrepreneurs predominated. Over half the allotments for which I identified a developer were begun by just two entrepreneurs, Brigeois and Penteuil. The majority of these developers worked out of Paris, and the rest often had offices in other suburbs. Only three developers I was able to trace were based in Bobigny, and each of these owned only one small allotment. Thus right from the start interests from Paris and other parts of the metropolitan region took over the local land market, a crucial step in integrating Bobigny into the larger region.[28]

Once he had set up an allotment, the developer then marketed it in advertising posters scattered over a wide area, especially in the more urbanized nearby suburbs like Pantin and Pré-Saint-Gervais, and in the northeastern areas of Paris. A typical poster publicizing lots for sale in Bobigny's largest allotment, Nouveau Village, promised land starting at 2.50 francs the square meter, with eight years to pay; it emphasized the allotment's proximity to public transportation. It also stated that there would be no payments for paving the streets and constructing sidewalks (*travaux de viabilité*) but did not explain that these improvements had not been made and would not be provided by the developer. Prices of land for allotments ranged from 2.50 francs to 9 or 10 francs, and the size of the individual lots went from 200 to 500 square meters. The fact that most allotments had no paved streets, sidewalks, water, or gas service was not mentioned in these posters. In any case, the posters performed their function well; many Parisians who had formerly come to the town on Sundays or holidays to enjoy its pastoral ambiance were now coming in response to the advertising posters to investigate the possibility of becoming suburban property owners.[29]

By the end of the first decade of the twentieth century the phenomenon of allotments had changed the appearance and population of Bobigny. The 1911 census showed roughly eight hundred people living in allotments, or one-fifth to one-fourth of the population. By 1921 this figure had climbed to about three thousand five hundred, just over half the population (or equal to its entire population in 1911); by 1931, when all the city's allotments had been established, the number of their residents approached eleven thousand; roughly two out of every three Balbynians were allotment dwellers.[30] This expansion of the allotments marked the physical appearance of Bobigny:

> around the market gardeners' fields, hemming them in more closely every day, one can see the roofs of the new little houses which continue on into infinity.... The little village of half a century ago has been entirely submerged; the old town center has not changed, with its badly paved streets, its decaying farm walls, and its dismal dirty gray-white façades; but

one can see toward the east an allotment, which has already more than seven thousand inhabitants and is still growing, known by the suggestive name "Nouveau Village," while a little farther to the north a second allotment, the "Village parisien," already houses almost six thousand.[31]

As the quotation suggests, most of the allotments were located in Bobigny's eastern section. At the turn of the century it consisted of farmers' fields. Since these *cultivateurs* were hard pressed by the competing market gardeners, and since their lands were generally cheaper, allotment developers often bought their property. As a result, this area was transformed in the first two decades of the century; thirty-five of the city's sixty allotments, including almost all the largest ones, were located in that section of Bobigny extending east of the Six Routes intersection. Twenty-six allotments, including giants like Nouveau Village and Village parisien, were established in the Pont de Bondy. This section symbolized the new Bobigny.

The new Bobigny was decidedly more proletarian than the old. As elsewhere in the Paris region, buyers of allotments in Bobigny tended to be either working class or lower middle class (*employés*). A sociological study of three Bobigny allotments in 1921 revealed that three-fourths of the residents belonged to these two groups. As the population of the allotments rose, the share of workers and employés in the city's population increased as well: in 1900 over half the people living in Bobigny were farmers and market gardeners; by 1911 they were workers and employés.[32]

In Bobigny as elsewhere, those who bought land in allotments had to provide the housing; most built their own. Purchasers would either camp out on their land or commute from a former residence to work on the new house. The quality of allotment housing in Bobigny varied greatly. In general, houses were simple one- or two-story structures with three or four rooms, a kitchen, and sometimes an indoor toilet. Some were fairly well built, especially those belonging to construction workers or their relatives. More often, however, they were ramshackle buildings that testified to their owners' lack of construction skills and money for materials of good quality. Abbé Ferret describes a typical allotment house:

> It is supported by four piles set into the ground, in rectangular position; two of these piles are higher than the other two facing them, which gives the roof a slope. The piles are linked by crossbeams, onto which are nailed or otherwise affixed all kinds of pieces of wood . . . then the four walls are formed by pieces of old billboards and doors, which have been joined together as much as possible; encased in the wall is one small window, very

used, bought for a few pennies at a secondhand store . . . the door is formed of an old, faded piece of fabric full of holes.[33]

Elsewhere in his account abbé Ferret even notes families living in tents and holes in the ground!

The discomforts of Bobigny's allotment dwellers did not end with the poor housing they were often forced to inhabit. Bobigny's allotments were defective: they lacked basic amenities of paved streets, sidewalks, sewers, water, gas, or electrical service. Of fifteen major allotments in Bobigny, twelve had no paved streets or sidewalks; twelve lacked sewers, and twelve had no water mains.[34] Included in the contracts of most allotments was a clause stating that the lot owners, not the developers, were responsible for all improvements. This stipulation usually came as a nasty surprise to the lot purchasers, who generally lacked the background to understand the legalistic writing of the contracts.[35]

Most developers chose to show their allotments to prospective buyers during the spring and summer, adding to the disillusion after a purchase. Camping out in a field in the summer seemed almost picturesque. The allotments presented a much less favorable appearance when the rains of winter turned unpaved streets into mud (a very frequent complaint among allotment dwellers) or caused floods, as in 1910. Moreover, walking to a streetside fountain to fetch the household's water supply was an onerous task once it turned cold.[36]

In any season, however, Bobigny's defective allotments in no way corresponded to the images their residents had cherished of life in the beautiful countryside. On the contrary, those who fled the slums of Paris found that miserable housing conditions accompanied them in their move to the suburbs. An official report on one allotment gives a good general view of these developments:

> These two streets . . . are unpaved, and have never been the subject of any improvements.
> Because of this situation, during rainy seasons they present the aspect of veritable cesspools; the rutted ground is covered by a thick layer of mud; because of the lack of drainage facilities, the water disappears slowly through evaporation or absorption into the soil.
> Moreover, because of the absence of facilities permitting the evacuation of waste waters, they are therefore poured onto the ground, where they stay. During the summer these putrid waters favor the breeding of mosquitoes and give off unhealthy odors.[37]

Not surprisingly, the proliferation of defective allotments in Bobigny resulted in poor health for their inhabitants, which was a paradox of suburbanization. Prompted to move by a desire to escape unhealthy urban living conditions and breathe fresh country air, many immigrants found instead health conditions as bad as, even worse than, those prevailing in the poorer neighborhoods of Paris. Basic health statistics from 1920 to 1924 for Bobigny and for the eighth and twentieth districts of Paris show this dismal contrast (Table 6).[38] In the slums of Paris, a major reason for high rates of disease was overcrowded housing, a problem in Bobigny also, even though its population density was lower.[39] But more than in Paris, in Bobigny's housing developments the lack of proper sanitation led to poor health conditions. Although the allotments were not the only source, they were a major factor in the unhealthy life in the community.[40]

The paucity of medical facilities also contributed to poor health. Before the Second World War, Bobigny's only hospital was the Franco-Moslem Hospital, founded in 1935, which was reserved for the use of Moslems. Other Balbynians who needed hospitalization were obliged to go outside the town to obtain it or to use the community's one small health clinic downtown. In the first decade of the century the only health practitioners in Bobigny were two midwives (*sages femmes*); no physician resided in the city until 1911. In 1922 a second physician opened a practice, and a third in 1930. By the end of the decade the community had five practicing physicians for its population of over seventeen thousand.[41] Bobigny's inadequacies in health care facilities and staff, combined with its defective allotments, thus resulted in a painful contrast to the image of clean country living held up to many of its new inhabitants.

TABLE 6

HEALTH STATISTICS FOR BOBIGNY

(per 10,000 persons)

	Paris−8	Paris−20	Bobigny
Pulmonary tuberculosis (birth−1 year old)	5.1	19.8	21.9
Pneumonia (40−59 years old)	3.2	5.3	7.2
General mortality (all ages)	109.6	161.2	172.3

SOURCE: Grégoire Ichok, *La Mortalité à Paris et dans le département de la Seine* (Paris, 1937), pp. 96, 127, 144.

An Inadequate Urban Structure

Traditionally, the image of suburbia predominant in France and America has been of communities whose primary function is to house people employed in a nearby city, to become ghost towns during the day when commuters are at work. Unable to compete with corresponding establishments downtown, in such communities commercial, industrial, and entertainment enterprises are underdeveloped and often lack cohesion and focus.[42] To see whether this image characterizes Bobigny in the early twentieth century, we must examine its commercial, industrial, and entertainment sector. Does the gap between growth of population and urban development that marked the allotments also exist here? This is a question not just of their aggregate numbers but of their characteristics. Also important is their location, to see how the geography of commercial and industrial enterprises reflects Bobigny's populations. How well do Bobigny's commercial establishments supply its goods and services?

The business sector in Bobigny expanded at a rate roughly comparable to that of the population until the 1920s. The spectacular growth in Bobigny's population that occurred in the 1920s was not matched in its new business establishments (Table 7).[43]

Food stores dominated the commercial sector: butchers, bakers, grocery stores (*épiceries*), and delicatessens (*charcuteries*) were the most important; the number of all food stores in Bobigny rose from nine in 1901 to one hundred two in 1939. Cafés and restaurants were numerous, constituting the largest single category; their ranks grew from ten in 1901 to sixty-two in 1931. The town's sartorial needs were

TABLE 7

GROWTH OF BOBIGNY'S BUSINESS SECTOR

(in percentages)

	Commerce[a]	Industry[a]	Services[a]	Entertainment[a]	Population[b]
1901	100	100	—	100	100
1911	233	300	100	270	188
1921	308	600	280	370	347
1931	675	957	500	660	893
1939	1308	1114	1040	880	908

SOURCE: Bibliothèque administrative de l'hôtel de ville, Paris: Annuaire de commerce —Didot Bottin, 1901, 1911, 1921, 1931, and 1939.

[a] 100% = initial number of establishments.

[b] 100% = population in 1901.

taken care of by its haberdasheries (*merceries*), which changed from one in 1901 to four in 1939. Bobigny households were provided with fuel by two coal dealers in 1901, twelve in 1939. Although Bobigny's commercial sector kept the same structure throughout the early twentieth century, by 1939 it had grown enormously, to nearly twice as many stores as in 1931.[44]

Service establishments, an important subsector of commerce, came into being in Bobigny after World War I, and their numbers remained small during most of the period. In 1921 the fourteen services included two hairdressers, two lawyers (*contentieux*), two pharmacists, one physician, and a real estate agent. Ten years later the number of physicians and hairdressers had tripled, and the town had added a dentist and a launderer to its services. By 1939 Bobigny had a flourishing services sector, indicating the development of an urban culture in the community.[45]

Commercial entertainment during this period was rudimentary. Aside from its two movie theaters, opened in the late 1920s, Bobigny's only commercial facilities devoted to social life were the cafés. These were either ordinary cafés and wineshops, or *vins-restaurants,* which served full meals and alcoholic beverages. Most cafés in Bobigny offered no music or other entertainment but were simply places to sit, talk, and drink.[46]

In general, from 1901 to 1939 the expansion of the business sector in Bobigny kept pace with population growth. During the 1930s, population growth halted while the number of establishments increased, compensating for its slow development in the 1920s. Even during the 1920s food stores, the most common businesses, grew at about the same rate as the population. Nonetheless, Bobigny's sparse service and entertainment facilities during the 1920s diminished the quality of life by making shopping there inconvenient.

The main deficiency of Bobigny's businesses was not so much their inadequate number as their uneven distribution throughout the community. During the early twentieth century the city center around the place Carnot had more stores than other areas did, a legacy of the earlier years when most of the town's population lived in the center. Its businesses simply did not spread out into the neighborhoods as quickly as the population did. A few outlying establishments opened during the 1930s, but most food stores, cafés, and other commercial shops remained located within a half-mile radius of the city center. On the town's eastern fringes, by contrast, the Pont de Bondy contained more than one-third of Bobigny's population by the 1930s but nowhere near one-third of its businesses. In 1931, for example, fewer than one-fifth of the city's food stores, fewer than a quarter of its cafés, and none of its service establishments were located in this neighborhood.

The Pont de Bondy's commercial structure presented a stunted appearance simply because it was growing so rapidly. But allotment developers added to its problems by neglecting to allocate space for future businesses when drawing up the plans of their allotments. As a result, the dreary suburban aspect that typified Bobigny in the early twentieth century was especially pronounced in this main area of recent settlement, eastern Bobigny. Its residents were put to more inconvenience by the shortage of stores than were other Balbynians; the experience of these prime representatives of the new, urbanized Bobigny sharply illustrates the uneven urbanization.

During the early twentieth century Bobigny's industrial establishments were mostly either artisans' workshops or small factories; throughout this period their growth kept pace with that of the large industrial concerns. Artisans' shops were about half of the industries in Bobigny; their number grew from six in 1901 to forty-four in 1939, when they included six shoemakers, four carpenters, three masons, and two watchmakers. Although the number of these businesses expanded, as a proportion of industry in Bobigny they declined. More than commercial businesses, artisans' workshops were scattered over the community, including several in the Pont de Bondy; however, the greatest concentrations remained in the center and in the industrial zone along the rue de Paris and the canal de l'Ourcq.[47]

The character of nonartisanal manufacturing, by contrast, did change greatly from 1901 to 1939. In number of businesses, the largest subcategory of industry in Bobigny was construction: from 1901 to 1939 the number of such firms increased from one to sixteen. The boom in the local construction industry was a function of the growth in Bobigny; although many new residents built their own homes, not all did, and new businesses usually resorted to private contractors. Rather than engage in construction, many businesses in this sector sold construction materials like bricks and lumber. The construction industry accounted for most of Bobigny's small industrial firms, which were often hard to differentiate from artisanal workshops.[48] By the 1930s, after the great wave of allotment development subsided, this sector stopped growing. The firms hired to implement improvements on the allotments under the Sarraut Law after 1928 came from outside Bobigny, whose enterprises were too small to handle such projects.

The two other large industries in Bobigny, metallurgy and chemicals, were more modern. From the 1840s, as noted in chapter 1, the chemical industry was suburban. It was the most common industry in Bobigny at the beginning of the century; in 1901 three of the five nonartisanal manufacturers were chemical firms. By 1931 the number of chemical establishments in Bobigny had grown to nine, including two manufacturers of lubricants, a wax factory, and a carbolic acid plant. Although this subsector expanded less rapidly than did the construction industry, it had more factories than semiartisanal businesses. The chemical industry was a major pollutant in Bobigny; many residents opposed its growth.[49]

Metallurgy was Bobigny's most modern industry and employed the most workers by the 1930s. The first factory was the Bocrie car plant, founded in 1903. By 1931 the city had nine metallurgical factories, including two car plants, a sheet iron manufacturer, and other smaller metal shops. Alone among Bobigny's industries and manufacturing, metallurgy continued to expand after the early 1930s. By 1939 the number of metallurgical establishments had doubled, and its eighteen plants included the Franco-Belge foundry and the Repiquet metalworks, both employing over one hundred workers. Most metallurgical plants in Bobigny were newer than the chemical plants, and larger than the average local manufacture. As in France as a whole, in Bobigny metallurgy symbolized industrial modernity.[50]

Like its commerce, Bobigny's industry was decentralized to a certain extent. At the turn of the century the only industrial zone was at the town's southern edge, extending along the canal de l'Ourcq. By the 1930s, it was still the largest industrial zone but manufacturing had spread. Several firms opened along the main streets of Bobigny—especially the route des Petits Ponts, but also the rue de la République, the route de Bondy, and the route de Saint-Denis; the Six Routes intersection was the third area of industrial concentration. By contrast, the Pont de Bondy or the other allotments had only scattered, individual industries, none of them large. Finally, as with the commercial sector, the growth of industry did not keep pace with increases in population in the 1920s and made up for this lag in the 1930s, by expanding the metallurgical sector.[51]

Bobigny's small industrial sector underscored the community's lack of autonomy. First, it meant that most working-class Balbynians had to find work outside their community. Comparing their life to the prospect of life in a more industrialized area like Aubervilliers, many inhabitants felt they had the advantage. Still, they had to deal with the inconveniences of commuting. Their modest average incomes combined with the lack of industry to produce a low tax base for the community, which increased the difficulty of developing adequate urban services and emphasized the city's economic dependence and its inability to benefit from the resources created by the labor power of its citizens.[52] Throughout Bobigny, examples of incomplete suburbanization—gaps and shortages in essential urban facilities and services—abounded. They were especially pronounced in the first two decades of the twentieth century, when local population growth far outstripped the expansion and modernization of Bobigny's existing amenities.

At the turn of the century Bobigny had only eleven paved streets, mostly in the center of town. Since the rest was agricultural fields, and since local farmers and market gardeners used their wagons for transportation, its unpaved streets were no inconvenience. As the population grew after 1900, however, these unpaved streets were more heavily used; few newcomers possessed farm wagons to negotiate the rutted thoroughfares. One of the worst was the chemin de Groslay, which formed Bobigny's eastern border with the suburb of Bondy. The construction in the Nouveau Village and Village parisien allotments had greatly increased the wear and tear on this road, once used only by farmers to reach their fields. In 1912 a local journalist described "the famous" chemin de Groslay as "transformed during the rainy season into a veritable lake. . . . From November on, the use of this road becomes absolutely impractical, although it is the only one that permits the inhabitants of Village parisien to go to their homes."[53] The fact that Bobigny and Bondy shared the chemin de Groslay made organizing its paving complicated; its location at the extreme eastern end of town helps explain why it was unpaved until 1920. The city council was able to pave most of Bobigny's public roads—those not belonging to allotments—by 1910. Although the allotments went unpaved, at least the main thoroughfares of Bobigny became negotiable.[54]

Beyond paving roads, Bobigny's city council did little until the 1920s to correct the inadequacies that growth created or exacerbated. Water service was one of the main problems. In 1903 the city government negotiated an agreement with the General Water Company to place four streetside water pumps (*bornes-fontaines*) in the center of town. A fifth one was added in 1906 in south central Bobigny, but no other beyond the center until 1912, when a sixth water pump was set up in the Six Routes area. The Pont de Bondy and some other neighborhoods never received water pumps at all and had to wait for water service until a municipal system of water mains was developed in the 1920s.[55]

There was little gas and electric service until the 1920s; Balbynians were without electricity until the Communist municipality developed its electrification project after 1925. Gas service in Bobigny in 1900 consisted solely of downtown street lighting, inadequate to the needs of growing numbers of commuters, many of whom had a fairly long walk to and from the tram. During the winter months commuters would arrive at the end of the tramline after nightfall to make their way home in the dark. In 1907 the city council considered extending street lighting from the downtown area to the Six Routes intersection but never followed through on the project. Gas illuminated only the downtown streets until the 1920s.[56]

Few facilities for education developed before the 1920s. At the turn of the century the community had a boys' and a girls' school, both located downtown. Although it enlarged them somewhat in the first two decades of the century, this expansion was far outstripped by the growth of the school-age population, which quadrupled between 1900 and 1921. No school existed in the Pont de Bondy neighborhood, which by 1913 had 220 school-age children; many parents paid to send their children to school in Bondy. The city council considered building schools in the Pont de Bondy and ratified the idea in principle before World War I; but again, nothing came of this until the 1920s.[57]

The first twenty years of the century provided other, less imposing, examples of the failure of Bobigny's institutions and services to compensate for the tremendous growth and change in its population. Residents of various neighborhoods said they wanted tobacconists or requested an expanded postal service; the city had no garbage collection service during the first decade. Overstrained local resources even involved the dead; although admitting the inadequacy of the town cemetery, the city council made no move to enlarge it until 1921.[58]

In general, municipal services failed to meet the needs of the newcomers who flooded into Bobigny after 1900. In contrast to the commercial and industrial sectors, public services lagged behind the growing population in the first two decades of the twentieth century; after 1920 the city government began to close the gap. All these problems arose from one source, the low average income of Bobigny's population. Moreover, since Bobigny lacked industry and commerce, it could not afford to expand municipal services from its limited tax base. All aspects of urban underdevelopment combined to magnify the inconveniences and difficulties for the working-class Balbynians with modest incomes. Life in this Parisian suburb had a grim, dismal air, which mocked the newcomers' hopes for a better life.[59]

The salient characteristic of Bobigny's suburbanization at the beginning of the twentieth century was the failure of urban institutions to expand at a rate equaling the growth of population. In many respects Bobigny retained the structure of an overgrown village well into the 1920s. The reluctance of the municipal government to upgrade its facilities certainly did not help matters; dominated by the market gardeners until 1920, the city council reflected their indifference to improvements they did not need. Not until the Communists, representing the community's newcomers, came to control did the municipality begin to address some of these problems.[60]

The deficiencies of Bobigny's suburbanization came both from its sluggish response and from its uneven development, as the contrast between the center and the peripheral areas of the community illustrates. In downtown Bobigny, urban institutions developed along with population growth: here commercial life flourished, tramway service was convenient, the streets were paved, and schools were nearby. Such amenities were less common and life was more difficult in the newly populated areas of eastern Bobigny like the Pont de Bondy. Yet it was here that the rate of population growth was greatest and the widening gap most evident. Moreover, these were the proletarian districts, whereas the local elite, mainly shopkeepers and artisans, tended to live downtown.[61]

It is true that the rapidity of Bobigny's population growth made it difficult, if not impossible, for the network of urban institutions to keep pace, no matter what the population was. As we have seen, the insufficiency of commercial institutions (rather than their uneven geographical distribution) became apparent only during the 1920s. The rapidity of Bobigny's growth was itself a consequence of the limited housing choices for the Paris area's working class; the wealthy had no problem in finding decent places to live without joining the workers' exodus to a community like Bobigny. New Balbynians could not stretch their low incomes to provide the amenities their community lacked.

Above all, the defective allotments constituted the major problem of Bobigny's suburbanization; they were residential areas without amenities or improvements. They arose in places that private real estate developers found unprofitable and in situations where governmental authorities were unwilling to intervene to make sure that the housing needs of people of modest means were met. As a result, in Bobigny thousands of people lived in places that remained simply farmers' fields. Their choice of an allotment was to a certain extent positive, but it was a choice conditioned by ignorance and severely limited by a lack of alternatives.[62] For workers, life in the allotments meant not just material deprivation but also a bitter sense of hopes betrayed. By and large they had expected life to be better in their new homes; that it was in some ways worse created profound disenchantment.[63] Bobigny's suburbanization did not just fail to erase class distinctions; it reinforced them dramatically.

The political implications that the allotments carried were not lost on observers of the Parisian working class in the 1920s. Rightist commentators like Wladimir d'Ormesson saw this issue as the key to Communist strength and thus as an urgent danger to the nation:

> The nerve center of French communism is Paris, or more specifically, its suburbs . . . the hordes of the Communist army consist of a few full-time fomentors of the jacquerie, the Fronde, the revolutions of Paris, surrounded by a large and increasing number of embittered, discontented, desperate souls who use the significant term *mal-lotis* to describe themselves. I would assert that out of every hundred Communists in the famous "Red Belt of Paris," for at least seventy-five of them communism is simply a question of the allotments.[64]

The crisis of allotments, combined with the shortages and scarcity of factories and workshops in Bobigny, made residential issues vitally important for the community's political life. The workers of Bobigny wanted more than anything else to shake off the mud of the defective allotments and create a decent place for themselves and their families to live. This desire, and the political terms in which they expressed it, would provide the foundations for red Bobigny.

CHAPTER 3

The People of Bobigny

On 20 December 1919, three weeks after his election as Bobigny's first Socialist mayor, Jean-Marie Clamamus undertook one of his more pleasant functions, officiating for the first time at a marriage ceremony. The groom was Jean-Paul Dupont, a twenty-two-year-old machinist from Paris, and the bride Claire Certeau, a twenty-year-old unemployed woman who lived with her parents in Bobigny. Claire Certeau and her family were typical Balbynians in several ways. Claire had been born in Nancy, her father's hometown; like many other immigrants from eastern France, her family arrived in the Paris area during World War I. Her parents, Pierre and Simone Certeau, settled in the La Favorite allotment of Bobigny, in the Anjou neighborhood north of downtown. Pierre Certeau periodically worked as a clerk or an unskilled laborer; like many other suburbanites, he was unemployed in 1931. His wife remained a housewife throughout the interwar period; at times she also worked as a foster mother, taking in infants from Paris.[1] The Certeaus—and their neighbors—typified working-class families in Bobigny, who were a majority of the population at the time of Claire's wedding and formed the local electoral base of communism in the interwar years. These new suburbanites were a key to the ability of the French Communists to forge a political consensus in the community.

Looking at the general population of Bobigny during this period, we are struck by the predominance of immigrants over native-born residents, and by the large working class. This young immigrant population of modest means lacked strong ties to any region of France and was already integrated into urban and industrial society. In short, Balbynians were people the PCF saw as its natural constituency and worked hard to attract.

Demography of the Paris Area

A look at greater Paris will give us some perspective on the population changes Bobigny experienced. This most economically developed part of the country experienced changes in population structure commonly associated with industrial growth more than the rest of the country.[2] The Paris area provided the greatest demographic contrast to the rest of France: whereas the nation was barely growing in the early twentieth century, the region around the capital was burgeoning. From 1906 to 1931 the departments of the Seine and Seine-et-Oise increased in population by 31 percent.[3] Their expansion was by no means the result of a high birthrate. Deaths exceeded births in the Department of the Seine, roughly as they did throughout the country. These statistics combine to show that immigration was a more significant element of the population in the Paris area than in the rest of France. From 1901 to 1931 the net figure for migrants into the Department of the Seine was over one million persons. This growth epitomized the increasing urbanization in the country.[4]

A low birthrate and a strongly immigrant population produced a very uneven age structure in the Paris area. Data for the city of Paris in 1931 show a population heavily concentrated in the productive years of adulthood. People under twenty and over fifty-nine formed a smaller percentage (about 30 percent) of the city's population than of the national populace.[5]

The occupational structure of the Paris area shifted during the early twentieth century, notably expanding the tertiary sector at the expense of traditional industry. While the latter portion of the economy grew by 32 percent from 1906 to 1931 (that is, at roughly the same rate as the population), the banking and commercial sector grew by 52 percent, liberal professions by 60 percent, and administrative services by 77 percent. This change was most noticeable in Paris, which was rapidly evolving from a city of workshops into one of offices; by 1931 the Parisian working class were only 31.5 percent of the city's population, as opposed to 40.7 percent in 1848. Yet the shift affected the suburbs as well; the class of industrial workers declined as a percentage of the

Paris area's population whereas lower level white-collar workers increased.[6] (Nothing we have seen of the occupational and class structures in Paris would predict success for political parties counting exclusively on a working-class base.)[7]

The population in the Paris suburbs was equally atypical for early twentieth-century France. Most important, the suburban areas of the Department of the Seine were growing at an even faster rate than Paris. For example, from 1911 to 1921 these suburbs grew at a rate of 17 percent while the capital achieved a rate of only 6.4 percent. As in the region as a whole, their growth resulted from migration, not natural increase by births. The rate of natural increase in the interwar suburbs was usually no more than 2 percent; by contrast, in the decade from 1921 to 1931 this area gained over 500,000 migrants while Paris lost over 50,000 citizens. Although many of these new suburbanites came from Paris or other parts of the metropolitan area, slightly more than 50 percent were of provincial origin. In general, they formed a young, low-income population, largely working class and lower middle class except in prosperous areas like Neuilly and Saint-Mandé.[8]

Births and Deaths in Bobigny

Many important changes in the population of greater Paris outlined above, such as the low and falling birthrates, arose from increasing urbanization. We might therefore expect such changes to appear in more exacerbated form in a community like Bobigny, which was one of the most extreme examples of urbanization during the interwar years. In some ways Bobigny followed, yet in others deviated sharply from, both national patterns and those of the Paris area.

It is the character of those deviations we must note. Between the wars Bobigny achieved recognition (for good or ill) primarily through its strong support for the PCF, a political deviation from the norms prevalent in France. Although the community's demographics did not explain its politics, they certainly had an indispensable part in the success of the Communists in Bobigny.

One characteristic of the population of the Paris area was low birth and death rates. As Bobigny was transformed from a largely rural community into a working-class suburb at the beginning of the twentieth century, its birthrate showed a steady decline. Although never as low as the average in the Department of the Seine, still less that in the city of Paris, in 1931, the rate dropped significantly.

Local rates of deaths changed more erratically. The rate of deaths in Bobigny increased sharply during the early twentieth century and fell in the 1920s; in 1931, however, it remained well above that average in the Department of the Seine (Table 8).[9] Like the population of the rest of France, Bobigny's population was failing to reproduce itself.

There is a correlation between the fall of the birthrate and the declining percentage of the population engaged in agriculture. As the urban percentage of Bobigny's population increased, the traditional predilection of urbanites for smaller or childless families affected the makeup of the general population. The poor quality of housing that the surge of allotments created may have helped to keep families small; overcrowding, not as serious as in the poorer areas of Paris, remained a fact for many Balbynians. Except for women married to farmers or market gardeners, wives often worked outside the home, which also tended to discourage a high birthrate as Bobigny urbanized (this pattern is discussed further below). Highlighting its conformity both to national patterns of birthrates and to classic patterns of urbanization, Bobigny's birthrate declined as its population increased.[10]

On the one hand, Bobigny's rate of deaths brings out more clearly the deficiencies of suburbanization in the community. The sharp increase in the town's deaths from 1900 to 1921 reflects the deteriorating health conditions that resulted from the construction and settlement of so many defective allotments and from the failure of health care facilities to keep pace with population growth.[11] The decline in the community's rate of deaths from 1921 to 1931, on the other hand, reflects the first fruits of attempts made by the municipal government to improve living conditions in the defective allotments, and to provide better drainage facilities for the whole community. In 1921, for example, Bobigny had no water mains; by 1931 it had more than thirty—for all the main streets and most of its outlying areas. In

TABLE 8

CRUDE RATES OF BIRTHS AND DEATHS IN BOBIGNY
(per 1,000 persons)

	Births	Deaths
1900	27.41	16.69
1911	22.68	26.50
1921	19.83	29.15
1931	15.60	19.00

SOURCE: Etat civil, Bobigny: Actes de naissances et de décès.

addition, the improvements begun in the mid-1920s greatly intensified following the passage of the Sarraut Law in 1928. These efforts certainly contributed to lowering the city's rate of deaths.[12]

On the whole, then, the rates of births and deaths in early twentieth-century Bobigny resembled those found in other French communities undergoing urbanization. Their extremes, especially the fluctuations in the rate of deaths, result from the very pace and conditions of the process in Bobigny. The decline in the rate of deaths after 1921 brings out the fact that urbanization is no impersonal, self-propelling steam-roller but an activity carried out by people, who must master its general direction and consequences.

Geographical Origins of Bobigny's People

Like the population of the Paris area (Map 4), that of Bobigny failed to reproduce itself after 1911. Yet at the same time the community was experiencing spectacular growth: the population of Bobigny grew by

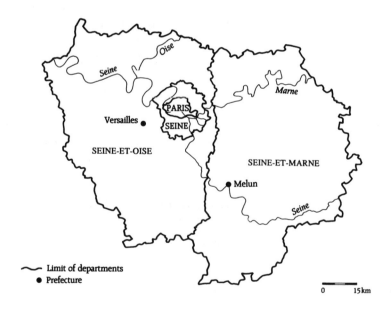

Map 4.   The Paris region in 1920.

475 percent from 1911 to 1931 (Table 9). Even more than other parts of the Paris area, therefore, Bobigny was dependent upon migration to replenish its populace. Throughout the period under study, the clear majority of Balbynians was born outside the community.

At the turn of the century close to one out of every three Balbynians had been born in Bobigny;[13] by 1931, this was true of little more than one in nine residents of the community (Table 10). Such a proportion diminished the importance of local traditions and opened local life to new outside customs.[14] Since Bobigny's new conventions were largely shaped by its immigrants, in evaluating their impact we must consider not merely the number of immigrants but their geographical origins.

As their birthplaces indicate, newcomers to Bobigny were neither just Parisians fleeing the city nor peasants escaping the rigors and limitations of rural life. At no point in this period did those who were born in Paris constitute even one-fourth of the population.[15] However, throughout the early twentieth century roughly half of the community's population was born in the Paris area; moreover, many people born in the provinces had lived in the metropolitan region from early child-hood.[16] Alain Raynaud, a twenty-seven-year-old coppersmith, was typical of these Balbynians who had grown up nearby. In 1921 Raynaud married Lucienne Clerc, who lived just down the street from him, in the rue Pré Souverain. Both were natives; Raynaud came from Pantin and Clerc had been born in Rosny-sous-Bois. Both were from working-class, not agricultural, families; Raynaud's mother was a lacemaker (*passementière*) and Clerc's father was a roadworker (*cantonnier*). They were certainly not Parisians but had no strong connection to rural France.[17]

A sizable proportion of the new Balbynians thus came from urban backgrounds; for them, adjustment to life in Bobigny would not pose the problems experienced by rural migrants to large cities in nineteenth-century France.[18] Their urban backgrounds meant that, as they dealt with the problems of urbanization, many Balbynians would use urban models of protest and organization. A common origin could explain why many Balbynians were drawn to the PCF, which had its strongest roots in urban France during this period.[19]

Against this possibility we must set the fact that from 40 to 50 percent of Bobigny's residents came from the provinces.[20] Because the census figures from 1911, 1921, and 1931 list only the towns in which people were born, not the departments, they do not show geographical patterns of migration to the community. I was able to estimate these patterns by using data from Bobigny's electoral lists, which do give the

TABLE 9

RESIDENTS BORN IN BOBIGNY

	Number	Percentage
1896	49	29.1
1911	75	20.5
1921	87	13.4
1931	197	11.5

SOURCES: For 1896—Conseil général de la Seine, *Etat des communes de la Seine à la fin du 19e siecle: Bobigny* (Paris, 1899), p. 32; for other years—Listes nominatives du recensement, Bobigny.
NOTE: The data in tables 9–16 and 18 are based on a 10 percent sample.

TABLE 10

BIRTHPLACES OF BOBIGNY RESIDENTS

	1896	1911	1921	1931
Bobigny	49 (29.1%)	75 (20.5%)	87 (13.4%)	197 (11.5%)
Paris	—	49 (13.4%)	132 (20.3%)	421 (24.7%)
Other Paris area	—	77 (17.8%)	85 (13.1%)	89 (11.1%)
Provinces	—	144 (39.5%)	313 (48.2%)	755 (44.3%)
Foreign	3 (1.8%)	7 (2.2%)	29 (4.5%)	139 (8.2%)
Not given	—	24 (6.6%)	4 (0.6%)	—

SOURCES: For 1896—Conseil général de la Seine, *Etat des communes de la Seine à la fin du 19e siècle: Bobigny* (Paris, 1899), p. 32 (only incomplete statistics available); for other years—Listes nominatives du recensement, Bobigny.

department of origin of the people counted (Table 11). The electoral lists are deficient, however, since they provide information only for adult males—and only for registered voters at that—a clear minority of the population of Bobigny. Still, their figures offer impressionistic evidence. The fact that the electoral and census figures agree on the relative proportions of Balbynians from the Paris region and from the provinces gives the electoral lists greater credibility. Among the regions of France represented in Bobigny's voting population, eastern France yielded the largest single cohort; the northern, western, and central parts of France also contributed significant percentages. But the south of France sent fewer people to Bobigny in the early twentieth century.

In their regional origins, Bobigny's migrants were similar to other residents of the Paris agglomeration. By the twentieth century immi-

TABLE II

REGIONAL ORIGINS OF VOTERS IN BOBIGNY

	1920	1927[a]	1935[a]
Paris region	75 (51.7%)	217 (44.4%)	219 (43.3%)
North	15 (10.3%)	56 (11.5%)	56 (11.1%)
East	32 (22.1%)	90 (18.4%)	96 (19.0%)
West	12 (8.3%)	43 (8.8%)	51 (10.0%)
Center	9 (6.2%)	55 (11.2%)	53 (10.4%)
South	2 (1.4%)	18 (3.7%)	17 (3.4%)

SOURCE: Listes électorales, Bobigny: 1920, 1927, 1935.
[a]Origins of the remaining voters were not listed.

gration patterns into the capital had become national. In 1931 the largest single group of people living in the capital who had not been born there were natives of the region; there were also large numbers of migrants from the north, east, west, and center living in the capital. Only the south was significantly underrepresented.[21]

Because of its size, the Paris area had well-defined and cohesive ethnic communities of people from Brittany, Auvergne, and other regions, who tended to preserve their own cultures and expand their influence in the metropolis.[22] Migrants in Bobigny were relatively evenly distributed and no particular regional culture had a definite presence there, since Bobigny was too small to have entire neighborhoods composed of natives from one particular province or region. It is doubtful, therefore, that provincial migrants to Bobigny were able to preserve much of their native traditions in their new community. Since roughly half its residents were from the Paris area, Bobigny's provincial migrants probably adopted Parisian customs, which new surroundings reinforced, rather than trying to hold onto the old.[23]

A final interesting feature of Bobigny's population in the early twentieth century is its changing proportion of foreigners. In 1931 this group was more than 8 percent of the population, having quadrupled its share from 1896. The community thus had a foreign population that was proportionately larger than that of France, 6.6 percent of whose residents were of foreign origin in 1931, but smaller than that of Paris, where foreigners made up well over 10 percent of the population by the mid-1920s.[24] This disparity resulted from the relative lack of industry in Bobigny until the end of our period, and from the small amount of cheap rental housing available. There were few of the *chambres garnis* that housed so many foreign workers in Paris; and the prospect of permanent investment in an allotment attracted few foreigners.[25]

With regard to their countries of origin, the foreigners living in Bobigny in the early twentieth century were representative of foreigners in France. The most numerous were Italians, followed by Poles, Spaniards, and Belgians. Almost all of Bobigny's foreigners worked in industry, especially in the metals and construction sectors. Some were skilled—many of the Italians were stonemasons, for example—but the majority seem to have been unskilled or semiskilled workers. Typical of these was Richard Pontin, a Belgian metalworker born in Liège in 1872. Pontin and his wife, Berthe, moved to the Paris area at the beginning of the twentieth century; in 1921 they lived with their son, daughter, son-in-law, and granddaughter in the allotment of rues Perron and Perruset. Like most of their foreign neighbors, the Pontins came from a country bordering on France. They also resembled many other foreigners in Bobigny in being a well-established family; although Bobigny had many transient single males in its foreign population, it also had people who had lived in their communities for years or even decades and were well integrated into local life.[26] The increasing number of foreigners worked in the local construction industry and in the industrial factories in Bobigny by the 1930s.[27]

The most striking characteristic of their origins was the percentage (86.6 percent in 1921) that was born elsewhere. More than in most communities, life in Bobigny was dependent on its migrant population, for whom the concept of traditional ways of life had little meaning, particularly after World War I.[28] Two other distinctive facts characterized this population: migrants from the provinces were evenly distributed and roughly half the town's population came from the Paris area. The first prevented the establishment of any strong regional subculture in Bobigny, which would have impeded the assimilation of provincial newcomers into the dominant local way of life; the second meant that the community's most important cultural pattern was an urban one.

These traits favored the chances of the Communists to win supporters in Bobigny. Local political traditions had little influence on the majority of the population by 1911, and the newcomers brought no strong political allegiances with them. Their politics were shaped more by their reactions to life in their new community. Given Bobigny's uneven urban development, these reactions were dominated by their frustrations as *mal-lotis,* to which the local Communists successfully appealed. Although the distribution of the population by no means ensured a strong Communist presence in Bobigny, it did facilitate its establishment.[29]

Age and Structure of Families

One striking demographic feature of the French population in the early twentieth century was its relatively advanced age. Even in 1931, only 30 percent of the population was under twenty, and more than 55 percent was between twenty and fifty-nine years old. Fourteen percent was aged sixty or older.[30] Since it is generally the young who migrate, we might expect Bobigny, a community undergoing rapid urbanization, to have a population younger than average.[31] Considering the distribution of ages in the population of the Paris area, we might also reasonably assume that there would be few children in the population; the high cost of living in the Paris area, especially for housing, acted to limit the size of families. However, these assumptions do not hold for Bobigny (Table 12). In fact, the ages were distributed in the local population as they were throughout France, although they deviated as a result of Bobigny's specific patterns of suburbanization.

As Bobigny grew, the percentage of children in the population declined and that of adults between the ages of twenty and sixty rose. In addition, our assumption about the population's relative youth in an area of intensive urbanization is borne out by the small size of Bobigny's elderly population. Here was its greatest difference from the ages of the general population.[32] A less dramatic but still noticeable difference was the large number of children. Even at its lowest point in 1931, the percentage of children in the community exceeded that in the

TABLE 12

AGES OF THE POPULATION OF BOBIGNY

	Birth–19 years	20–59 years	Over 60 years
1896	59 (36.0%)	94 (57.3%)	11 (6.7%)
1911	125 (35.1%)	210 (59.0%)	21 (5.9%)
1921	214 (32.4%)	388 (58.8%)	58 (8.8%)
1931	537 (31.5%)	1,058 (62.0%)	112 (6.5%)

SOURCE: Listes nominatives du recensement, Bobigny: 1896, 1911, 1921, 1931.

Paris area and in the general population, a phenomenon for which two explanations come to mind. First, since the middle and the upper class had lower birthrates in France, Bobigny's large working class may have accounted for its large youthful population.[33]

More significant, however, was the character of the community as a residential suburb where the majority of residents owned their homes. Many had decided to move to the suburbs for the well-being of the families they had (or planned to have). Moving to suburbia would not constitute proof that families in Bobigny had lots of children; but since in Paris the average family had fewer than two children, any community that seemed to favor families with children would probably have a disproportionate number in its population.[34]

Bobigny was not however a haven for big families. A large number of households included only a single individual or a couple living alone. Families with more than three children were few (Table 13).[35] Some of the difference between the large number of children in Bobigny and the relatively small households results from the fact that a large minority (41.7 percent in 1931) of adolescents did not live at home and that a number of two-person households consisted of one adult and one child. Moreover, because there were few elderly people in Bobigny, the other age groups were proportionally larger. The average size of households declined from 1896 to 1931 (except that of 1911). The percentage of households of one or two persons increased while that of six or more members declined: households of one to three members increased from 50 percent in 1896 to 59.8 percent in 1911, 61.5 percent in 1921, and

TABLE 13

SIZE OF HOUSEHOLDS IN BOBIGNY

Size	1896	1911	1921	1931
1	2 (4.5%)	12 (11.2%)	13 (6.8%)	60 (11.1%)
2	8 (18.2%)	27 (25.2%)	59 (30.7%)	153 (28.3%)
3	12 (27.3%)	25 (23.4%)	46 (24.0%)	159 (29.4%)
4	8 (18.2%)	18 (16.8%)	38 (19.8%)	84 (15.5%)
5	7 (15.9%)	9 (8.4%)	19 (9.9%)	46 (8.5%)
6	4 (9.1%)	9 (8.4%)	7 (3.6%)	20 (3.7%)
7+	3 (6.8%)	7 (6.5%)	10 (5.2%)	19 (3.5%)
Average size	3.4	4.1	3.3	3.1

SOURCE: Listes nominatives du recensement, Bobigny: 1896, 1911, 1921, 1931.

68.8 percent in 1931. Beyond these characteristics, the data reveal no clear trends.

This shift toward smaller households paralleled Bobigny's increasing development and stemmed from two factors: the community's falling birthrate and its decreasing number of extended family households. The declining birthrate had greater impact on the size of households; urbanization decreased the number of extended families as market gardeners—who often included in their households people who were not part of the immediate family—declined as a percentage of the population.[36]

The Humbert household was characteristic of Bobigny's market gardeners. In 1896 Claude and Clémence Humbert grew vegetables on their own land at 8, rue de Blanc-mesnil, in the heart of Bobigny's community of market gardeners. Their household included one daughter and an unrelated individual who worked in their fields. By 1911 the family had added two sons; except for the younger son, all members of the family worked their land. By 1921 the older son, François, had married and lived with his wife and her son on a farm next door to that of his parents, at 10, rue de Blanc-mesnil. As the community urbanized, such households typifying the old, rural Bobigny were increasingly rare.

With the reduction in extended families came an increase in single-person households, most of them elderly individuals who in more traditional communities would have lived with their children or other relatives.[37] Women living alone were a majority of the elderly single householders. Added to women heading families, they made up over 10 percent of Bobigny's households during our period. The large numbers of elderly women living along reflected both the traditionally longer life of women in industrial society and the decline of the extended family. Many other households were headed by younger women, who usually worked outside the home; often these were the widows of soldiers who fell during World War I. In 1921 they were 14.1 percent of the households.[38] Yet the war distorted the gender ratio less in Bobigny than in France as a whole; the ratio of men to women remained stable: 1.20 in 1896, 0.98 in 1911, 0.87 in 1921, and 0.99 in 1931.[39] In 1921 the ratio shifted slightly toward women, but this increase had disappeared by 1931. This unusual situation derived from three factors. First, a greater proportion of rural Frenchmen fought and died in World War I than did their urban counterparts; the percentage of male Balbynian casualties was correspondingly smaller than the French norm.[40] Second, most of Bobigny's interwar population was born elsewhere and came to buy land in an allotment; the new homeowners were largely couples or families, not single men or women. Bobigny did have a large number of individuals living alone, but they remained a minority. Moreover, this group included as many men as women, the many elderly women counterbalanced by young foreign men, single or married, who lived alone (in 1931 they accounted for half the men under age fifty living alone). The presence of a large foreign male population in Bobigny was thus a third reason for the balanced sex ratio of the town's population.

One pronounced change in the structure of Bobigny's households was in the number of persons employed. The percentage of households with more than one wage earner declined from 1896 to 1931 (Table 14; the small data base causes the figures to fluctuate slightly). Although their percentage declined to a minority, even by 1931 these households remained an important segment of the population. Many women, both wives and daughters, were employed; the large number of two-person families, mostly married couples with jobs, bears this out. Sometimes the additional wage earners were adolescents, the majority of whom had jobs and lived with their parents. As this fairly traditional arrangement shows, local adolescents lacked an autonomous "youth culture"; of those who did not live with their parents, the majority were married with households of their own.[41]

In general, Bobigny's households evolved in the early twentieth century from the pattern of large families with several wage earners toward that of the nuclear family, with one wage earner. Though a sizable percentage of families remained that did not conform to the model, this trend marks Bobigny's urbanization and the cultural *embourgeoisement* of the working class, as it moved toward middle-class ideology and mores.[42]

One would normally expect such a cultural trend among the electorate of Bobigny to hurt the prospects of a militantly class-conscious political party like the PCF. Imitation of middle-class life-styles does not necessarily mean identification with the middle class, however, especially in politics.[43] Judged from its family structure, the working class of Bobigny in this period resembled that of the Paris suburbs after World War II, certainly more than it did the nascent proletariat of nineteenth-century France. The electoral geography of the Paris suburbs after 1945 showed that such a working class was not immune to the appeals of the PCF. Therefore, though the modern,

TABLE 14

HOUSEHOLDS WITH MORE THAN ONE PERSON EMPLOYED

Size	1896		1911		1921		1931	
2	5/9	(55.6%)	16/26	(61.5%)	24/61	(39.3%)	68/161	(42.2%)
3	11/14	(78.6%)	17/26	(65.4%)	24/44	(54.5%)	62/157	(39.5%)
4	5/6	(83.3%)	12/15	(80.0%)	25/36	(69.4%)	26/84	(31.0%)
5	4/6	(66.7%)	6/10	(60.0%)	11/21	(52.4%)	28/45	(60.0%)
Average size	71.4%		66.2%		51.9%		41.0%	

SOURCE: Listes nominatives du recensement, Bobigny: 1896, 1911, 1921, 1931.

middle-class structure of many families and households did not necessarily increase the opportunities of Bobigny's Communists, neither did it prevent them from forming a popular base there.[44]

Bobigny at Work

More than its demography, Bobigny's patterns of employment determined the shape of the community's political life. Since they changed greatly during urbanization, they merit an analysis in depth— a basic portrait (in Table 15, below) of the distribution of occupations among the population from 1896 to 1931.

The most striking aspects of this occupational distribution are the decline in the number of market gardeners and the increase in that of working-class Balbynians. In 1896 market gardeners were the majority in the community; by 1921 the working class was. More than any other change, the reversed positions of the market gardeners and the workers dramatized the urbanization of Bobigny.

The market gardeners took control of the municipal government from the farmers by the last decade of the nineteenth century but saw their power challenged and overthrown as Bobigny urbanized and its population took on a more working-class character. Their ranks declining, market gardeners and farmers were forced to form a tactical alliance to preserve even a modicum of political influence. As part of the traditional population of Bobigny, the agricultural groups and the shopkeepers owned businesses, such as cafés, restaurants, and food stores, usually in the center of town.[45] Despite the population's growth, the number of shopkeepers increased little. The newcomers were poor and lived in migrant neighborhoods far from the city center where most

TABLE 15

DISTRIBUTION OF OCCUPATIONS IN BOBIGNY

	1896	1911	1921	1931
Farmers	6 (6.3%)	9 (4.2%)	4 (1.1%)	7 (0.9%)
Market gardeners	52 (54.2%)	67 (31.3%)	61 (17.2%)	48 (6.0%)
Shopkeepers	5 (5.2%)	18 (8.4%)	22 (6.2%)	33 (4.1%)
Employés	6 (6.3%)	15 (7.0%)	34 (9.6%)	91 (11.3%)
Professionals	1 (1.0%)	3 (1.4%)	11 (3.1%)	22 (2.7%)
Service staff	5 (5.2%)	8 (3.7%)	9 (2.5%)	47 (5.8%)
Manual workers	20 (20.8%)	94 (43.9%)	214 (60.3%)	557 (69.2%)

SOURCE: Listes nominatives du recensement, Bobigny: 1896, 1911, 1921, 1931.

shops were located; many new Balbynians commuted to work and could make some purchases elsewhere.[46] Not all shopkeepers lived in the city center, however. In 1921 Brigitte Delmas owned a café in the avenue Edouard Vaillant, in the small commercial section of the Pont de Bondy. A few years later she and her family moved to the Grande Denise allotment near Six Routes, where she opened up a café with her husband, Marc Delmas, a carpenter. By 1936 the Delmas were running a grocery store, having abandoned the café business.[47]

The group of professionals were teachers, medical personnel, and a few owners of small factories. The most interesting characteristic of this group was its small size; the largest cohort, that of 1921, consisted of only twenty-two people (mostly teachers and medical personnel). Since Bobigny contained few factories during most of this period, the few industrialists preferred to live in Paris or in other, more attractive, locales.[48] I have come across no evidence that professionals had a significant role in local life, either before or after the Communists gained control of the city government: they never appeared as guests of honor at public festivals; they had no streets named after them in any neighborhoods. The striking weakness of a group that usually enjoyed authority and prestige in French urban life illustrates one feature common in interwar suburban development, the lack of elites.

The employés, or lower level white-collar workers, were the other major group in Bobigny besides manual workers to expand consistently during the early twentieth century. A large number worked as railroad clerks at the station in nearby Noisy-le-Sec. Many employés were clerks in industrial offices, department stores, and government offices, generally located in Paris. The growth of this group is therefore linked to that of the tertiary sector in the Paris area.[49] The social status of the employés was only slightly superior to that of manual workers; they were "brain" rather than "hand" workers, but their levels of pay and working conditions were little different from those of manual workers.[50] In Bobigny the similarities were emphasized by comparable living conditions. Both groups settled in Bobigny's developing allotments. The employés living on the defective allotments experienced the same housing and sanitation problems there as their working-class neighbors. Therefore, in spite of differences in social status, they found in their equally frustrating living conditions a commonality of political interests and attitudes.[51]

Service staff formed a smaller, more traditional group than the employés; it included domestic servants, concierges, and others who provided direct services. This group declined from 1896 to 1921 because the number of domestics decreased, as did the percentage of agricultural families, who were their most frequent employers in Bobigny. In 1931 it consisted of concierges and *gardiens*, or caretakers. Throughout the period this sector was almost exclusively female and, because of its small size, had little impact on the political life of the community.[52]

This service sector did not employ all local women who worked in nonhousehold occupations. It is important to note that the percentage of women employed outside their homes dropped from a high point of 73.4 percent in 1911 to 49.0 percent in 1921, and then to 41.5 percent in 1931. In Bobigny as elsewhere in France, urbanization reinforced the conviction that a woman's place was in the home. Part of the decline in the employment of women came from the decreasing proportion of Balbynians in agriculture. Census records for most farming families registered wives in the same occupational category as the male family heads, especially that of market gardeners (and somewhat less so that of shopkeepers). Therefore, as these groups became smaller, so did the numbers of women they employed.[53]

Even if we do not count those employed in agriculture, the percentage of women with jobs outside the home declined in Bobigny as in interwar France generally, a sharp contrast to the contemporary stereotype of independent women leaving their kitchens for offices or workshops. Although patterns were similar, the percentage of women employed was slightly greater in Bobigny than elsewhere in France; in 1921 the numbers were 49 percent and 42 percent, respectively.[54]

In looking at the jobs in which Bobigny's working women were employed (Table 16), we note the predominance of working-class jobs and the decline of agricultural ones. To a greater extent than the laboring population at large, Bobigny's employed women had unskilled jobs: *journalière* was women's most common occupation. Also worthy of note is the increase in employées, especially after 1921. These women were secretaries and clerks, whose increasing presence in Bobigny's female labor force reflected the changing patterns of women's work in France.[55] Women who worked outside the home were usually not married: adolescents living at home, heads of households, or single women. A significant number, but fewer than half of married women, was employed—31.9 percent in 1921, for example. More often young working women would quit their jobs when they married.[56] Quite typical was a person like Claudine Chevalier, of the rue de la Tour d'Auvergne. While her husband, André, was employed as a railway worker, she worked as a housewife. After André's death, however, when Claudine was fifty-seven, she found a job as a streetsweeper.

A final characteristic of the local occupational structure was that it had little social mobility. Four out of five Balbynians had jobs with the same level of status as those of their parents throughout the early twentieth century (Table 17). The fact that most workers had working-class parents meant that in Bobigny they found no new proletarian training ground but a familiar industrial landscape.[57] Their lack of social mobility reinforced class identification. Among the many at the bottom of the social scale it promoted the belief that self-improvement through individual initiative was an unlikely prospect. Emphasizing class consciousness and collective, not individual, advancement through political activity, the PCF spoke directly to such feelings.[58]

TABLE 16

WOMEN'S EMPLOYMENT IN BOBIGNY

	1896	1911	1921	1931
Professionals	—	3 (3.2%)	1 (0.8%)	3 (1.1%)
Shopkeepers	—	12 (12.8%)	11 (9.1%)	4 (1.5%)
Farmers	25 (58.1%)	34 (36.2%)	27 (22.3%)	21 (7.9%)
Manual workers	18 (41.9%)	43 (45.7%)	78 (64.5%)	200 (74.9%)
Employées	—	2 (2.1%)	4 (3.3%)	36 (13.5%)

SOURCE: Listes nominatives du recensement, Bobigny: 1896, 1911, 1921, 1931.

TABLE 17

INTERGENERATIONAL SOCIAL MOBILITY IN BOBIGNY

	1900	1911	1921	1931
Unchanged	18 (85.7%)	43 (91.5%)	88 (89.8%)	125 (86.8%)
Upward	3 (14.3%)	3 (6.4%)	2 (2.0%)	10 (6.9%)
Downward	—	1 (2.1%)	8 (8.2%)	9 (6.3%)

SOURCE: Etat civil, Bobigny: Actes de mariages 1900, 1911, 1921, 1931.

Since the working class constituted the absolute majority of the population by 1921, it dominated the city's politics, alone or in alliance with other groups. More than any other factor, the preponderant working-class population of Bobigny after World War I determined the community's life and enabled the local Communists to gain great influence in Bobigny. It was working-class people who moved into the defective allotments and suffered the inconveniences of life there, who commuted to work in Paris or other suburbs, who sent their children to overcrowded schools, and who generally voted for the PCF as a way of dealing with these problems.

Not all French workers voted for the PCF during the interwar period; if they had, it would have been a much stronger party. Therefore we must look at the character of their work, to see if there was something about its composition that moved them toward radical politics (Table 18).

The process of urbanization in Bobigny enlarged some working-class occupations and limited others. The clothing and food sectors were the most obvious examples of the latter. Although the number of clothing workers, mostly laundresses, grew throughout this period, it was outstripped by other groups and declined as a proportion of the population; the same was true in the food business, most of whose workers were employed in grocery and other food stores. Few members of these groups commuted to work, so their opportunities for employment were limited to the expansion of shops in Bobigny itself.

Not surprisingly, the growth in construction was tied to the progress of urbanization in Bobigny, and the development of the allotments in the 1910s and 1920s gave a clear boost to this occupation. Its decline after 1921 was a function both of the slower expansion of allotments and of the faster growth of other working-class occupations.

TABLE 18

OCCUPATIONS OF BOBIGNY'S WORKERS

	1896	1911	1921	1931
Food	4 (20.0%)	4 (4.3%)	7 (3.5%)	26 (4.8%)
Clothing	6 (30.0%)	16 (17.0%)	25 (12.4%)	63 (11.6%)
Transportation	—	1 (1.1%)	14 (6.9%)	43 (7.9%)
Construction	1 (5.0%)	15 (16.0%)	33 (16.3%)	77 (14.2%)
Metals	4 (20.0%)	11 (11.7%)	34 (16.8%)	112 (20.7%)
Unskilled work	4 (20.0%)	34 (36.2%)	67 (33.2%)	180 (33.3%)
Other	1 (5.0%)	13 (13.8%)	22 (10.9%)	40 (7.4%)

SOURCE: Listes nominatives du recensement, Bobigny: 1896, 1911, 1921, 1931.

By contrast, the sectors of transportation and metals clearly expanded over the period. Unlike construction, they relied on opportunities for employment in the Paris area rather than in Bobigny alone. The transportation workers were drivers of cars and trucks, or employees of the area's public transit system. The metals sector of the labor force ranged from highly skilled jobs like tool fitters (*ajusteurs outileurs*) and tracers to unskilled or semiskilled positions like molders (*mouleurs*).[59]

Like employment in transportation and metals, unskilled work in Bobigny grew significantly after 1896, although after 1911 its percentage of the labor force remained constant. This was the most difficult sector to analyze, since census data merely list "unskilled" (*manœuvre*) for the occupational category and rarely give any idea of where it took place.[60] For example, a large number of Bobigny's unskilled jobs were probably in the chemicals industry, which tended to use unskilled labor; there were many chemical factories in nearby suburbs like Aubervilliers.[61]

The large size of the unskilled sector is our clearest indication of a general characteristic of the working-class population: it was composed mostly of unskilled or semiskilled workers. Although we cannot determine exact percentages for each sector, the census data reveal that working-class occupations had few skilled workers, except in construction. This was certainly true in the food and clothing sectors; many local metalworkers held semiskilled jobs. It was the factory operative, therefore, not the craftsman or skilled worker, who was the most representative of Bobigny's working class.[62]

Lacking thorough analysis of the sources of the PCF's support in the interwar period, we cannot determine to what extent the particular configuration of Bobigny's working class helped the PCF to win in 1920.[63] Because no single occupation monopolized the working class, its members would be unlikely to unite as carpenters, laundresses, or ditchdiggers, but rather as workers.[64] Perhaps more important, however, was the simple fact that the majority of Bobigny's work force was unskilled or semiskilled. Until the Popular Front of 1936, workers were usually unorganized and had little influence over the conditions in their workplaces. To vote Communist in a local election could be a way to exercise control over their community in compensation for their helplessness on the job.

One powerful barrier against communism had little place in Bobigny: the community lacked a strong elite class committed to the status quo and exercising significant local influence.[65] Thus from 1896 to 1931 Bobigny differed most from other communities in two striking characteristics of class structure—the preponderance of its working class and the almost complete absence of elite social groupings. Their limited contact with local elites did reduce the workers' conflict in everyday life; they were not elbowed off the sidewalk by wealthy bourgeois. Yet the difficulties of life in the allotments and the entrepreneurs' responsibility for developing the lots were more than enough to convince many Balbynians of the hostility of the capitalist class. As the following excerpts from a letter to Mayor Clamamus in 1925 indicate, hostility was expected and reciprocated:

> Residing in the chemin de la Madeleine, part of the allotment of La Favorite, we have written to Monsieur Brigeois asking him to repair our road or at least help us with the costs of such repairs. However, M. Brigeois, like all allotment developers, prefers to leave us hanging. . . .
>
> Therefore I request that you take the necessary steps to constitute us into an association conforming to the law of 1912; we intend to use all possible means to bring these swindlers (*mercantis de la terre*) to justice.[66]

The community's heavily working-class character also favored the PCF, since to control local political life it needed to win only the votes of a majority of its natural constituency. Members of the working class, in France or anywhere else, do not automatically vote Communist. But the class structure of Bobigny meant that if the PCF could win anywhere in France, it would do so here.

By far the most important deviation—in demographic and sociological terms—of Bobigny's population from that of other communities in France was in class structure. Bobigny was a homogeneous community. The increasing segregation of the population within greater Paris, which consigned the area's industrial workers to the suburbs, made it so. Between the wars the working class composed a clear majority of the community's population, with no significant elite; this structure went a long way toward enabling the PCF to gain a strong foothold in the municipal politics of Bobigny. More than most places in France, the class structure in Bobigny corresponded to that envisaged by orthodox Marxism for advanced industrial societies; it was only natural that the PCF, operating with this ideology, should feel at home.

Other aspects of Bobigny's composition also favored the Communists. Migrants from all over France increased the population and overlaid earlier local traditions, so that no one group was able to impose its traditions on the community. This situation tended to make Balbynians receptive to new beliefs, such as those advocated by the PCF.

Finally, since migrants to Bobigny in the early twentieth century often came from an urban industrial background, PCF's ideology appealed to them. Far from the "primitive rebels" of eighteenth- and nineteenth-century Europe, working-class Balbynians were largely assimilated into industrial society. An ideology condemning industrialism in toto and preaching a return to preindustrial utopia was not likely to hold them. In contrast, the PCF espoused a revolution against the capitalist class who monopolized the fruits of industrial society. It is not surprising that Bobigny's working class should take its grievances and complaints about urban life to a political party that did not plan to overthrow industrial society but to realize its potential.[67]

By the 1920s workers constituted a proportion of the population of Bobigny large enough to ensure the political dominance of any party they supported. The PCF's strength was based not just on them, however, but also on the employés. What united the two groups were the poor living conditions in the community—specifically, the crisis in the allotments—a combination of sociological and urban factors that provided a propitious climate for community-based politics. By focusing on such issues, the PCF was able to bring the two groups together in a political coalition that proved impregnable.

PART TWO

The Origins
of Suburban Communism

CHAPTER 4

Electoral Politics in Bobigny

The first part of this study outlined the development of Bobigny into a working-class commuter suburb in the early twentieth century, focusing on the characteristics that allowed the French Communist party to gain a dominant position in local political life after 1920. To assert that these characteristics made it inevitable that Bobigny would become a Communist fief, however, would be to fall into a rigid historical determinism. Other Paris suburbs, especially in the northeast of the Department of the Seine, experienced urbanization similar to that of Bobigny between the wars and yet offered far less support to the PCF or the Left.[1] To analyze what favored the PCF's influence in Bobigny is important, but to complete our history of the community we must describe the evolution of political forces and political life.

Electoral politics in Bobigny during the early twentieth century was above all urban: the issues and structures, the advantages and disadvantages of suburbanization underlay all political contests and furnished their dominant electoral themes. The positions people took on such issues usually reflected their social class. In more than one respect, therefore, politics and suburban development in early twentieth-century Bobigny marched in step.

Republicanism in Bobigny: Dominance and Disunity

At the start of the Second Empire in 1852, Bobigny voted solidly, sometimes almost unanimously, for the official conservative candidates.

This situation began to change at the end of the next decade; in 1869, liberal Republican forces were able to gain almost as many votes in Bobigny as the monarchist Party of Order, while a small minority of local electors cast their ballots for representatives of the Radical Left. The growing strength of the Republicans in Bobigny correlated with the influx of the market gardeners; the social divisions between these newcomers and the farmers mirrored and reinforced their strong political differences.[2]

The Franco-Prussian War of 1870 and the Commune of 1871 disrupted the community. Because Bobigny lay directly on the invasion route from Germany to Paris, Bobigny's entire population was transferred to Paris in 1870 and returned only after the defeat of the communards. The experience of the war and the founding of the Third Republic in 1871 eliminated the prewar political extremes from Bobigny. In sharp contrast to the rest of France, Bobigny gave the monarchist Right only token support after 1871, but the Radical and socialist Left was temporarily forced out of political activity by governmental repression after the Commune. Henceforth politics in Bobigny was dominated by the Republicans.[3]

Although the national traumas of 1870 and 1871 altered the mode of political expression in Bobigny, they did little to change a fundamental conflict between the old rural community headed by the farmers and the newly arrived market gardeners. The farmers, shopkeepers, and other traditional Balbynians now identified with and voted for the conservative republicanism symbolized by Adolphe Thiers and the national government of the Third Republic. Just as they had under the Second Empire, these social groups continued to support those political forces that stood for the defense of property and order.[4]

The political allegiances of the late nineteenth-century newcomers to Bobigny were less defined: the market gardeners, wage earners, and other "outsiders" supported Boulangists, Radicals, and different socialist factions. This political heterogeneity arose not so much from local causes as from the difficulties that French political forces to the left of center experienced in coalescing and elaborating a direction and sense of purpose. Despite this diversity of political expression, however, the market gardeners usually opposed the conservative Republican farmers.[5] As the market gardeners became the majority of the population, so the leftist republicanism they championed became the dominant force in local politics. By 1900, three-quarters of Bobigny's city councillors were market gardeners. Though the farmers and other traditional social groups kept some local influence, by the 1890s they had ceded political dominance to the market gardeners. Since the late nineteenth-century political allegiances in Bobigny so neatly paralleled social divisions, they foreshadowed the early twentieth-century rise of socialism and communism in the community.[6]

From 1900 until the outbreak of the First World War the domestic politics of the Third Republic was dominated by the Republican Left, a loose coalition of the Democratic Alliance, the Radicals, the Radical Socialists, and the socialist parties of Jean Jaurès and Jules Guesde. Stemming from the Dreyfus affair, this coalition was united in its desire to safeguard the republic and foil the political ambitions of the church, the army, and other conservative forces in French society. It produced the strident, and popular, anticlericalism of the government of Emile Combes but was profoundly divided over social questions. The growing socialist strength, and the climate of labor militancy that led to clashes like that at Draveil in 1908, indicated that the hegemony of liberal republicanism would be threatened from the Left as well as the Right.[7]

Bobigny followed the nation's lead in political affairs. In 1900 forces that identified themselves as Radicals or Radical Socialists, supported by the market gardeners and by some wage earners and other nontraditional groups, controlled political life. Not a unified political party, they had a common viewpoint on many issues of importance to the people of Bobigny. They concurred with the protests of the Republican Left against the privileges of the wealthy and advocated greater concern for the rights of small independent producers. They were strongly patriotic and approved of the national government's secular stance.

In local affairs, Bobigny's city government emphasized a passive, go-slow approach to developing and expanding the community; it was generally cool toward projects to tamper with the quality of life in Bobigny, especially if they involved large municipal expenditures. Except for the tramway line linking Bobigny with Paris, which many Balbynians desired, the city government did little in this period to upgrade municipal services or promote the growth of the town.[8] The issue of growth weakened the de facto political coalition of market gardeners and wage earners against the traditionalist old guard. Bobigny's working and lower middle classes were still small; their members favored the town's growth and expansion of municipal services. Their political representatives spoke out against what they saw as the government's lack of dynamism. In 1902 a correspondent for the suburban newspaper *Paris-Est*, which often favored the progressive

Republicans in Bobigny, attacked the municipality in the following terms:

> The population of Bobigny is growing and changing every day and the old city councillors are becoming less and less adequate to the task of guiding the city along new paths. In their opinion, everything is as it should be, and nothing should be changed. For them, it is always nostalgia for the good old days, but we doubt that this nostalgia is shared by the majority of the population.[9]

This belief in change and progress, which for Bobigny in 1900 meant advocating greater suburbanization, soon divided the dominant Radical forces in the community and gave rise to a more progressive strain of radicalism. Although this latter grouping included fewer market gardeners among its supporters than the more traditional Radicals of Bobigny, the difference between the two groups was not a simple function of class divisions or a split between rural and urban factions. A sizable minority of Bobigny's market gardeners supported the progressives. Moreover, although the dispute over modernization was the main issue between the two political groups, it was not the only one. The minority, progressive Radicals of Bobigny viewed their traditional opponents as less firm in their commitment to democracy and the Third Republic.

> The city councillors are certainly honest people, but it is not easy to understand their political opinions. They call themselves Republicans, but that is difficult to believe. They are Republicans along the lines of the Boulangists and Nationalists who criticize everything that the government does and who are always ready to accept alliances whose goal is the overthrow of the republic. . . . They are Republicans who regret the passing of the empire, or who would gladly cry "Long live the king!"[10]

In effect, the progressive Radicals of Bobigny felt that there was little difference between the mainstream radicalism that dominated the city council and the conservative republicanism of the farmers and their community's old guard. Their progressive radicalism eventually failed in Bobigny. But the group represented an interesting aspect of the early phases of Bobigny's integration into the Paris metropolitan area. It attempted to go beyond the class-based politics that characterized the town. While it rejected the attempts by market gardeners to shore up their dominant position in the community, it also opposed the control of city politics by the working class. Some members of the group were willing to go a long way in working with Socialists, especially before

1908, but most rejected a political landscape in which the working-class Left would occupy the primary position. Many members, including their leader, Paul Peysson, belonged to the urban middle or lower middle class. Had progressive Radicals been a larger percentage of the population, they might have been an urban alternative to working-class socialism. Unfortunately for Peysson and his followers, they lacked a solid constituency in the allotments.[11]

Although the progressive Radicals formulated their political position by the turn of the century, they took longer in putting together a formal organization. Certain adherents formed a committee in 1901, but it quickly fell apart because of differences of opinion among its members. Judged from newspaper reports, these differences concerned both ideology and strategy.

> The democratic Republicans are far from being in agreement as to individuals, ideas, or the means of waging the struggle. Some would prefer to fight with their colors openly displayed, whereas others would prefer to play hide-and-go-seek with the city council. . . . As for the leadership . . . the discord is so complete that, during the last elections, it could not even agree upon a titular leader for an electoral list.[12]

Somewhat shakily, these progressive Radicals did manage to pull themselves together in 1902 to back Adrien Veber's campaign for election to the national legislature from a suburban district that included Bobigny. Veber, who was president of the General Council of the Seine, was well known as a socialist. The willingness of Bobigny's leftist Radicals to support him indicated both the diffuse organization of socialism in France before the formation of the Section française de l'Internationale ouvrière (SFIO) and their identification with all progressives in opposition to enemies of the Third Republic. Certainly Veber's campaign, which was backed by an organization named *Concentration républicaine*, was not that of a fire-breathing Marxist. At an electoral rally in Bobigny held by the Veber committee less than a month before the election, the candidate and his supporters declared themselves Republican Socialists and emphasized their commitment to the defense of the republic.[13]

Veber won his race and was elected to the legislature in May 1902, but he lost in Bobigny. His Nationalist opponent, Goussot, outpolled him by a score of 185 to 136 on the second round of the election. The vote nonetheless demonstrated that Bobigny's progressive Radicals could marshal support in the community to compete with the traditional Radical establishment, which had supported Goussot. Because of this, Peysson and his colleagues considered the Veber campaign a victory:

> Bobigny has proved herself worthy of the republic on the second round of the vote. In spite of 40 new abstentions, the Republicans won 35 votes over the first round and the reactionaries lost 46. We hope that the municipality will understand the significance of such a result and that it will finally decide to devote itself to progress.[14]

Understandably, the leftist Radicals did not wait for such a change of heart on the part of the municipality. Within a year they were organizing themselves to compete for political control of Bobigny in the 1904 municipal elections—a difficult task, as the leftist Republicans of the town had been unable to agree. Some, such as the local arrondissement councillor Collardeau, while criticizing the passivity of the city government, associated themselves with it on some issues; others, such as Peysson, condemned the city councillors as monarchists in Republican clothing. A key source of discord between the two factions was that the latter tended to emphasize social issues and to collaborate with the Socialists, from which Collardeau and his colleagues often demurred.[15]

Despite their lack of unity, the leftist Radicals put together an energetic campaign for the municipal elections. In March 1904 this group finally managed to form its own organization, the Republican Committee for City Interests; its introductory manifesto emphasized the committee's concern for the well-being of Bobigny's market gardeners and demanded to know what the city council had done for them lately. A majority of the committee's members were market gardeners, although employés and small businessmen were also represented.[16] Peysson, as the committee's candidate for mayor, took the lead in waging this group's electoral campaign. He used his connections with the newspaper *Paris-Est* to write a stream of articles attacking the city government and commenting on the ideas and progress of the progressive Radicals; he was most responsible for defining the committee's campaign platform. Not surprisingly, the major issue at which Peysson and his colleagues hammered away was the municipal administration's failure to modernize Bobigny. Not only did most progressive Radicals see this as the most important issue, but it was one of the few questions on which they could agree.[17]

The municipal administration of Mayor Antoine Boyer, who was up for reelection, defended its record energetically. The Union of Patriotic and Liberal Committees, the organization of the traditional Radicals, emphasized how judiciously and impartially the Boyer administration had run the affairs of the city. It stressed the important contacts Boyer had developed with the prefect of the Seine and other national officials to promote the well-being of Bobigny. Without directly replying to the charges by their opponents that city government had become stagnant and wary of progress, the traditional Radicals accentuated the stable, peaceful character of city government during their term in office.[18]

The supporters of the Boyer administration also vociferously attacked Peysson and his followers. First, they charged that the leftist Republicans were spendthrifts without a proper sense of the responsibilities involved in running a city government. Second, the traditional Radicals accused the progressive Radicals of lacking patriotism and of opposing the French military, even though Peysson had at one time been an army officer. However, the most frequent reproach that Boyer's supporters aimed at Peysson and his colleagues was that they were either dupes of the socialists or socialists themselves. The traditional Radicals focused upon the support their opponents gave to Veber during the legislative campaign of 1902 as proof of a commitment to "collectivism." In contrast, Boyer and his supporters tried to portray themselves as upholding the rational political center, against both the antirepublicanism of the extreme Right and the socialism of the extreme Left represented by Peysson.[19]

Peysson and the progressive Radicals waged an energetic campaign but lost the municipal election. Out of a total of 430 votes cast, 239 were for Mayor Boyer to 178 for Peysson. This victory in 1904 represented a last hurrah for Boyer; the days in which his supporters controlled Bobigny's political life were numbered, as the race for the arrondissement council in the canton of Noisy-le-Sec a year later demonstrated. In Bobigny the candidate of the Republican Committee, Renault, came in first with 79 votes, followed by a Socialist with 71, and a Nationalist with 69. This election was important in pinpointing political trends in Bobigny: it showed the strong position of the leftist Radicals, the dramatically increasing strength of the Socialists, and the growing distance between the two groups.[20] *Paris-Est* explained the results:

> For the first time in Bobigny the Republicans have obtained a majority, and if the Socialists had kept the promise they had made to marshal all Republican votes behind the candidate who won the most votes on the first round, against a Nationalist candidacy, we would have opposed 150 Republican votes to 69 Nationalist ones.

Although the Radicals came in first place, it was the Socialists who registered the greatest success, which they obtained through an energetic campaign.[21]

The progressive Radicals never won political hegemony in Bobigny, which had seemed in their grasp until 1905. The rise of the Socialists fundamentally changed the rules of the political game. Before 1905, the progressive Radicals had viewed the socialists as another kind of Republicans, as allies and followers in the primary struggle against the traditional Radicals.[22] But in 1905 the unification of the SFIO, with a more clearly defined Socialist doctrine, and the growing Socialist strength in Bobigny changed their perspective; by 1912 the majority of the community's progressive Radicals considered the Socialists to be the main enemy.[23]

This political shift gained momentum in 1906 during Veber's campaign for reelection to the legislature. Many leftist Radicals who supported Veber in 1902 refused to do so again after a strike by agricultural workers against market gardeners in Bobigny and other northeastern Paris suburbs. This strike in March and April of 1906 brought home to many market gardeners the dangers of supporting a strongly pro-union party like the SFIO, and *Paris-Est* was firmly hostile to it. The fact that the SFIO had introduced a bill into the national legislature to enact the eight-hour day for industrial *and* agricultural workers did not help either. Veber won the election, but in Bobigny his conservative opponent beat him by 239 to 134 votes.[24]

From 1906 to 1912 local politics in Bobigny was preoccupied by the growth of the progressive Radicals, and their increasing distance from the Socialist Left. In October 1906 a group of dissidents criticized the hostility of Radical Socialist leaders to Veber; by 1908 this group had formed its own political organization, the Republican Association for City Interests (ARIC). ARIC soon moved to the right, however, displaying the same hostility to the Socialists as had the Radical Socialist leadership. In the legislative election of 1910 Veber was opposed for the first time by a Left Republican, who won a majority of the vote in Bobigny. The results of this election, added to ARIC's failure to establish a distinct leftist Radical presence, marked a gradual rapprochement of the Radical factions in Bobigny.[25]

The municipal elections of 1912 both illustrated and reinforced the results of 1910. For the first time the SFIO ran its own separate list and thus made a bid to govern Bobigny. Most of its members were new to municipal politics in Bobigny, although a few, such as Peysson, had run as Democratic and Socialist Union candidates in 1908. Some would later prosper in local politics, like Jean-Marie Clamamus, the future mayor, who was running for the first time.[26]

Yet the most notable aspect of the municipal campaign in 1912 was not the entry of the SFIO but the unification of the Socialists' opponents that the campaign provoked. At the end of 1911 a correspondent for *Paris-Est* had predicted that there would be four competing slates in the municipal elections, two of Republicans, one of independent Republican Socialists, and one of Socialists. By the following spring the two Republican lists had merged, however, cumbersomely and confusingly, into the Republican Radical Socialist Union. This slate included most of the outgoing city councillors as well as several former ARIC members, mostly market gardeners. Out of the twenty-three candidates on the list, sixteen were market gardeners and two were farmers, the rest being members of the urban middle classes. The slate excluded Bobigny's working class—at this point more than two-fifths of the population. It embodied a political coalition among Bobigny's farmers, market gardeners, and middle classes to ward off the growing political challenge posed by local workers.[27]

The results of the 1912 municipal election made the need for such a coalition even more apparent. Although its list represented forces that dominated the political life of Bobigny, the Republican Radical Socialist Union obtained only 40 percent of the votes cast. The remaining 60 percent was divided between the SFIO slate and a group calling itself Republican Socialist. Since the Republican Radicals had won a bare plurality, the head of its list, outgoing Mayor Montigny, was reelected. The new city council consisted of fourteen members from the list and seven from that of the SFIO.[28]

The municipal election in 1912 signaled the end of the era in which the rivalry between farmers and market gardeners dominated politics in Bobigny and expressed itself in electoral battles among Radical factions. As *Paris-Est* recognized, city government in Bobigny would no longer be the same.

Has something changed in Bobigny? We would respond with the affirmative.

The group controlling the old city council, almost entirely composed of market gardeners and farmers, has lost seven seats. That is to say that the newcomers, who only yesterday represented a negligible fraction of the community, today easily represent as large a proportion as the old population.

> In consequence, we estimate that each neighborhood of the city is
> represented and we note with pleasure that allotment areas like la Folie, the
> Pont de Bondy, and Six Routes have their own councillor at city hall.[29]

The elections demonstrated that the progressive Radicals of Bobigny
had failed to transcend class politics or create a middle ground between
traditional republicanism and socialism. Although the Independent
Republican Socialists had done fairly well, they lost importance after
1912. Other representatives of the leftist Radicals either made their
peace with the traditional old guard or else, like Peysson, temporarily
cast their lot with the SFIO. From 1912 to 1919 the contest between
these two groups was to dominate political life in Bobigny.[30]

The Rise of Socialism in Bobigny

Before 1905 there was little distinction between socialists and leftist
Radicals in Bobigny. Even the local organization that supported Adrien
Veber's legislative campaign in 1902 was not a strictly socialistic one.
As late as 1904 a local commentator suggested that Bobigny's socialists
had no realistic prospects for electoral success.

> The socialists are agitating confusedly in Bobigny. Up until the present all
> their efforts have only succeeded in demonstrating their impotence. They
> challenge the Republicans who are determined not to give up any of their
> present gains. . . . Even with the protection of M. Veber, there is no chance
> that the red flag and the "Internationale" will be displayed in our streets. . . .
> Let us return to our fields, with the firm conviction that the republic will
> continue to triumph against the revolution in our city.[31]

Yet the views of this commentator were soon refuted by the surprising
strength of Bobigny's Socialists. In 1905 they scored their first electoral
gains, when the SFIO candidate came in second in Bobigny in the race
for the arrondissement council. Much of their success came from the
energy and organization with which they waged their campaign.
Another telling factor was the working-class background of Robillard,
the Socialist candidate. Because of it, many working-class voters who
had voted Nationalist switched their support to the SFIO.[32]

The SFIO's electoral gains, in the first year of its local founding,
came from the growing working class and its newly articulated class
consciousness. The workers and their families who moved into the
community after 1900 were isolated both physically and socially from
the other major population groups. It is not surprising that working-
class politics should reflect this isolation, all the more since neither

traditional nor progressive Radicals sought to include working-class representatives in their electoral slates. This situation helps to explain why many Bobigny workers had voted Nationalist at the beginning of the century; they were voting against the Radicals and the market gardeners. In forming a self-proclaimed working-class political organization whose candidates would be workers, the SFIO of Bobigny not only enabled local workers to vote for their own but spurred the growth of class consciousness among them.[33]

A growing working-class population boosted the Socialists' political strength in other Paris suburbs before 1914. Socialists controlled municipalities in substantial working-class communities like Ivry and Saint-Ouen before 1900. In Montreuil-sous-Bois, whose population was roughly one-third working class in 1912, the SFIO doubled the vote total of the Radicals and nearly won a plurality in that year's municipal elections. In Drancy, the SFIO candidate for the legislature in 1910 won the election with nearly two-fifths of the vote.[34]

In 1906 the SFIO section of Bobigny devoted most of its efforts to reelecting Veber to the legislature. In contrast to 1902, in this campaign Veber ran as a Socialist in Bobigny and received much less support from leftist Radicals and market gardeners than he had four years previously. Veber won, but his local campaign—a Socialist effort—did not. Other than this campaign and the legislative election of 1910, the SFIO took little part in local electoral politics until Bobigny's municipal election of 1912.[35]

It is hard to say whether the SFIO's minimal electoral participation in Bobigny from 1906 to 1912 derived from lack of resources or from greater emphasis on other aspects of organizing and community politics. In these years the Socialists did become involved in important community issues. In 1909, for example, they founded a local branch of the SFIO's Commuters' Federation, to press for improvements in Bobigny's tramway service. This effort led to conflicts with the progressive Radicals, who had been agitating over the same issue in their community organization and who regarded the local SFIO group as interlopers. The Socialists began to develop neighborhood groups; in 1912 they held a meeting to explore a possible section of the SFIO's People's University for Bobigny.[36]

In May 1910, in the aftermath of Veber's successful legislative reelection campaign, the Socialists of Bobigny issued their first position paper since the founding of the local section. In this document they elaborated SFIO's approach to dealing with community problems.

Comrades and small property owners—
You came to Bobigny fleeing the high rents of Paris and seeking to emancipate yourselves from the rapacity of bourgeois who exploit you in all possible ways.

Unfortunately, in our city you have found only high taxes, absurdly poor means of communication, rutted streets, insufficient lighting, mounds of garbage, and no drinking water. . . . On the other hand, you have a city administration that is very costly and incapable of making any social progress.

The schools have neither day-care centers nor lunch rooms, and your children have to wade through the mud in the winter in order to come home for lunch. . . .

In cities dominated by Socialist elements, they make the effort to create means of social education, such as *patronages laïques* [youth clubs], scientific conferences, and so forth.

For these reasons we invite you to join us and examine with us those municipal issues that are of greatest interest to you.[37]

From the first words of their manifesto, the Socialists of Bobigny identified their constituency as the working-class residents of the allotments, the *mal-lotis,* who had come to the community to realize their dreams of owning homes in the country and had instead been confronted with life in suburban slums. The manifesto ignored the farmers, market gardeners, and middle-class residents of Bobigny. Unlike the propaganda of the leftist Radicals, it emphasized that the SFIO was primarily a working-class party.

The other striking characteristic of this document was its strong emphasis on local issues and living conditions in Bobigny, as opposed to national questions and work-related grievances. The Socialists stressed the working class's immediate and omnipresent grievances, which they ascribed to the capitalist system, and gave less priority to the national struggle to implement socialism. The emphasis on living conditions over workplace issues reflected the experience of Bobigny, already largely a working-class commuters' suburb. Stressing the inadequacies of suburban life, the local SFIO mapped out a strategy that it and the Communist party used to great effect for a political base in early twentieth-century Bobigny.[38]

In 1912 the municipal elections put the SFIO on the political map. In their first attempt at winning control of Bobigny, the local Socialists recorded about one-third of the vote and elected seven of their members to the city council, the first Socialists to sit there. This vantage gave them the opportunity to develop their popular base by demanding improved tramway service and introducing petitions from their districts for better water and electric service, and other changes. Moreover, the elections marked the first time that Bobigny's Socialists campaigned independently of, and against, the progressive Radicals. In more ways than one, the 1912 elections indicated the maturation of the SFIO section in Bobigny.[39]

Special municipal elections in August 1914 provided dramatic proof of this growth. In July, after a wave of resignations from the city council, byelections were called to replace five of its members. Four lists contested, one of traditional Radicals, one of leftist Radicals, one of independent Socialists, and one of the SFIO. The split between the Radicals (who had united in 1912), as well as the continued divisions between the SFIO and independent Socialists (some of whom had been on the SFIO list in 1912), seemed to presage a return to the politics that preceded the SFIO's upsurge in 1912.[40]

Yet the electoral results showed that local politics would not return to the past. Four out of five of the SFIO's candidates were elected to the city council, in the first four places; the party's fifth candidate placed seventh. Except for city councillor Guieu, who defected to the independent Republican Socialists, the elections gave the Socialists control of ten out of twenty-one seats on the city council. Their stunning victory in the elections of 1914 resulted not from better electoral organization or strategy, but above all from the increasing percentage of their working-class constituency. It came at a momentous time: the elections took place on 1 August, the day after the assassination of Jean Jaurès and two days before France plunged into World War I. That night Balbynians sang the "Carmagnole" and the "Internationale" in the streets, as both Bobigny and France as a whole prepared to face a future they could not have predicted.[41]

The Triumph of Socialism

Municipal elections were suspended in France for the duration of the First World War. Politics seemed to come to a standstill as the country prepared communities for the war and then tackled the problems it caused. The first elections after the end of the war, in 1919, resulted in the complete triumph of the SFIO in Bobigny and ushered in an unbroken sequence of city administrations controlled by the Left. Although such a victory had been foreshadowed by the striking progress the Socialists achieved in Bobigny from 1905 to 1914, it was not automatic. During the war the representation on the city council they had gained in 1912 and 1914 became more valuable: without elections and with much of the press closed or censored, the activities of their city councillors were almost the only means the Socialists had to demonstrate their capabilities and intentions to the working people of Bobigny. The Bobigny SFIO's city councillors made a major effort to soften the impact of war on the people of the community, and this effort was not forgotten in 1919.[42]

The two basic wartime problems the city council had to deal with were food and fuel, especially coal. Early in the war the municipality formed an emergency coal stockpile, from which it sold coal to city residents.[43] Socialist councillors said the city was overcharging people for its coal, especially given the large quantities stored. They also transmitted citizens' complaints over the quality of coal distributed.

> M. Vasseur brought to the attention of the tribune of the council the complaints of a large number of people having affirmed the lack of equity in the distribution of coal, and he noted that he had confirmed that some people have received coal that was 95 percent powder, whereas others got large chunks.
> M. Beaugé joined his protests to those of his colleague Vasseur and advised that equity in the distribution can only exist when the practice of tipping has been suppressed.[44]

Food, or preventing shortages of food, also became a major political issue. One of the council's first acts in August 1914 to prepare the community for war was to establish municipal soup kitchens in the schoolhouse, which served meals for twenty centimes, approximately the cost of a pound of bread. As the war dragged on, the SFIO city councillors began protesting that this was not enough, that measures should be taken to reduce the inflation of food costs for the majority of the population who did not use the soup kitchens.[45]

Socialist members of Bobigny's city council tried to ensure that public transportation ran smoothly and frequently pointed out inadequacies of service, especially in the number of working-class trams. They also lobbied for a city workhouse, which was headed by the SFIO city councillor Pierre Adam. It manufactured pants and, employing mostly women with children, slightly eased wartime unemployment in the community.[46]

Most of their wartime activities Socialist city councillors devoted to protect the living standards of their working-class constituents. There were exceptions, however, including a motion in 1916 that put socialism on the map in Bobigny. Noting that Bobigny was one of the few Republican municipalities in the Department of the Seine that had not honored Jean Jaurès, the assassinated Socialist statesman, Jules Vasseur proposed to rename the rue de Romainville, avenue Jean Jaurès. In spite of protests from local shopkeepers, many with shops located in the rue de Romainville, the city council voted to adopt the change—the most visible sign of increased Socialist influence in municipal affairs during World War I.[47]

Although not caught up in the wave of revolutionary enthusiasm that swept central and eastern Europe in 1919, French politics immediately after the war displayed a decided tendency toward extremes. On the Left, sympathy for the Russian revolution and protests against wartime inflation created massive strikes in 1919 and 1920. In both the labor movement and the SFIO, radicals were clearly on the offensive, forming the French Communist party in 1920 and causing a schism in the Confédération générale du travail in 1921. On the Right, members of the Party of Order joined with many Radicals frightened of bolshevism and resentful of the Treaty of Versailles to form the Bloc national, which scored a landslide victory in the legislative elections of November 1919.[48]

In the same month, Bobigny held its first full municipal elections in seven years. Aside from the SFIO's impressive rise in the community since 1905, many indications pointed to a Socialist victory. By the end of 1919 both the national SFIO and its union ally, the Confédération générale du travail, were growing rapidly. Although the national SFIO did poorly in the legislative elections, it scored close to 30 percent of the vote in the Paris suburbs of the Department of the Seine; in Bobigny the Socialist candidate won a majority of the vote for the first time in the city's history. Moreover, 1919 was a year of heightened revolutionary expectations all over Europe, registered even in Bobigny.[49]

In contrast to the elections in 1912 and 1914, in 1919 municipal elections in Bobigny were contested only by two slates, the SFIO and the Republican and Social Union. The Socialist list included most of the party's city councillors, plus politicians, such as Léon Rouberty, who had earlier belonged to independent socialist groupings, and political neophytes, such as Léon Pesch, who would affect Bobigny's political future. Almost all were running as candidates for the first time; of the twenty-three individuals on the SFIO list, four were incumbents and only one, Robert Saunier, had been elected before 1914.[50]

The candidates on the Republican and Social Union list were equally new to electoral politics in Bobigny; only two were incumbents. The newness of the candidates on both lists and the fact that there were only two slates indicated the beginning of a new political era in Bobigny. World War I served as a great divide; before 1919 the working-class Left possessed only marginal influence in city politics, whereas after 1919 it achieved permanent control of the municipality. During the war the city's Socialists had strengthened their appeal and increased their natural working-class constituency. The municipal elections were their opportunity to show how well they had used this time.

The municipal elections, the first round of which took place on 30 November 1919, were not even close. Under France's new system of proportioned voting, each ballot could contain as many votes (in this case, 23) as there were positions to be filled. Out of 1,089 ballots cast, the top SFIO candidate won 609 votes, while the one at the bottom of the list won 588. The vote totals of the representatives of the Republican and Social Union list, by contrast, ranged from 432 to 463. These municipal elections, unlike the legislative elections a month earlier, were a general success for the SFIO. In the Department of the Seine the number of city governments controlled by the SFIO bounded from seven to twenty-five, and in the provinces for the first time the party took control of important centers like Toulon and Lille.[51]

Among the reasons for the local victory of the Socialists in 1919 is one of national dimension. Balbynians shared the desires of their fellow citizens all over France for a better life and for social equality after many years of hardship and sacrifice; the SFIO articulated these desires for its working-class constituency. Certainly the SFIO's vigor at the national level immediately after the war also contributed to the Socialists' victory in Bobigny.[52]

Yet by far the most substantial reason for their victory in Bobigny was the increase in the community's working-class population, to which the Socialists succeeded in forming strong links. From 1911 to 1921, when the desperate wartime housing shortages occurred in Paris and the allotments expanded phenomenally, the working-class percentage of the population of Bobigny rose from under 44 percent to over 60 percent. By 1921 the employés were another 10 percent of the population, whereas the farmers and market gardeners together made up only slightly over 18 percent. These statistics made victory certain for any party that could win the loyalty of most of the former groups—the Socialists' appeal to Bobigny's *mal-lotis* won city hall.[53]

In 1912, moreover, competing for control of the municipality had been two socialist lists, which divided the majority of the vote they won. The disappearance of the independent Republican Socialists, some joining the SFIO and others leaving local politics, figured in the victory of the SFIO in November 1919. Some leftist Radicals, such as Paul Peysson, who had adopted socialist ideals and causes, were unable to make the transition from a political faction supported by market gardeners and employés to a group based on the working class. In addition, the independent Socialists lacked ideological coherence and national organization; they posed little obstacle to the SFIO's successful struggle for the allegiance of Bobigny's working class.[54]

The municipal elections of 1919 were a great success for the SFIO in the Paris suburbs and marked the beginning of the Red Belt. The Socialists retained the seven city halls they had previously won, took over eighteen new ones, and established strong minority positions in six more. The combination of intense industrial mobilization in the Paris area and unprecedented housing shortages in Paris during World War I had created the working-class base for the Socialists' success of November 1919.[55]

Well before the SFIO rose to importance in Bobigny, the community's political life had reflected the social split between farmers and market gardeners. The Socialist electoral victory in 1919 showed that, although the dividing lines had moved, local politics remained largely based on class. This fact was demonstrated in the 1920s and 1930s by the PCF, successor to the SFIO, which regularly received a majority of the vote in this predominantly working-class community.[56]

The SFIO had power in Bobigny for only one year before the Congress of Tours split the old party in two to form the new French Communist party. But the Socialists nonetheless made it clear that their victory would bring changes to Bobigny, as their enemies noted with sarcasm.

> It is generally clear that something has changed in Bobigny. In other times, when the "bourgeoisie" held the pot handle, it was rare to see official papers pasted on the walls. The public's attention was called upon only when it was indispensable to do so, and the city authorities tried to be as brief as administrative form permitted.
>
> Now this is no longer true. The former city councillors worked and did not talk. In their place the electors have preferred orators, citizens capable of speaking for an hour without saying anything.[57]

During its year in office, the SFIO municipality began work on a number of important city projects. These included paving the avenue Jean Jaurès and the chemin de Groslay, bringing electricity to the community, and constructing schools for the Pont de Bondy district. One of the first acts of the new administration in 1920 was to vote to install a bust of Jean Jaurès (paid for by individual city councillors, not the municipality) in the council chambers.[58]

From Socialism to Communism

Although a majority of the SFIO's members voted to affiliate with the Third International and the new PCF in December 1920, only a minority of Socialist officeholders—including municipal officials—approved the decision. In the Paris region, however, of the twenty-five SFIO city administrations in the Department of the Seine, sixteen chose to join the new party; they included Bobigny's Socialists. Their choice in 1920 was not atypical.[59] More unusual was their ability to keep the municipality in the hands of the PCF over the next few years. For members of the PCF, these were years in which the new party was being recast along more Leninist principles; many who had originally joined out of vague sympathy with the Russian revolution became disillusioned and often left or were expelled from the PCF. For municipal officials, the Communist leadership's insistence on their subordination to the national Party was an onerous consequence of the Congress of Tours. As a result, many city administrations that had declared themselves Communist in December 1920 soon revolted: in October 1922 an influential mayor, Henri Sellier of Suresnes, led eight suburban municipalities in the Department of the Seine to quit the Party. By 1925, on the eve of the first municipal elections contested by the PCF, it retained only three city halls in the Seine: Bobigny, Saint-Denis, and Villetaneuse.[60]

The experience of Saint-Denis exemplifies the chaotic first years of PCF municipal government. In December 1920, seven Saint-Denis city councillors rejected the choice of the majority and voted to stay with the SFIO. More significant was the refusal of most of the new Communist city councillors to follow the directives of the Saint-Denis PCF section; they held to the traditional autonomy of municipal officials. In July 1921 these councillors elected one of their own as mayor, removing Saint-Denis from PCF control. The PCF regained city hall in May 1922 after byelections, only to lose control of it again in February 1923, after several of its city councillors were expelled from the Party. Not until the regular municipal elections of May 1925 (and just barely then) did the PCF succeed in wresting definitive control of Saint-Denis from a coalition of Socialists and dissident Communists.[61]

Although in Bobigny the hold of the PCF over the city administration was never seriously contested during this period, discord among city councillors did lead to resignations from the Party and the city council. For example, Pierre Beaugé, one of the four SFIO city councillors elected in 1914, sent two letters to the prefect of the Seine in April and July 1921, alleging that Clamamus was abusing his functions as mayor. Beaugé then stopped coming to city council meetings. Refusing a summons to explain his actions to the council, he resigned his position in October.[62] In a similar, though less dramatic, case, Jules Vasseur, another SFIO candidate elected in 1914, clashed with the mayor and his fellow city councillors over the relations between the municipality and local Communist organizations. At a March 1923 council meeting Vasseur protested Clamamus's endorsement, in the name of the Bobigny municipality, of a dance held by a Communist sports society, La Prolétarienne. Other councillors attacked Vasseur's position, one stating that it was natural for the mayor to grant municipal approval to a working-class organization.[63] Vasseur and others like him did not last long in the new Bobigny. The slate that the Bobigny PCF ran in the 1925 municipal elections contained mostly newcomers. Out of twenty-two candidates, only eight had been elected in 1919, and only one (Clamamus himself) in 1914. Thus the PCF that fought the elections in 1925 was not the same political party as at the beginning of 1921.[64]

And yet despite these changes in Bobigny the PCF had managed to hold onto the municipality from December 1920. By the 1930s Bobigny was the only city in the Department of the Seine to have achieved this record without a break. Why was Bobigny unique? Structural explanations do not suffice. It is possible, for example, that the newness of Bobigny's Socialist administration allowed its members to accept the PCF; they had not had time to get used to the traditional autonomy of municipal officials, and the PCF's stricter guidelines might not have seemed burdensome.[65]

More significant were the attitudes of the suburban mayors toward the new PCF. I have not analyzed the political history of every Parisian suburb in the early 1920s, but of those I have, in each case a Socialist suburban mayor led a majority of his city councillors in opting for either the new PCF or the SFIO. In Puteaux, the first Socialist administration was elected in 1912 and reelected in 1919; the municipality split in 1920, yet Mayor Charles Auray stayed in power as a Socialist, and the return of three city councillors from the PCF to the SFIO in 1924 assured him and his party full control of the city council. More typical were the experiences of Montreuil and Drancy. In both communities the first Socialist municipality was elected in 1919; following the local mayors, the councils joined the PCF overwhelmingly in 1920 and left the Party at the end of 1922. Moreover both mayors, Poncet of Montreuil and Duchanel of Drancy, dominated local politics until the Popular Front of 1936.[66]

Bobigny provided another example of this trend. The consistent emphasis that Bobigny's Socialists placed on local rather than national issues certainly kept their organizations intact amid national and international schisms in the workers' movement. Yet their emphasis resulted less from structural factors than from individual personalities, above all that of Mayor Clamamus. As mayor of Bobigny throughout the 1920s and 1930s, Jean-Marie Clamamus was the city's preeminent Communist leader; to many inside and outside the community, he *was* red Bobigny. In 1920 Clamamus did not personally dominate politics as he would ten years later, but his prestige was sufficient in 1920 to cause his colleagues on the city council to follow his choice between the two leftist parties (unless they dropped out of politics). Unlike many other suburbanites, few who left Bobigny's city council and the PCF in the early 1920s rejoined the local SFIO, which between the wars remained weak, almost inexistent. Clamamus's stress on local concerns, above all the problems of the *mal-lotis*, meant that Communists who disagreed with national policy would keep their party membership without continuous, total adherence to the exact Party line. The local PCF was able to maintain the consensus reached at the Congress of Tours during the Party's stormy infancy, thanks to the political astuteness of the city's mayor.

Interwar Electoral Politics

Compared to that of the French Communist party and of many Communist municipalities, Bobigny's history of electoral politics between the wars was uneventful; nothing challenged the dominant position of the local PCF. Of the three municipal elections during the 1920s and 1930s, the PCF handily won those of 1925 and 1935; in 1929 it was unopposed. The legislative elections presented a similar picture. Clamamus was elected to the national legislature for the first time in 1924 from a district including Bobigny and most of the northeastern suburbs of the Department of the Seine. He was reelected in 1928 and 1932; he stepped down in 1936, having been elected to the Senate, whereupon he was replaced in the legislature by Gaston

Monmousseau, also representing the PCF. Only in 1928 did Clamamus face significant opposition.[67]

The power and stability of Bobigny's PCF were unusual in the Paris Red Belt in two respects. First, Communists in other suburbs generally faced more formidable opposition, especially from the Right. In Ivry, for example, the PCF outdistanced the rightist slate by only three percentage points in the second round of the 1925 municipal elections, and by one percentage point in the second round of the 1928 legislative elections; not until 1936 did it win a majority of the vote on the first round.[68] Second, many PCF suburban municipalities—including Clichy, Saint-Denis, Villetaneuse, Malakoff, and Pierrefitte—were taken over by Communist dissidents at one point or another between the wars. The solidity of the PCF's base in Bobigny was in fact more typical of the Red Belt after 1945 than in the 1920s and 1930s.[69] Their electoral power was indomitable, based on local issues and networks, not on national politics. Even when the PCF was in poor straits elsewhere in France during the late 1920s and the early 1930s, in Bobigny it continued to receive solid majorities over all opponents (Table 19). The fact that many Balbynians identified themselves as Communists (not necessarily militant or activist), added to the achievements of the PCF municipality and the personal popularity of Mayor Clamamus, explained the interwar political situation in Bobigny better than specific political issues or campaigns.

TABLE 19

THE PCF'S PERCENTAGE OF THE VOTE IN BOBIGNY ELECTIONS

	Legislative Elections			
	1924	*1928*	*1932*	*1936*
Bobigny	59.6	66.8	65.7	70.3
Electoral district	35.7	33.1	38.7	56.1
	Municipal Elections			
	1925	*1929*	*1935*	
Bobigny	47.0	76.3	69.8	

SOURCES: For legislative elections—Annie Fourcaut and Jacques Girault, "Les conseillers municipaux d'une commune ouvrière et communiste," *Cahiers d'histoire de l'Institut Maurice Thorez* 19 (1976): 66; for municipal elections—Annie Fourcaut, "Bobigny, banlieue rouge," *Communisme* 3 (1983): 14.

The PCF drew a large share of the vote in the electoral district (most of the northeastern suburbs of the Department of the Seine) and all over Bobigny; it was strongest in the Pont de Bondy. In the 1928 legislative elections, it won 72 percent of the vote in this neighborhood and received 65 percent in central Bobigny. Conversely, the Right received 21 percent of the vote in the center, but only 10 percent in the Pont de Bondy. Although the central voting district contained many allotments, it also held Bobigny's few shopkeepers and market gardeners, two population groups hostile to the PCF.[70]

Even though the working class's general identification with the interests of the PCF largely determined the outcome of local elections, there were aspects of the local Communists' electoral strategy that improved its prospects. One of these concerned the class background of the candidates whom the Communists backed. In all three municipal elections of the interwar period, a majority of the PCF candidates for the Bobigny city council were of working-class background, and many of the remainder were employés. The PCF was not unique in this strategy, nor was it imposed by the national PCF during its *bolchévisation* campaign. (In 1919, 70 percent of the SFIO's candidates in Bobigny were also from working-class backgrounds.) By the 1930s it was evident that an electoral list without working-class candidates had no chance in Bobigny, so that even the Right proposed a predominantly working-class list for the 1935 municipal elections. Nonetheless, the PCF was more consistent in giving the workers of Bobigny a chance to "vote for their own." Similarly, including employés on the Communist electoral slates reflected both the local party's ties to Bobigny and its conscious attempts to maintain its support there. It was this attention to the sensitivities of its constituents that sustained the crucial sense of identification between the Communists and the people in Bobigny.[71]

Campaign literature featured prominently in the PCF's electoral strategy. In addition to the usual propaganda, I uncovered two lengthy manifestos for the municipal elections of 1929 and 1935, both of which praised the achievements of the Communist municipality. In language almost identical to that in the 1929 manifesto, the 1935 document argued that the high quality of the PCF's municipal administration justified a vote for its candidates.

> When in 1925, once again asking for your votes, we examined the achievements made since 1919 by your working-class elected officials, we did not fail to indicate to you the great difficulties we would encounter in trying to carry out the program that we presented to you.

Today, in spite of the difficulties that have occurred, resulting from the general financial situation created by the Bloc national and the Cartel des gauches, we are proud to affirm that this program has in large part been achieved.

None can even dream of denying the excellence of the city administration of Bobigny.

On every side, in the legislature, in the central government (despite the latter's constant struggle against communism), people acknowledge the impeccable financial management, the imaginative initiatives, and the audacious achievements of the Communist municipal elected officials of Bobigny.[72]

Both manifestos had subsections dealing with the municipality's achievements in financial management, welfare, public instruction and hygiene, public works, and so forth. Neither manifesto, nor any other campaign literature put out by the Bobigny PCF, centered on the workplace or the significant ideological change in the national PCF from the "class against class" period to that of the Popular Front. From time to time the PCF would indicate these shifts: for example, in 1935 it put out a small brochure detailing the effect of the depression on small shopkeepers and its proposals to help them. It did not show such concern for shopkeepers in the late 1920s and early 1930s.[73]

Concentrating for the most part on local issues, Communist electoral propaganda avoided doctrinal differences in municipal elections. Even in legislative elections, the local PCF emphasized loyalty to a political party that had done so much for the workers of Bobigny. In any electoral campaign the competing parties will naturally emphasize their most impressive achievements; for the Communists of Bobigny those were the achievements of the municipality. For the PCF militants and the average voters of Bobigny alike, communism was above all a local affair; their common viewpoint was reflected in the consistent electoral success of the PCF in Bobigny.

In conclusion, the electoral history of Bobigny in the early twentieth century supports our contention that residential issues, not workplace concerns, dominated the community's political life. At the beginning of the century the major political debates centered on the way Bobigny should develop. Right from the start, Bobigny's Socialists stressed their determination to amend the poor living conditions of the city's workers. The communists inherited this approach to local politics and carried it to fruition in the 1920s and 1930s.

From the late nineteenth century until the Second World War, political allegiance in Bobigny paralleled social class. Before 1900 the open-field farmers supported the Party of Order, whereas the market gardeners voted for the Radicals. The arrival of a suburban population reinforced this general pattern, as the workers and employés solidly backed their own political party, the Socialists and then the Communists. For workers and employés social class related more to similarities in urban structure than to differences in workplace. Farmers, market gardeners, workers, and employés represented different degrees of urban development; conflicts among the latter three groups, for example, arose not at the point of production but rather from the contrasting needs and desires of rural and suburban populations. Political class conflict in Bobigny thus assumed a distinctly urban flavor.

Its urban background explains why Bobigny's history of elections was so undramatic: to a large extent political conflict reflected its gradual suburbanization. One reason why Communist politics in Bobigny did not reflect the weakness or volatility of the French labor movement in the interwar years was its link to urban change; as the pace of suburbanization stabilized after the mid-1920s, so did local communism. The correspondence between the arrival of a new urban and working-class population in Bobigny and the shifts in its political life is so strong that these changes could almost be seen as an autonomous process.

Yet that was not the case. The crucial factor in the success of the Socialists and then the Communists in Bobigny was that they *won* the allegiance of the city's working class. The isolation of that class from community life tended to promote class solidarity, but such feeling did not automatically translate into votes for the Left. The Left worked to win this allegiance; it did so by using its control of the municipality to improve local living conditions and by developing an extensive network of community associations that shaped residential life in Bobigny. It was into these areas, rather than electoral politics strictly defined, that the PCF put the bulk of its efforts in Bobigny. Electoral politics was responsible for the slogan "red Bobigny"; it was municipal policies and community activism that made that slogan a reality.

CHAPTER 5

The Communist Municipality of Bobigny

The Communist party's long-term control of Bobigny's municipal government made the community unique in the Paris area. In analyzing such a political formation, we should consider whether its existence as a Communist entity made any difference to the town's inhabitants. It existed within a capitalist system; if Stalin could not create socialism in one country, Mayor Clamamus had no hope of doing so in one city. Yet the people of Bobigny consistently elected a Communist city government; in seeking to discover why, we must consider its actions and achievements.

One fact that emerges from our previous discussion is the municipality's overriding concern with urban issues. Just as the problems of suburbanization dominated political debate in Bobigny, so the need to resolve those problems governed activities of the Communists. By no means did they see themselves simply as a party of municipal reform; they linked their ideological agenda to the most pressing daily concerns of their working-class constituents. In Bobigny such concerns were urban issues, a fact the PCF city government astutely grasped and acted on.

Municipality, State, and Party

Before looking at the accomplishments of the Communist municipality of Bobigny in the interwar period, we must bring into context two constraints on its activities. The French national government strictly limited the powers of municipal governments; the French Communist party, like the French state, was a centralized national organization and left as little as possible to local initiative. They did not act in concert, but both forces influenced the policies of Bobigny.

The law of 5 April 1884 created the regulations that governed French municipalities, continuing the highly centralized government established by Napoleon. The responsibility of overseeing the work of city officials fell to the prefect of each department. Appointed directly by the president of the republic, the prefect was a department's administrative head and worked under the minister of the interior. The prefect's broad range of powers over municipal government was perhaps most significant in city finances; all city budgets had to be approved by the prefect. Moreover, if the city government failed to include enough funding for necessary services like police or education, the prefect had the power to add these to the budget and force the municipality to levy additional taxes to cover their cost. This policy allowed him a part in determining what programs a municipality could undertake.[1]

Finances were by no means a prefect's only avenue of influence over city governments. The prefecture administered programs for education and relief of poverty with little input from local municipalities. Although city governments paid for police services, police commissioners were usually appointed by the prefect or the president of the republic. The prefect had the general right to annul any city council decision that he judged to be beyond the parameters of municipal concerns. Finally, the prefect had extensive disciplinary powers over municipal governments. In the case of illegal actions by city officials, he could temporarily suspend them from their functions or expel them from their positions.[2]

Although not applicable to the city of Paris itself, the law of 1884 did cover its suburbs and the rest of the Department of the Seine. In the Seine, however, in contrast to other departments, suburban municipalities had not one but two prefects to deal with; they were also subject to the decisions of a prefect of police. This official had jurisdiction over all matters of public order and safety in the suburbs, such as surveillance of public places, control of vagrants, and maintenance of prisons. The function was justified by a greater need for security in the capital, and by the natural turbulence of large cities.[3]

These strict prefectural controls meant that major aspects of life in Bobigny lay beyond the influence of its Communist municipality. The city council could not change the curriculum in local schools to reflect Marxist ideology, for example. The relative powerlessness of French municipal government explains the PCF's pessimistic view of its possibilities: the PCF rejected the concept of "municipal socialism" within a capitalist state and constantly emphasized national political issues over local concerns.[4]

The Communists were not the first leftist political party to grapple with socialism's implications for municipal government. In 1881 the "Possibilist" party of Paul Brousse published a program advocating municipal autonomy from the central government, municipal ownership of public utilities like gas and water, and local control of unemployment relief and other services. Other socialists, notably Jules Guesde, attacked this program as simply reformist. In rejecting municipal socialism, therefore, the PCF adopted much of the prewar critique by the Guesdists.[5] This attitude toward city government was not restricted to Communists in France; for the Comintern, municipal issues definitely had secondary significance. The Second World Congress of the Communist International, held in Moscow from 19 July to 7 August 1920, indicated its view of the relation between communism and municipal government by devoting a single paragraph to the subject:

> 13. Communists, if they obtain a majority in municipalities, should: a) form a revolutionary opposition to the central power of the bourgeoisie; b) try by all possible means to serve the interests of the poorest part of the population (economic measures, creation of or attempts to create an armed workers' militia, etc. . . .); c) use every opportunity to reveal the obstacles raised by the bourgeois State against all radical reforms; d) develop on this basis energetic revolutionary propaganda, without fearing conflicts with the bourgeois State; e) replace, in certain conditions, municipal governments with soviets of workers' deputies. All the action of Communists in the municipalities should be integrated into the general task of the disintegration of the capitalist system.[6]

Aside from specific instructions, such as replacing municipal governments by soviets, which reflected the revolutionary hopes of the era, this Comintern document clearly expressed the view that all specific actions by Communist municipalities should work to overthrow capitalism. It referred to concrete reforms that Communists in control of city governments could make to improve the material conditions of the working class only obliquely, in one phrase, "economic measures." It devoted greater attention, in subsections (c) and (d), to using the municipality to embarrass and hinder the central government. Even in its single paragraph on local issues, the Comintern emphasized the primacy of national politics; this remained a central theme of the PCF's programs for municipal government.[7]

Throughout the 1920s and 1930s certain broad themes character-ized the Party's policies on city government. First and foremost—in line with the Comintern document—all municipal activity must be subor-dinated to the main task of challenging the capitalist system on a national level; municipal socialism was simply reformist or unrealistic. The municipality could serve the interests of the working class only by helping to prepare the socialist revolution; without this clear perspec-tive any reforms it achieved could harm those long-term interests by delaying the development of revolutionary class consciousness. PCF propaganda constantly pointed out the limits that the French state imposed on municipal activities, as in an article on the Communist city government of Clichy. After listing all the material improvements implemented, the author noted,

> Certainly, the workers are still exploited by capital just as much in Clichy as elsewhere. And that which a municipality can do in the bourgeois state, under the yoke of bourgeois power, is nothing in comparison with what should be done—*with what cannot be done until the proletariat holds state power in its hands.* Certainly, what a municipality can do is nothing in comparison to what the soviet will do tomorrow.
>
> The example of Clichy shows nonetheless that Communist workers are capable of managing the interests of the workers much better than the bourgeois who administer city halls for the profit of *their* class.[8]

Aside from general revolutionary theory and strategy, a more immediate reason for the national leadership to downgrade municipal issues was its determination to ensure that local Communist politicians remained firmly under the control of the Party. Where the PCF controlled a city government, a Communist mayor could build up a personal base of support and thus challenge the Party's leadership.[9] Traditionally, political parties in France were loosely structured orga-nizations, with little effective control over the activities of their elected officials. This was particularly true at the municipal level, where a politician's activities often had more to do with his position in local society than with his party affiliation. In trying to create a new kind of political party in France, party leaders rejected the traditional auton-omy of French politicians; they feared moreover that municipal officials immersed in local affairs would lose sight of the broad lines of PCF policy and gradually lapse into reformism. Therefore the goal was to

keep Communist mayors and city councillors on a short leash; but this
was easier said than done.

Circular on the Control of Municipal Activity

In spite of precise directives repeated a hundred times, there are still some
municipalities that try to evade the control of the Party, or district
organizations that neglect their duty to control the municipalities.

We remind you that this control is an absolute obligation and also that
the actions of municipal councillors cannot be overseen from a distance, but
only by working closely with them. If this is not done, the municipal
councillors can hide behind the excuse of artificial technical difficulties, or
else comrades may ignore real technical difficulties and commit mistakes.[10]

In general the organizational methods devised by the PCF to manage
municipal politics seem to have functioned sporadically, if at all.[11] They
were part of the larger organizational structure decreed by the policy of
bolchévisation, which tried to increase the role of working-class
militants and the control of PCF leaders over all aspects of Party life.[12]
Yet in spite of the plethora of dummy committees, commissions, and
sections, the PCF asserted effective control over its city governments. It
did so by ensuring the uniformity of all municipal electoral
campaigns;[13] most important, it expelled Communist municipal politicians who failed to adhere to the Party line. In 1929 there was a wave
of expulsions of local officials who had refused to accept the PCF's new,
ultraleftist "class against class" position.[14] The PCF's ability to regain
control of Saint-Denis after expelling Jacques Doriot clearly showed its
success in changing the traditional relation between French political
parties and their elected representatives, and in dominating municipal
policy.[15]

Involvement in city politics benefited the Party, especially when the
PCF gained control of a municipality. First of all, the Communist
municipality was useful in providing an electoral base for Party leaders,
such as Maurice Thorez, mayor of Ivry (or Doriot, mayor of Saint-
Denis). The PCF also used city payrolls to provide sinecures for
important Party activists; for example, a police report of March 1933
noted that the Communist militant Suzanne Girault had been appointed a mayoral assistant in Vitry.[16] The leaders of the young
Communist party considered control of a city government gave its
organizers on-the-spot training in administrative skills. By training and
closely supervising the work of Communist municipal officials, the
Party could exercise greater control over them and create the adminis-
trators for the workers' state of the future.[17]

From time to time the PCF called on city governments to challenge the national government, to defy "bourgeois legality." By going beyond the juridical bounds set for municipal government, PCF local officials would show workers how those legal limits worked against their class interests. Workers would then, the Party hoped, draw the lesson that only by destroying the bourgeois state that set and enforced those limits could they improve their condition.

> We must always keep in mind that this program and the revolutionary municipal action that it entails will inevitably break the limits of bourgeois legality and that it will come up against the repressive measures of the bourgeois state and its apparatus (prefecture, police). Thus every time that the authorities place obstacles before our [workers'] class policy, and harass or imprison our elected officials, we should seize the occasion to denounce to the masses more vigorously than ever before the constraint, the repression, and the dictatorship of the bourgeois state, to undertake a vast campaign of agitation and mobilization of the masses for the defense of *their* Communist municipality and *their* Communist party.[18]

The Party expected Communist mayors, for example, to close their city halls in observance of its general strikes, to show that they were not simple politicians like any others but were above all servants of the revolutionary interests of the working class. In January 1930 the Party censured the PCF mayors of Clichy and Chambon for "capitulating before the bourgeoisie" when they agreed not to hold Communist meetings at their city halls if the local prefects agreed not to send police into their communities during the PCF's general strike on 1 August 1929.[19]

Perhaps most useful in winning over the vast numbers of workers unaware of revolutionary class consciousness, Communist municipalities could enact reforms to improve the material standards of the working class. They could demonstrate at once their administrative competence and their working-class credentials. The Paris suburbs, which had more people living under PCF governments than any other part of France, were key to this strategy. The Communist municipalities of the Department of the Seine thus became the PCF's laboratory for testing its municipal policies.[20]

Communist city governments in the Paris suburbs did devote a lot of attention to improving local living conditions. Bobigny and Vitry took the lead in dealing with the problems of their defective allotments, of vital concern to suburbanites. Saint-Denis, the largest suburb controlled by the PCF, was especially active in building new urban facilities and upgrading old ones. During the 1920s and early 1930s the city built an entire new school complex, repaired or enlarged many other school buildings, built a swimming pool, a day-care center, a city library, and set up a summer camp for the city's children. And such activities built the long-term bases of PCF electoral strength in the Paris suburbs.[21]

A related aspect of the PCF's municipal policy was the concept of Communist city governments as "bastions of socialism." PCF municipalities were expected to use their governmental powers to aid unions and other working-class organizations.

> We must create, or at least try to create, a proletarian municipal policy, whose principal tasks were determined by the last presidium of the Communist International: . . . support the economic struggles of the workers by the vote of subsidies to strikers, by the organization of soup kitchens for the strikers and their families, by the organization of colonies for their children.[22]

One instance was the massive sitdown strikes of June 1936, the largest of the interwar period, when Communist municipalities organized soup kitchens for the striking workers. During the depression PCF city governments were instructed to help committees of local unemployed workers, by letting them hold meetings in municipal buildings, for example.[23]

For us, the PCF's interwar municipal policies are more than a record of events, however significant: they give us the key to a fundamental characteristic of the Party, its centralized structure. To a greater extent than in socialist groups before 1914, decisions within the PCF were made by the leadership and imposed on Party members. The leadership took this structure from Moscow, believing that such centralization made the Party more effective in fighting capitalism. But the structure also mirrored that of the highly centralized French state. Especially for municipal policy, the structure of the PCF was both a result of Soviet directives and a distorted reflection of French government. "Fighting fire with fire" in working for the revolutionary overthrow of the French government, the PCF reproduced the French hierarchical structure within itself.[24]

Ideological Actions of Bobigny's Communist Municipality

As a Communist stronghold during the 1920s and 1930s, Bobigny offers an excellent example of how the national Party's instructions concerning municipal governments worked at the local level. Much of the Communists' success came from the city administration's ability to resolve the concrete problems resulting from Bobigny's chaotic and overrapid urbanization; still, Bobigny's Communists were not just "sewer socialists." The city council did take many overtly political positions and in general attempted to use the Bobigny municipality to serve the broader revolutionary goals of French communism.

One service expected from Communist municipalities was to put the resources of the city government at the disposal of the national Party and of Communist causes. Among the numerous allegations that the city government of Bobigny subsidized the work of the PCF—both the local section and the national organization—were those made by the right-wing *Journal de Saint-Denis,* a newspaper which covered the northern Paris suburbs. Yet the *Journal de Saint-Denis* was not the only observer to note these practices at Bobigny's city hall. In 1928 a police report stated that the municipality had purchased a Citroën, which was used exclusively to transport PCF candidates to electoral rallies. Given the widespread use of Communist municipalities for similar purposes, this was almost certainly no isolated incident.[25]

At times PCF city governments aided the clandestine activities of international Communist officials. For example, Mayor Clamamus was able to give Jules Humbert-Droz, a Swiss Communist working for the Third International, falsified papers with the identity of a painter residing in Bobigny.[26] As Clamamus later confirmed, this was not the only time he used his official position to perform services for Moscow: "I hid in Bobigny . . . the first agents from Russia, Diegott for example, who came at the same time as Richard Schuller, to prepare for the arrival of Clara Zetkin. They were friends. . . . Others came afterwards. I never asked them their names."[27]

The Bobigny municipality tried to help the work of local Communist organizations, often allowing them to use city buildings for meetings and rallies. The Edouard Vaillant marketplace and the *maison du peuple* on several occasions served local Communists for informational meetings, showing films, and similar activities. The city sometimes cosponsored demonstrations with the PCF section. One very solemn instance occurred in 1938 when the city government, with every Communist and sympathetic organization in Bobigny, held a public funeral service to honor two young citizens of the community who had died while serving with the International brigades in Spain.[28]

In addition, Bobigny's Communist municipality displayed solidarity with PCF national actions. To honor the general strike against fascism called by both the PCF and the Socialist party on 12 February 1934, the city government permitted the picketing and closing of the local schools. On 12 October 1925, the Party sponsored a one-day general strike to protest the French government's repression of Moroccan independence fighters in the Rif. Mayor Clamamus closed Bobigny's city hall and gave all city workers the day off while he went on working in his office. Disregarding Clamamus's protests that he was not responsible for a municipal walkout, the prefect of the Seine charged that "in officially announcing the halting of public services, M. Clamamus has gravely failed in his duties" and suspended him from his functions for one month.[29]

The PCF condemned this decision as a politically motivated attack against communism in general. During a session of the Chamber of Deputies dealing with the suspension of PCF mayors after the 12 October general strike, Clamamus spoke.

> The measures taken against certain Communist mayors are arbitrary . . . *these mayors can be reproached with nothing more than having participated in an antiwar demonstration.* To suspend a mayor because, independent of his will, city services did not function, is arbitrary. . . . Your decisions are class decisions. The workers of the suburbs will not accept them. No matter what you decide, the people of the suburbs will oppose your arbitrary exercise of power.[30]

In fact, what lay behind this participation by Communist municipalities in general strikes was not the belief that such aid would bring about their success. In part it was a desire to show that Communist city officials were not like other politicians, that they did not always accept the rules of the game. More important, as Clamamus's statement demonstrates, Communists hoped that such actions would discredit the government in the eyes of the working class and win over the workers to the PCF. In this instance, therefore, the contribution asked of a Communist municipality like Bobigny was not so much material as symbolic and didactic.

By far the most significant project to further the national PCF was the establishment of the Bobigny Lenin School in November 1924; the police raided the school at the end of the year, more than anything else confirming Bobigny's reputation as a solidly Communist suburb. The Bobigny Lenin School was the first national school the PCF set up to train the leadership of the future. In the early 1920s in several local schools the PCF had attempted to train its working-class members in Marxist theory and the history of workers' movements. Bolchévisation began in 1924 and required among other things that most PCF candidates for public office come from working-class backgrounds; a national PCF training facility was needed for these new working-class politicians, many of whom, far from having a sophisticated knowledge of Marxist dialectics, could barely read or write.[31]

Most of the roughly sixty students at the school were young men from working-class backgrounds, many with responsible positions in their own unions or Party organizations. While at Bobigny, students were required to participate in local Communist cells for part of every day.[32] The majority stayed there only briefly; some students did complete their studies and go on to important positions in the PCF. The most illustrious Lenin School alumnus, Jacques Duclos, described it in his memoirs.

> The school had been installed in Bobigny in a barracks put at the disposition of the Party by the Communist municipality. This barracks was located very close to the present maison du peuple, not far from city hall. At the time Bobigny was a small suburban community where everything that touched upon daily life was immediately noticed. . . . We came every morning in a bus and ate our meals in a small restaurant near the school, which in that part of Bobigny created an unaccustomed excitement.[33]

Party leaders did not intend to make a top secret establishment of the Lenin School; still they preferred to locate it in friendly territory. Yet by the mid-1920s this was getting rather difficult to find in the Paris area. Clamamus had already shown his reliability by sheltering Communist agents. Naturally the PCF leadership decided to locate the Lenin School in Bobigny. " 'We are supposed to create a Marxist-Leninist school,' explained [Louis] Sellier. 'Orders from Moscow. You are the only mayor worthy of confidence that we have left. That's why we thought of Bobigny.' "[34]

It was not long before the Bobigny Lenin School, attacked by the rightist Action française as "a nest of Red Guards," attracted the attention of the national government. As part of a series of attacks against PCF targets in the Department of the Seine, the Paris police raided the Lenin School on 6 December 1924. Over 150 police agents surrounded the school's barracks, ordered all students and teachers outside, confiscated their books and notes, and searched the building. Several foreign students, Belgians and Italians, were arrested and soon deported.[35] To the PCF, the raid exemplified the general right-wing offensive by the newly elected government of the Bloc des gauches; the PCF accused Prime Minister Edouard Herriot of having been pushed into the police action by pressure from Charles Maurras, leader of the

Action française. The raid also brought home the disadvantages of not having municipal control over the police.[36]

In 1925 the Lenin School moved to Clichy, which had just elected a Communist municipal government; but for many years people linked the Lenin School with Bobigny. In agreeing to shelter the school, Bobigny's municipal government proved that it was interested not just in building more sidewalks but in expressing one of the PCF's most important principles of city government.

Direct aid to the PCF was not the only way Bobigny's city government sought to demonstrate its ideological character. It took many positions and actions that, without necessarily strengthening the Party's organization, expressed the municipality's adherence to PCF doctrine. One example was the "political" motions passed by the city council, decisions that dealt not with business as usual but expressed a clear ideological viewpoint. Because these actions involved only the municipal government, they clearly show its support for Communist party doctrine.

The council's political resolutions often took the form of subsidy grants.[37] In September 1921 the councillors voted a subsidy of 500 francs to aid the victims of famine in the Soviet Union. In 1936 the council allocated 350 francs to a committee commemorating the one-hundredth anniversary of the death of Claude-Joseph Rouget de Lisle, author of the "Marseillaise"; it granted an equal amount the following year to a group planning to build a monument to Paul Lafargue, an eminent prewar French socialist and son-in-law of Karl Marx.[38] None of these subsidy grants or the brief motions passed to approve them expressed an exclusively PCF point of view; after all, neither Rouget de Lisle nor Lafargue was a Communist, and the PCF was not the only group in France to aid people starving during the Soviet Union's civil war. Yet the acts did identify the Bobigny municipality as an integral part of the French Left.[39]

At times the city council expressed its political point of view by denying requests for subsidies. When asked by the city council of Saint-Mandé, a wealthy Parisian suburb, to donate money to create an endowment for the children of French war hero General Mangin, the city councillors of Bobigny responded forthrightly:

Considering that a working-class city council should not spend the pennies of its taxpayers on subscriptions for the children of generals.

That generals who died in their beds while millions of workers and peasants fell on the field of battle have no right to solidarity from their victims.

That the pensions given to generals' families are quite generous when compared to the dole received by the widows of simple soldiers and the miserable allocations accorded to mutilated veterans.

Refuses, for these different reasons, to take part in the envisaged subscription.

Affirms its intention to reserve its solidarity for the workers who were victims of the Great War, and also for the young French workers and peasants who are dying today in Morocco and Syria for the greater profit of the financiers.[40]

The Bobigny municipality used this subsidy request to condemn the First World War as a class conflict and also—anticipating by five days the PCF's general strike against the French campaign in Morocco's Rif mountains—to attack all French military engagements in Morocco and Syria on similar grounds. On another occasion, in a resolution allocating 4,000 francs to victims of flooding in southwestern France the council condemned "capitalist cupidity" as responsible for the tragedy and for good measure lambasted the government's handling of the reconstruction of regions devastated by World War I. It directed moreover that the subsidy be given to the Comintern's International Workers' Aid, an "organization of proletarian solidarity, alone qualified to ensure the distribution of these funds to the workers and peasants of the region, who alone interest us."[41]

In contrast to the motions cited earlier, these last two express a more strictly Communist viewpoint. The overriding theme of both is class conflict and solidarity; the monies of a working-class municipality should be used only to benefit other members of that class. Given this viewpoint, it is not surprising that several of these subsidies went to striking workers. For example, in 1931 the Bobigny city council voted to give 1,000 francs to the town of Halluin for the welfare bureau, which was out of money because of the demands on it for striking textile workers; their vote stipulated that the funds be given to strikers no matter what their political opinions were. In June 1926 the council voted to send 250 francs to the British miners' union, which had stayed out despite the collapse of the general strike a month earlier.[42]

Although the spirit guiding these subsidies to strikers was that of abstract class solidarity, when possible the municipality directly connected such grants to the immediate interests of the workers of Bobigny; thus Clamamus justified his request for aid to the clerks involved in the strike of 1925 against Paris banks: "The Mayor explains to the council the situation of the bank clerks as a result of the strike that they were forced to declare to obtain a wage increase, and the situation of clerks living in Bobigny thus deprived of resources. . . . The council . . . in solidarity, votes an indemnity of 500 francs to the bank clerks' strike committee."[43]

Before ending this discussion of the political resolutions voted by the Bobigny city council, I must make two points. First, the number of such forthrightly ideological resolutions was very small. In searching through the city council's records from 1920 to 1939, I found that fewer than twenty resolutions met this criterion (the council met twice a month and discussed up to fifteen items of agenda, many routine). The motions remain significant for us: they show what positions the council took and what issues it chose when it expressed its politics in such a direct manner. Yet they also demonstrate that the municipality considered such overt ideological statements to have minor importance.[44]

Second, much of the money voted by the Bobigny city council subsidized either Communist organizations or causes the PCF favored. Like the money voted for the victims of flooding in southwestern France, the funds for starving Russians in 1921 were handed out by a PCF official, M. Stratta (presumably Emile Stratta, the secretary of the Bobigny PCF section). The PCF put a great deal of effort into supporting the strike against Paris banks; and red Halluin, like red Bobigny, had a Communist municipality.[45] As for the struggle of the British miners, after the moderate leadership of the Trades Union Congress abandoned the general strike, it became a favorite cause of the Comintern. We must recall that for French Communists in the 1920s, the most meaningful aid to the working class *was* aid to the PCF, because only the PCF was fighting to liberate the proletariat. Still, we might add that the Bobigny municipality's political subsidies were made less in a spirit of disinterested class solidarity and more in the desire to assist various Communist endeavors. In granting political subsidies, the city government united its goals of nourishing other branches of the Communist movement and of proclaiming its ideological convictions.

The municipality did not limit itself to subsidizing strikers in other areas; at times it aided striking workers in Bobigny itself. As with the political resolutions, examples of such aid are few, primarily because Bobigny was a residential suburb; having few factories, it had few strikes. The aid for local strikers took two forms: demonstrations at the picket site, and soup kitchens for the striking workers. An example of the former occurred in 1932; during a brief strike by ditch diggers at the Versille workshop in Bobigny, Mayor Clamamus led a delegation of unemployed workers to join the strikers picketing at the work site.[46]

The city government had meals served to the families of strikers; it sometimes arranged arbitration between striking workers and management and let unions use the city facilities to hold meetings.[47]

The Budgets of the PCF Municipality

By a variety of political activities, the city government of Bobigny sought to broaden the sense of identity between it and its constituents into a more expansive feeling of solidarity between the French Communist party and the national and international working class. Its symbolic resolutions in favor of strikes, however, did not account for the average worker's consistent vote for the PCF municipality. It won workers' loyalty by the concrete improvements it was able to make in their living conditions.[48] The major achievement of the city's PCF government was that it provided Bobigny with an urban structure commensurate with the size of its population.

One way to form a picture of the municipality's achievements is to look at the city's budgets. A full-scale analysis of budgets from the Communist takeover in 1920 to 1939 does not fall within the scope of this study, which offers a brief description of their basic structure and evolution during the 1920s and 1930s.[49] The most elementary fact to note about the budgets is their spectacular growth. From 1921 to 1936 the total expenses of Bobigny increased from 579,304 francs to 12,710,937 francs—nearly twenty-two times; they grew at an average annual rate of over 140 percent. Of course, the city's population also grew substantially, but its increase of roughly 284 percent from 1921 to 1936 hardly explains the budget's expansion. The municipality was spending a lot more money per capita in 1936 than in 1921: this fact alone indicates the development of city services and of the public sector by the PCF city government.[50]

The taxes that provided the ordinary receipts for French city governments fall into three categories: the *octroi*, the *centimes additionnels*, and other taxes, in descending order of importance. The *octroi* was a sales tax on all goods brought into the community; it was often the largest source of revenue in many suburban municipalities. The *centimes additionnels* were a surcharge based on direct national taxes; if a municipality levied a total of twenty centimes additionnels, its taxpayers paid an amount equal to 20 percent of their national taxes to the city (in addition to the national taxes). The state restricted the number of centimes additionnels a municipality could impose to eighty during the interwar period, but this limit went largely unenforced. Finally, municipalities could and did impose a number of less important taxes, including those on dogs, on commercial performances (*spectacles*), and on funerals. We can include in this category revenues from renting city property or spaces in city markets, sales of hunting licenses, and similar charges, though they are not strictly taxes.[51]

Within this city tax structure, the most unusual characteristic of Bobigny's local taxes was the absence of the octroi. For years the French Left had harshly criticized it as outmoded (it was created in the Napoleonic period), cumbersome, and—above all—highly regressive. Both the Socialist and Communist parties called for its abolition.[52] Yet even a wealthy municipality was loathe to abolish a major source of revenue, and PCF city governments were anything but wealthy. Therefore most Communist municipalities continued to collect the octroi. Because Bobigny was small it never had an octroi before the PCF came to power. In 1921 the town's population reached six thousand, the number needed to establish an octroi; Bobigny's Communists could more easily refuse to begin levying one than other similar municipalities could abandon a tax inherited from previous administrations to search elsewhere for funds. Nonetheless, refusal to levy the octroi was seen as a major step toward greater fiscal egalitarianism, one to which the Communists pointed with pride in their electoral propaganda.[53]

The money it failed to take in with an octroi Bobigny made up in ordinary receipts, principally by collecting a large number of centimes additionnels. The number of these imposed "because of insufficient revenues" rose from 640 in 1921 to 811 in 1936, by which time they accounted for well over half of all ordinary receipts. As an income tax, the centimes additionnels were more progressive than the octroi, since parts of them would not affect taxpayers of moderate income.[54] Thus Bobigny's general tax structure partially justified the PCF's claim that its city governments redistributed the tax burden away from the working class.[55]

Even more than its receipts, the expenditures of a Communist municipality were to demonstrate its sensitivity to and identification with the interests of the working class and poor. In its program for the 1929 municipal elections, the Communist party of Bobigny emphasized the municipality's efforts in public assistance, unemployment relief, and education. In actual fact the Bobigny city government used a small share of its budget for public assistance; 11 percent of the ordinary expenditures of the 1921 budget was the highest amount I discovered for the 1920s and the 1930s. By contrast, public instruction was a major budgetary item, from a low point of 20 percent of total ordinary expenses in 1921 to nearly 40 percent of city expenditures in 1931. In a sense, Bobigny's PCF municipality made a decision to use the present to feed the future.[56]

The PCF valued unemployment relief as an important service that Communist municipalities provided their constituents. By 1936 Bobigny was spending more than six million francs (or 45.4 percent of total expenditures) on unemployment relief a year; most of this sum came, however, from subsidies by the department and the state rather than city revenues. The subsidies covered obligatory expenses for unemployment relief; anything extra was paid by the municipality. And like other Communist municipalities, Bobigny did make extra efforts to deal with the crisis.[57] In January 1936 the PCF newspaper, *La Voix de l'Est*, reported that Bobigny had given out five hundred tons of coal to the local unemployed since the start of the winter.[58]

All in all, the Communist city government of Bobigny gave its constituents well-developed social services, in spite of its rather meager public assistance. The PCF neither initiated nor restructured such day-to-day services, however; its major innovation in Bobigny was to develop an urban structure for the community. Its extraordinary expenditures are that section of the city budget that most accurately shows the extent of this effort. Aside from unemployment relief funds, this section consisted of debt service payments on loans contracted by the municipality to pay for projects in city improvement. For example, the extraordinary expenditures of the 1931 Bobigny city budget include these payments:

Payment on 50,000-franc loan to purchase land for a new school	2,808 francs
Payment on 82,075-franc loan to construct new schools and enlarge the city cemetery	4,609 francs
Payment on 176,803-franc loan to enlarge the cemetery	14,970 francs
Payment on 60,000-franc loan to improve the chemin de Groslay	5,031 francs
Payment on 33,053-franc loan to enlarge the post office	1,867 francs

In 1931 such payments totaled almost 1.5 million francs, or 61.3 percent of the amount for that year's ordinary expenditures.[59]

In the four annual budgets I studied from 1921 to 1936, debt service payments had the largest share of expenditures in 1931, which is not surprising, since the Sarraut Law of 1928 added impetus to the cleanup of the allotments. Moreover, in 1931 the Great Depression was beginning to weigh on city resources. Yet in all four budgets, extraordinary expenditures were a significant component. Their symbolic importance was greater: it was to carry out the projects that these expenditures stood for that the people had elected a Communist city government. What did the people of Bobigny get for their money?

Dealing with the Allotments

The crisis in the allotments confronted Bobigny with its greatest problems at the beginning of Communist municipal control in 1921. The frustrated *mal-lotis* were largely responsible for the victory of the old SFIO in the 1919 municipal elections. To retain the allegiance of local voters, the young PCF would have to improve the living conditions for this critical constituency. Before 1928 the national legislation on the allotments was the overriding obstacle to their improvement. The law passed by the legislature in 1919 gave municipal authorities no powers to enforce the law's standards on allotment developers; the 1924 law did not apply to those allotments finished before its passage. Since municipal authorities could not force developers to provide their allotments with certain basic amenities, before 1928 the Communists of Bobigny devised two strategies to cope with the problem. They applied existing legislation as strictly as possible and worked with allotment residents and developers to undertake the necessary improvements; after 1924 this local strategy intensified. The second strategy, which Mayor Clamamus carried out at the national level as parliamentary deputy, publicized the problems with allotment developers and worked for more equitable legislation that would make the developers pay.[60]

Though the 1919 law was unenforceable, the Bobigny city council did demand that developers follow its provisions and submit all plans for allotments to city hall for approval. Speaking before the council in 1921, Mayor Clamamus explained the city's requirements, since most roads opened by developers would become city streets.

> All owners of land converted into allotments that would require the opening of roads destined to be included in the city street network will be required to furnish for their allotment plan a dossier detailing the length and width of the streets, as well as a proposal for paving streets and building sidewalks, to be submitted to the city council for approval.[61]

In this early period the Bobigny city council occasionally committed its own funds to cleaning up the allotments. For example, in November 1924 the council voted to pay part of the expenses of a sewer leading from the chemin de Groslay to the avenue Edouard Vaillant. Since the sewer would serve the Pont de la Madeleine allotment, its developer was asked to pay the remainder of the cost. In the long-term struggle to improve conditions in the allotments, the municipality tried to get allotment residents to form *associations syndicales,* or property owners' associations, to equip their allotment roads.[62]

In theory, the law of 1924 gave the city government of Bobigny greater powers over the allotments and their developers. It was not retroactive, and the municipality could still do little for most of the *mal-lotis.* The 1924 law did at least give the city power to approve or reject new allotments. Within the first year after the law's passage the city council ruled on the applications of eighteen new allotments, reaching the crest of this wave at its session of 1 August 1925, during which it considered the applications of nine allotment developers.[63] Of the eighteen applications reviewed, fourteen were approved, on the basis of investigations by the departmental Hygiene Commission. The main criteria for evaluating allotment applications were their drainage facilities and water service. Thus, in rejecting the application of the Clos Billard allotment, the Bobigny city council stated:

> The Council . . .
> Considering that this terrain is far from all paved streets and sidewalks; that the only access is provided by a small, impractical road; that water service can be assured only by wells or pumps; the lot buyers would be forced to use cesspools to dispose of waste waters, which would risk contaminating the ground water and thus lead to epidemics. . . .
> Gives an unfavorable decision.[64]

Since there are no dossiers in the Bobigny municipal archives on associations syndicales for allotments begun after 1924, we can assume that the city council made sure that the allotments it approved were all adequately equipped.

The municipality acted to ease the sufferings of its citizens in defective allotments, where flooding occurred frequently during the winter. It was not the allotment developers but the city that dealt with these floods. In the spring of 1926, for example, severe flooding in the Anjou neighborhood of Bobigny prompted the municipality to rent three automatic water pumps, which it ran almost continuously for several weeks to clean up the mess. On another occasion, the city council voted 250 francs in emergency aid to the residents of Les Vignes to help them pave the allotment's roads and construct an adequate drainage system.[65]

The case of the widow Renaud showed the gravity with which the Bobigny municipality weighed its approval or rejection of new allotments. Mme Renaud was a developer who opened up an allotment, sold individual lots, and began to build houses on a few of them, all without getting the city's approval. The allotment failed to meet the standards mandated by the law of 1924; the Bobigny municipality responded by bringing a civil suit against Renaud under the provisions of the 1924 law.[66] Apart from the suit's value in deterring similar actions by other developers, it showed that the local authorities would not tolerate the problems they would face in a defective allotment.[67]

Yet for most of Bobigny's *mal-lotis*, city suits and water pumps changed nothing; they provided no general method to organize and fund work to bring allotments up to standard. Given the paltry resources of most allotment residents (and of most municipalities with allotments), this work could be done only by the national government. Such was the opinion of the Bobigny city council; in February 1924 it made a formal protest against the developers' activities, appealing to the public authorities for aid in resolving the problem.[68] Except for this appeal and other protests, Mayor Clamamus took primary responsibility for bringing the problems of Bobigny's *mal-lotis* into the national political arena. By the end of the 1920s Clamamus was recognized as the French Communist party's leading specialist on the allotments. His parliamentary district was Noisy-le-Sec, which had the greatest concentration of allotments in the entire Paris region; as its deputy, Clamamus gave the issue a great deal of attention. Yet Bobigny was his political base, and the place he knew best; he came into closest contact with the problems there and, as mayor, had to answer the *mal-lotis'* questions on when they could expect assistance. Because of Clamamus's dual role, the *mal-lotis* occupied a strategic place in the PCF's position on the allotments.[69]

The Communist party's position on the allotments was simple and straightforward: contracts or no contracts, the developers bore sole responsibility for the poor living conditions that existed on the allotments; they should therefore be required to pay for all necessary improvements.[70] A poster the PCF put up in the early 1920s to warn workers against the allotments' developers made this point quite clearly:

By lying promises, the sellers of lots and houses prey upon your savings; and once you have signed the contracts that they offer you, it is too late to react.

The "allotment developers" promise you pretty streets and avenues, but they rarely keep these promises. . . .

We demand that these mercenaries be forced to clean up the allotments and to make the streets and avenues passable (the present price of land would still bring tidy profits).[71]

Throughout the 1920s and 1930s, and especially in the 1920s, Clamamus wrote articles for *L'Humanité* and the local PCF press on the crisis of the *mal-lotis*, the burden allotments placed on municipalities, the role of the national government, and other aspects of the phenomenon. In many of these articles he drew from his experiences as mayor. For example, in a March 1926 article in the local PCF newspaper, *L'Aube sociale*, "How to Regulate the Allotments," Clamamus attacked the national government for failing to provide enough financial aid to communities like Bobigny.

If concerning the allotments certain municipalities, especially Communist municipalities, have made fruitful initiatives to reduce to a minimum the evil done by allotment developers speculating on the needs of the workers . . . the administration, respectful of form and legality, makes it its business to defeat their efforts, as in the case of Bobigny. . . .

Five years ago, the city submitted a project for a collector sewer, asking the department to pay for it.

The administration has opposed this project, pretending that it is of purely local interest and that therefore the city should pay for it, whereas the major part of the floodwaters in the allotments come from neighboring communities.[72]

As a deputy to the National Assembly, Clamamus could go beyond merely criticizing the government's lack of effective action to propose alternative ways of dealing with the problem. On 3 March 1926 he proposed a law to regulate the allotments, one of several the assembly considered between 1924 and 1928. Clamamus proposed that the national government distribute a total of 50 million francs to municipalities in the departments of the Seine, Seine-et-Oise, and Seine-et-Marne for allotments completed before the law of July 1924. City governments would not be required to contribute anything to these funds, which would provide the allotments with sewers, water mains, and other equipment.[73]

Clamamus estimated the national government's 50 million francs to be about one-third of the money required for the allotments. The developers were to pay the remaining two-thirds. The project thus dealt more severely with this group than other proposed laws did. Unlike them, it also gave a precise definition of an allotment developer. It included a provision for mandatory associations syndicales for residents of allotments (with most costs to be paid by the developers) and regulated the resale of lots to inhibit speculation.[74]

The Sarraut Law of 1928 declared once and for all how the government would deal with allotments. Clamamus led the French Communist party's opposition to that law, charging that it let the developers off scot-free. The law stipulated that the government and the associations syndicales of the allotments' residents each pay roughly half the cost of providing defective allotments with the necessary services. The Party attacked the rules on establishing the associations syndicales as being so complicated that many residents would not bother to set them up; they would consequently receive no government subsidies to clean up their allotments and their problems would continue. In an article in *L'Humanité*, Clamamus denounced the new law in fiery terms:

> *Electoral bluff*, we said; scandalous and hypocritical *demagogy*, we denounced.
>
> Means of coercion and repression against communism, such is the essence and the specific meaning of this so-called Sarraut Law, which in its present form and spirit cannot give satisfaction to the *mal-lotis*. . . .
>
> *The mal-lotis have not yet seen the end of their pain and their misery.*[75]

The phrase "means of coercion and repression against communism" was partly an allusion to the harshly anti-Communist policies of the law's sponsor, Minister of the Interior Albert Sarraut. It was Sarraut who announced in 1928, "Communism, there is the enemy!" Clamamus feared, however, that the law might convince the *mal-lotis* that their problems were solved, weakening the PCF's strong position among them and its prospects in the 1928 legislative and 1929 municipal elections.[76] More important, the PCF feared that allotment residents, disenchanted by the Sarraut Law's slow and unsatisfactory action, would turn their frustrations against their local officials—especially in a Communist municipality like Bobigny where the allotments were a burning issue.[77] Either way, the government would be able to use the Sarraut Law to drive a wedge between the PCF and one of its most important constituencies.

As it turned out, however, the issue did not bear out this fear. Roughly two months after the Sarraut Law's passage, the Bobigny city council met to plan out how it would correct the problems of the city's defective allotments. It drew up a list of the twelve allotments that the Sarraut Law would benefit. After 1928 the municipality would continue to rule on applications to open allotments (it reviewed twenty

ap᾿   9) and would occasionally undertake
m   on defective allotments.[78]
                     ᾿ents had no direct role in implementing
              ᾿ many indirect ways in which they could
           ᾿bigny's municipality demonstrated. First, it
           ᾿ associations syndicales, which involved a
          ᾿ndated by the law of 1912 on associations.[79]
          ᾿ments had to put together a dossier containing
         ᾿mation, such as a report on hygiene conditions in the
         ᾿ copy of the allotment's contract (*cahier des charges*), and
        ᾿ry account of the constitutive meeting of the association.
       ᾿ver, the structure of the association followed a certain form, and
       ᾿rs were to be elected.[80] Given this state of affairs, the PCF's
      ᾿est against the Sarraut Law's overcomplicated provisions made a
      ᾿d deal of sense. Far from understanding how to follow all the steps
      ᾿ law mandated, most *mal-lotis* probably had only the haziest idea of
      ᾿ow it was to function. All they knew was that the law was supposed
   o solve their housing problems.[81]

In Bobigny, the pattern for setting up these associations syndicales ran somewhat as follows: a group of allotment residents would write to Mayor Clamamus for help in cleaning up their allotment. Clamamus or another member of the city council would write back, explaining how the Sarraut Law worked and proposing that they set up an association syndicale. If the residents seemed willing, the municipality would set a date and time for a general constitutive meeting and inform all prospective members. A municipal councillor would preside at the meeting and explain to those assembled what had to be done to qualify for the association's government subsidy.[82] Once an association had been constituted, the mayor and the municipality continued to help; Clamamus would work with the association's officers to put together a formal dossier and send the loan application to the prefect. The prefect dealt not with the associations but through the intermediary of the mayor, as association officers did with the prefect; in effect, Clamamus coordinated the whole process. On occasion the mayor intervened more directly into the associations' affairs: I have come across one case where he pushed a rather negligent association officer into organizing the allotment's cleanup.[83]

Typically, everyone turned to Clamamus for help with problems on the allotments: to obtain their governmental subsidies and clean up their allotments; to deal with residents who did not wish to join their associations, with developers, and with construction firms. In arranging to fix Bobigny's defective allotments, when any parties involved in the project had problems or questions they usually wrote to him, not to each other. Finally, the Bobigny city council would sometimes lend money to associations so that they could begin repairing especially serious problems before the departmental subsidy came in. Thus in October 1933 the council decided to loan the association of La Bergère 38,046 francs to pay for laying water mains under the rue des Coquetiers.[84]

Relations between the municipality and the associations syndicales were not trouble-free. Residents often complained to the mayor that the work of cleaning up their allotments was delayed in starting or was taking a long time to complete. Usually the tone of these complaints was not hostile; rather than accusing Clamamus of being derelict in his duties, they were merely asking him to help them:

> I have the honor to inform you that the inhabitants of the rues Perron, Perrusset, and Herzog request that you convoke them in a general meeting, to inform them as to the current situation re the equipping of their streets.
> In effect, Your Honor, we are very surprised that since February, when our association was formed, and given the good will shown by all in making their payments, work has not yet been started.[85]

The *mal-lotis* sometimes turned their frustrations against the mayor and his administration, however. The long, drawn-out process of upgrading Bobigny's defective allotments did not always enhance the municipality's image in the eyes of its constituents, as the following letter from a local Communist to Deputy Mayor Léon Pesch indicates.

> I am receiving demands from residents of the allotment of La Renaissance who are faced with flooding and ask what is happening with the project for their street. They object to the slowness of the formalities to be dealt with; they were supposed to be convoked into an association at least six months ago and yet they have heard nothing. Because of this bad weather they are knee-deep in mud and they blame us, figuring that it is our fault.[86]

Despite their complaints, the constituents kept their good opinion of Bobigny's Communist municipality and especially of Clamamus personally. Their occasional disenchantment with the municipality's role in cleaning up the allotments resulted from their high expectations when the process began. Disputes that did arise were more like a family quarrel than a sharp break. In any case, no evidence indicates that the Sarraut Law cost the Clamamus administration much support among the *mal-lotis;* there was no significant fall in the PCF's percentage of the vote in the 1929 municipal elections. It seems therefore that the Sarraut Law posed no real threat to the Communists' popular base in Bobigny. Legally, the Bobigny city government had no direct responsibility for helping to clean up the defective allotments. Yet it did so, and its participation was crucial.[87]

Lighting the Lamps of Bobigny

To French Communists in the early twentieth century, adequate utilities were not just a convenience but symbolized progress and modernity as well. After all, Victor Hugo had said that democracy equaled universal suffrage plus electricity; amplifying the French novelist's definition, Lenin had recently proclaimed that socialism plus electricity produced communism. Bobigny's Communist municipality viewed the development of utilities as a strategic element in improving local working-class living standards and pointed with pride to its achievements.

The municipality's projects to provide water, gas, and electrical service were an important part of cleaning up the defective allotments, giving the *mal-lotis* such services—especially drinking water. Bobigny's utilities were poorly developed when the Communist administration began in 1921, and it had to provide them for most of the community.

Of the three utilities, water service took the greatest time and energy to develop. Before the 1920s the community possessed few water mains; most residents got their drinking water from local fountains and in some areas lacked even those facilities.[88] The Communist municipality's effort to provide drinkable tap water began in 1924. In December the city council approved a plan to equip eight streets in central Bobigny with water mains. The next major extension of water service occurred in 1926, when the municipality began laying water mains under eleven streets. Unlike the 1924 project, it equipped peripheral areas; one street was the avenue Edouard Vaillant, the main thoroughfare of the Pont de Bondy and thus vital to the PCF's constituency in Bobigny. Not all the streets to receive water in 1926 were in such friendly areas; the rue de Blanc-mesnil had one of Bobigny's largest concentrations of market gardeners.[89]

The municipality worked hard to equip the city's streets with water mains from 1928 to 1935. In 1928 eleven more streets were so provisioned, including the streets of the allotment of rues Perron and Perrusset, and several others. By 1929 the local PCF could claim that on most of the city's main arteries, mains supplied residents with drinking water. In consequence, the city council decided to start removing water fountains from central Bobigny in November 1929, claiming that fountains were no longer needed since the area was now amply supplied with water pipes.[90] Most of the streets in Bobigny that did not get full water service until the early 1930s were small and located far from the center of town. Moreover, a large number were private allotment roads, technically outside the jurisdiction of the authorities. In dealing with such streets the city council usually worked through the associations syndicales; for example, the municipality supplied the rue Butté with water by lending the money for the operation, 35,880 francs, to the Chemin de Fer allotment's association.[91]

By 1935, at a meeting of a community organization in the large Nouveau Village allotment, Léon Pesch could claim that all of its streets had been provisioned with drinking water. Nouveau Village had been a prominent example of the new working-class Bobigny and of the crisis in allotments; the fact that it was now completely provided with water service constituted an important symbolic victory for the municipality. From 1929 to 1934 nineteen kilometers of Bobigny's streets had been equipped with water mains, at a total cost of just over 1.5 million francs. Providing drinking water for the people of Bobigny was to figure prominently in local Communist propaganda as a concrete achievement of the municipality.[92]

Providing gas and electrical service for home use and public lighting required less effort and expense than did the construction of a system of water mains and took less time. Bobigny had installed gas lighting for the streets in the center of town in 1896. In its first year in office, the Communist municipality extended gas lighting to the avenue Jean Jaurès, running from the industrial area along the canal de l'Ourcq through the city center to the Six Routes intersection, and to the avenue Edouard Vaillant. By the end of 1923 other major thoroughfares in the city, such as the rue de Paris, the route de Saint-Denis, and the route des Petits Ponts, also had public gas lighting.[93]

In July 1922 the Bobigny city council and the Suburban Gas Company had meanwhile negotiated a contract to provide all of the city's households with gas service; the work of laying the gas mains was well under way by 1924 in the outer areas of the city. The work went rapidly because many of the streets concerned in the peripheral areas and allotments were already torn up for laying streets and sidewalks or water mains. Between 1924 and 1928 almost all of Bobigny's streets were provided with gas mains for household gas service. In 1924 more than sixty streets, in all parts of the city, were equipped with gas mains. Ten more streets were equipped in 1925, and for the next few years about four streets (mostly minor ones by this point) acquired gas mains every year. By May 1929 the Communists claimed, "At present, all streets, without exception, are provided with gas mains."[94]

The process of providing the city with electrical power took somewhat longer and began much later. The Communist municipality had to start from scratch; the city had no electricity before the 1920s. Following a complicated series of negotiations between the city government of Bobigny and two different power companies, the Suburban Gas Company and the North-East Parisian Power Company, the municipality finally decided to proceed with the electrification project in 1925.[95] As the *Journal de Saint-Denis* was not slow to point out, this decision came on the eve of the 1925 municipal elections, the first time Bobigny's Communist city government would have to face the voters.[96]

As with the development of gas service, electrification entailed providing for both household and public lighting. In this case, however, the former came first; the replacement of street gas lamps by electric lighting began only at the end of the 1920s. The contract with North-East Parisian stipulated that electricity for household use would be introduced into Bobigny in three stages: first the city center would be furnished with power, then eastern Bobigny, and finally western Bobigny. The first stage was largely complete by the middle of 1928; eastern Bobigny acquired electric power by the following year—just in time for the municipal elections.[97] The western area of the city, around the rue d'Anjou and the chemin de la Madeleine, took a little longer because its terrain was not flat as in the rest of the city; it was finished by the mid-1930s.

Before completing this process, the municipality began equipping the main streets of the city with electric lighting. In 1928 the city council investigated the possibility of providing electric lights for the route des Petits Ponts, but only two years later did the avenue Edouard Vaillant become the first street to be electrified. By 1935 so were the route des Petits Ponts, the avenue Jean Jaurès, the place Carnot, and several other main streets. The PCF's claim that year that all of Bobigny's main thoroughfares had been electrified was a bit exaggerated—the rue de la République did not get electric lights until 1938, for example. Nonetheless, when World War II began this project had been completed.[98]

Although the municipality could claim success in developing utilities service, how much most Balbynians benefited from the service is less clear. Without precise statistics for Bobigny we can only form an idea based on patterns of their use prevalent in France. Water service was certainly the most widely used, offering Balbynians rudimentary indoor plumbing facilities like a cold water tap and a Turkish toilet. Electricity and gas service, on the other hand, were considered luxuries and were probably not utilized for more than simple household lighting in interwar Bobigny.[99] Therefore, aside from water service, the development of utilities in Bobigny assumed a significance that was as much symbolic as real. The municipality's programs did bring its constituents concrete benefits, and they demonstrated that Communist Bobigny was a forward-looking community vitally interested in enabling ordinary people to enjoy the benefits of technological progress.

A New Urban Structure

The Bobigny municipality's efforts to improve local living conditions went beyond its reaction to the population explosion—repairing the defective allotments and developing adequate utilities. Much of the city council's work involved the expansion of traditional city institutions and above all signaled the PCF's success in leaving its imprint on the city.

Bobigny's population in the first decades of the twentieth century outgrew the local market system. In 1921, Bobigny had only one covered marketplace, located in the place de l'Eglise at the city's center. It was owned by the city government and managed by private firms; the annual rent on the market concession was 500 francs. This was a paltry sum, according to the new Communist administration, which felt that the city could do better on its own. In January 1922 the municipality therefore cancelled the lease and began managing the marketplace directly, making it the only large example of municipal socialism in Bobigny.[100]

Whether privately or publicly operated, however, the market quickly showed itself inadequate to the needs of the new Bobigny. Later in 1922 Clamamus broached to the council the idea of building a second city market, noting that many peddlers had begun to work in the Six Routes area and that he had received a number of requests for a new market from the area's residents. He argued that the success of this market would be helped by its location, since Six Routes was the terminus of a major tramway line.[101] Building a market in the Six Routes area was more catching up with the present than building for the future. In fact, the city council's decision in 1922 did not create a market at this location—one had come into existence spontaneously—but rather equipped and formalized it. Yet the council's passive role showed its sensitivity to the needs of the local population; rather than impose a rigid structure on the city's development, the Bobigny municipality showed itself willing in this instance to be a participant in that process.

Construction of the market proceeded quickly. It opened for business the day after Christmas. The new market prospered and in ten years had to be moved to a new site (in the same area), having outgrown the old one. In the meantime, however, the municipality began considering building a third city market for Bobigny. From 1921 to 1926 the local population had bounded from less than seven thousand to over eleven thousand; by 1926 the new Six Routes market was too small for the marketing needs of the people of Bobigny. Late in 1926 the city council therefore decided to consider building a third marketplace in Bobigny, on the avenue Edouard Vaillant. The Pont de Bondy area was a logical site. Much of the recent population increase had occurred there, farthest from the markets in the center and in Six Routes. The proposal to build a market for the Pont de Bondy also expressed the council's desire to provide urban services for that area of town which embodied working-class Bobigny and the core of popular support for the Communists.[102]

The lag time between the city council's first proposal and this project's completion was considerably greater than that for the Six Routes market. The final decision to build the fixed marketplace on the avenue Edouard Vaillant was made in November 1935, and the construction of the market took almost two years. As with the Six Routes project, a spontaneous market had grown up on the site when construction began, so again the municipality's action modified and gave official sanction to what already existed.[103]

By the end of the 1930s the Bobigny municipality could point with pride to its system of markets, which more than tripled the space available in covered marketplaces, accessible to people in all parts of the city. We must, however, grant pride of place to the city government's expansion of the educational system. This was its most impressive accomplishment. Since Communist propaganda for its municipalities laid heavy emphasis on raising the next generation, we can understand why a large portion of the PCF city budgets for Bobigny should be devoted to public instruction.[104]

It was less ideology than the explosive growth of Bobigny's school-age population that motivated the investment in the city's educational system. From 1911 to 1921 this age group expanded from 780 to 1,400, almost doubling in size; by 1931 it had increased to 2,630. The city government had given a certain amount of attention to its inadequate school facilities before and during the First World War; but by 1920, when the Communists took power in Bobigny, it had accomplished little.[105]

At the end of 1920, responding to widespread discontent among Pont de Bondy residents over the lack of local schools, the municipality set up temporary facilities in an old army barracks left over from the war.[106] At roughly the same time the city government began negotiating with the national government and financial institutions for funds to build a group of schools in the neighborhood and for land. In April 1926 the city council approved the project, which was to consist of a boys' school, a girls' school, and a nursery school. For years the city had been looking, without success, for funds to finance its school construction project; in 1926 it also decided to build smaller schools to make their construction feasible. Meanwhile the schools in the center of Bobigny grew more and more crowded; the boys' and girls' schools increased their total enrollment from eight to ten classes in the early 1920s.[107]

The primary hold-up in the construction of the Pont de Bondy schools was negotiations between the Bobigny municipality and the prefecture of the Seine over the granting of a state subsidy. In a later interview on the subject, Clamamus bitterly commented on the complicated procedure:

> [The process of building new schools] starts by the deliberation of the city council, which decides the purchase of land for the envisaged school group. Then it establishes plans and constitutes a dossier. Five to six months are needed.
>
> The dossier thus constituted is sent to the prefecture. Upon its arrival it receives a number; when its number comes up, the commission examines it and—if it is accepted—sends it back to the city. At least a year is necessary for this.
>
> But the tribulations of our dossier are not yet finished; it is then sent to the Subsidies Commission of the Ministry [of the Interior] . . . then a year later, its turn has arrived, the commission shakes off the dust that has accumulated on our dossier and examines it.[108]

Construction did not begin on the Pont de Bondy group of schools until 1927; the boys' and girls' schools opened only in 1929. By then they had to accommodate 500 students, or 25 to 50 percent more than they had been built for.

With the Pont de Bondy boys' and girls' schools completed, the municipality shifted its attention to nursery school facilities. In 1931 the municipality opened two nursery school classes in the Pont de Bondy girls' school.[109] The following year the city council finally decided to go ahead with plans to build a separate nursery school in the area, to consist of seven classrooms plus sleeping rooms, gardens, kitchens, and a playground; construction began in 1937. On 19 May 1939, before a crowd of three thousand spectators, the opening ceremonies for the new Pont de Bondy nursery school at last took place. The Pont de Bondy finally had its schools.[110]

The city government did not rest on its laurels. In 1937 it voted to proceed toward the development of a similar school group in the rue d'Anjou, about halfway between the Pont de Bondy and the city center. In February 1939 the municipality also decided to build a school group for the neighborhood of La Courneuve, in the northwestern part of the city. Neither project had been started by the end of the decade and thus cannot qualify as an achievement of Bobigny's Communist city government in the interwar period. But they confirm the great importance of education to that government.[111]

Perhaps the most colorful program in the educational system was its summer camps. The idea was first proposed early in 1919 by the Socialist city councillor Laporte, but nothing came of the matter at that point. Once the Communists had taken over the city administration they acted quickly on this issue, opening the city's first summer camp in 1921 in the community of La Machine in the Department of the Nièvre.[112] La Machine's camp received one hundred children during its first year of operation and increased this number to almost three hundred by the mid-1930s. Because of the program's popularity, in 1933 the city council decided to begin operating a second summer camp and bought a piece of property on the Ile d'Oléron, a popular resort area on the southern Atlantic coast. The Ile d'Oléron's camp opened during the summer of 1934. Children from six to thirteen years old were sent to La Machine, while adolescents went to the Ile d'Oléron.[113]

Both summer camps lasted forty-two days, and their fees were low. In 1930, for example, a summer at La Machine for a young Balbynian cost 150 francs, plus 4 francs a day for food; as late as 1936 this remained the basic fee. The Ile d'Oléron's camp was more expensive; in 1936 the fee was 295 francs per camper; unlike La Machine, the Ile d'Oléron was a true residential camp and thus cost the municipality more to maintain. Campers' fees could be paid in installments over a period of several months; moreover, children of unemployed Bobigny residents were admitted free. (For working-class parents, with average salaries of 5 to 7 francs per hour, it would take one to two hours of labor to send a child to camp for a day—roughly the cost of a dozen eggs.)[114]

The main purpose of the camps was to expose working-class children of Bobigny to the fresh air of the countryside, and to give them a respite from the miserable existence of the poor in the suburban slums surrounding Paris (a somewhat ironic comment on life in Bobigny, since their families had moved there to escape city slums). Camp activities consequently emphasized outdoor pursuits like soccer, basketball, fishing, and hiking. As an article on La Machine in the local PCF press noted, however, good health was not simply an end in itself:

> Our working-class city councillors have well understood the truth of the old Roman adage, which indicates that it is necessary to have "a sound mind in a healthy body." The one complements the other, and the working-class child, taught from early age the harsh necessities of the class struggle, whose consequences he experiences daily in his family, draws from the fresh air of the countryside the physical strength that will make of him a conscious worker, *capable of defending himself in all situations,* and that will make of him a fighter for the revolutionary combat.[115]

There can be no doubt that Communist politics was an integral part of young Balbynians' camping experience, particularly in the Ile d'Oléron, because the children spent more of their time together and under the supervision of the municipality's counselors than at La Machine. The Ile d'Oléron's camp proclaimed its politics with two prominent hammers and sickles over the entryway. The Bobigny Communists gave a great deal of publicity to campers' letters to their parents—often publishing the letters in *La Voix de l'Est*—which usually contrasted idyllic life in the countryside with the dreary surroundings of workers exploited under capitalism. A correspondent for the newspaper of Jacques Doriot's French People's party gave his right-wing view of the Ile d'Oléron's camp in 1937:

> In full view of the little cabin where I live, floats the oriflamme of the Bobigny summer camp. The venerable senator—whom everyone here simply calls Father Clama—personally directs, like a good father, this little beehive

of young drones. Guided by this illustrious luminary of Moscow, the children march along the beach singing the "Internationale" and the more attractive "Young Guard." . . . The militants who accompany and direct them submit them every day to unceasing propaganda that, if not counteracted, must certainly lead to the germination of the evil Bolshevik grain in this virgin soil.[116]

Clamamus's presence at the camp indicates how important Bobigny's Communists considered the program. They valued it with reason, for it very effectively transmitted their ideas to the future generation of working-class Balbynians.

In addition to its major endeavor, Bobigny's Communist municipality undertook many smaller projects to improve the quality of life. In 1936 it built a new *maison du peuple* for the use of the city's trade unions and community organizations. For hygiene and health care, it built Bobigny's first public baths in the early 1920s, built another in the Pont de Bondy, and at the end of 1937 voted to modernize and expand the municipal health clinic in the center of town. In the 1920s and 1930s the city government installed new fire hydrants in various areas such as the Pont de Bondy, which before the mid-1920s had no fire hydrants at all; it got about half of these. The municipality also installed mailboxes in all peripheral areas, especially the Pont de Bondy, and encouraged the opening of tobacconists' shops in those neighborhoods as well.[117]

The Municipality Versus the Prefecture

The PCF considered Communist-controlled municipalities useful not just for helping the local working class but also for protesting. In Bobigny protests did not limit themselves to ideological questions but took up more concrete matters, usually involving the prefecture. The single most important source of contention was the public transportation system, which the national government had taken over in 1910. The functioning of working-class trams provoked numerous protests; in the early 1920s the city government made several complaints about the shortage of working-class cars and their poor scheduling during commuter rush hours.[118]

The extent of service was the subject of most correspondence between the Bobigny municipality and the tramway company (STCRP), and the source of constant requests that more bus and tramlines be created or rerouted to serve Bobigny. In October 1922, for example, the city council passed a resolution requesting the extension of tramline no. 51 (Pantin–Paris) to Six Routes in Bobigny, and attacking the temporary suspension of service between Bobigny city hall and Six Routes on tramline no. 99 (Bobigny–Paris). In 1925 it requested (and was denied) a stop in Bobigny on the Paris–Strasbourg railway line, so that local workers could use the train for commuting. In 1930 it asked that the public authorities create a bus line linking the northeastern and eastern suburbs, so travelers would not have to waste time going through central Paris to get from one place to another within the same area. Such persistence sometimes got results: in 1936 Clamamus persuaded the STCRP to add two extra working-class cars on the no. 51 tramline.[119]

Unemployment relief also created tensions between the municipality and the state. In line with general PCF policy, the Bobigny city government attacked the limits that the national government placed on unemployment relief, as the city council did in 1927 in a resolution proposed by Ivry's council:

> Considering that the decision of the public authorities suppressing public relief for all those unemployed longer than 150 days . . . has hurt a great number of workers, especially those who have suffered the most . . . because for 150 days they have had no income other than that provided by unemployment relief; that elimination of such aid could lead these workers . . . to commit reprehensible acts; that the latest prefectural circular makes people dropped from unemployment relief the financial responsibility of the municipalities . . .
>
> Requests that those on unemployment relief for 150 days be granted an extension of their benefits.[120]

On another occasion, the city council asked the prefect of the Seine to grant it an extra 25,000 francs for unemployment relief. In both cases, the municipality was concerned with the plight of the unemployed and also with its own fiscal solvency.[121]

Finally, Bobigny's PCF city government did what it could to protect the environment by protesting dangerous or noxious industrial operations on or near its territory. Since such installations usually required the approval of the prefect of police of the Seine, protests on this issue were addressed to him. In 1929, for example, the city council sent a resolution to the prefect of police attacking a gut factory (*boyauderie*) just over the city line in Drancy, which was causing problems of air pollution for the adjacent Bobigny neighborhood.[122] And in a virtuoso move, Clamamus managed to attack both noxious pollution and militarism by a protest against a military fortification in nearby Aubervilliers:

The mayor called the attention of the council to the danger of fires at the Aubervilliers fort adjoining the city of Bobigny.

He noted that the accumulation of a large quantity of explosives and asphyxiating gases in this fort is a permanent danger for the neighboring Bobigny population, and asked the council to register an energetic protest against such a situation caused by this militaristic administration's lack of foresight.[123]

In linking local issues with a more general PCF position, the protest against the Aubervilliers fort was exceptional; for the most part, the Communist municipality stuck to specific issues. In this sphere, as in so many others in red Bobigny, practical concerns and ideological positions were usually kept separate.

The practical problems of residential life concerned the people of Bobigny, and consequently the Communist municipality worked most at making Bobigny a better place to live. Arranging for matching funds to repair defective allotments, sponsoring summer camps, and trying to get better tram service, Bobigny's red city hall focused its attention on community-based politics. Clamamus and members of the city council did support strikes and back local unions, but as far as municipal action in Bobigny was concerned, sidewalks counted far more than strikes.

Among the activities and accomplishments of Bobigny's Communist municipal administration in the interwar period, one characteristic that stands out is its adhesion to national PCF prescriptions on city government. The Bobigny municipality often helped the work of the national leadership and was in general not afraid to proclaim its political coloration. This is not to suggest that the city councillors did nothing but wave red flags all day; local officials seemed at times ambivalent about linking their roles as Communist militants and city politicians, and the atmosphere around city hall seems to have been decidedly businesslike. Political activities were a small but important proportion of the total accomplishments of the municipality and served to underline the difference between a Communist city government and its bourgeois homologues. Given the record of Bobigny's municipality on this score, it is not surprising that Clamamus was so respected by the PCF hierarchy. Much of this respect stemmed from the municipality's ability to solve concrete problems for the community's residents, and the dividends of political loyalty from these accomplishments. Impressive though the accomplishments were, they were not unique; the Communist municipalities of the Paris suburbs in general worked to deal with the overrapid urbanization and improve the living conditions of their working-class constituents.[124]

A number of non-Communist municipalities in the Paris suburbs also improved local living standards. Antony was one, on the southern edge of the Department of the Seine; like Bobigny, Antony was severely affected by the allotments crisis. During the 1920s and 1930s, the Radical administration of Mayor Auguste Mounié made strenuous efforts to repair the defective allotments and provide utilities service for them; moreover, the municipality put up posters warning prospective buyers about the allotments. Mayor Mounié was known as "le père des mal-lotis" throughout the Paris area because of his actions on this issue.[125]

The most active city administration in the Paris suburbs was that of Henri Sellier, Socialist mayor of Suresnes from 1919 to 1945. An internationally recognized urban planner, Sellier put his skills to work in reshaping Suresnes. Under his leadership the city council had built a *cité-jardin* of 2,500 housing units, an innovative school (including both indoor and outdoor swimming pools), a city dispensary, a cultural center, and an office of hygiene. In 1937 Sellier drew up a plan of urban development (*plan d'aménagement*) that made Suresnes a model for many other French cities.[126]

Earlier socialist municipalities had done much to improve urban facilities and living conditions. In his study of Limoges during the nineteenth century, John Merriman has described how the socialist government elected in 1895 undertook extensive renovations of the working-class neighborhoods of the city, building sewers, paving streets, and expanding medical service for the poor. Nor did the Limousin socialists neglect politics: they observed May Day at city hall, renamed local streets after famous progressives, and, most important, worked hard to support local strikes.[127]

Clearly, then, Communist municipalities did not hold a monopoly on urban development in the interwar Paris suburbs. What a particular city administration accomplished depended more at times on the individuals in charge, the problems to be faced, and the resources available to deal with such problems, than on the political coloration of the administration. And yet Mounié and Sellier were more exceptions in the Radical and Socialist parties than was Clamamus in the Communist party. One benefit of the tight control the PCF exercised on its municipal officials was their greater consistency in attacking urban problems compared to suburban mayors from other political parties.[128]

The achievements of Bobigny's municipality during the interwar period were nonetheless impressive. By 1939 the Communist administration had closed the gap between the needs of the city's population and the size of its urban facilities that existed when it took office in 1920; its efforts for the Pont de Bondy were particularly noteworthy. These achievements proved that French Communists could attend to urban issues despite an ideology that downplayed these in favor of issues of the workplace. They also showed that these urban issues had overwhelming importance.

To assume that local residents cared nothing about Communist ideology and only wanted their allotments cleaned up would be going too far. Although the municipality usually separated its ideological from its "bread and butter" activities, in both spheres it identified itself with the interests of the working class. Thus, its changes in the material quality of life in Bobigny had a primary place in building a Communist political consensus.

CHAPTER 6

Culture, Politics, and Community in Communist Bobigny

In *The Long Revolution*, Raymond Williams defines popular (or "social") culture as "a description of a particular way of life, which expresses certain meanings and values not only in art and learning but also in institutions and ordinary behaviour."[1] This description of the daily lives of ordinary people is a central task of the social historian, to show the patterns underlying peoples' lives and how they perceive them.

This chapter describes working-class popular culture in Bobigny during the early twentieth century and focuses on the role of the French Communist party in daily life. As yet there are few historical studies of popular culture in twentieth-century France, especially its interwar period, a topic to which I hope to contribute. My primary concern is not popular culture itself but how it interacted with Communist politics and ideology at the local level, how working-class consciousness in Bobigny related to the local PCF. Two questions occur here: to what extent did the popular culture of Bobigny affect the PCF's electoral strength in the community? Was the PCF able to create and popularize a specifically Communist culture in Bobigny?

I contend that there was a culture of communism in Bobigny that helped to form the PCF's political strength and was reinforced by it. I do not mean that daily life in the community perfectly corresponded to Communist ideology; the average Balbynian was no real-life version of the brave proletarian hero or heroine found in much of the period's left-wing fiction. Rather, Communist culture in Bobigny was a broad, deeply felt working-class consciousness that arose out of popular culture but was influenced by the practices of the local PCF.

The core of this culture was a strong spirit of working-class solidarity. Encouraged and channeled by Bobigny's Communists, this spirit was the product of an increasing split between production and consumption and of a growing social segregation. Both trends helped form class consciousness in Bobigny. Its distinctive spirit constituted the raw material of the culture of communism, which local activists molded into a definite political formation. Through political symbolism that was often astute, Bobigny's Communists were able to make their ideology a part of daily life. Perhaps more important, they linked the social and urban marginality of the suburban working class to the political marginality of the PCF. This affinity in turn allowed many Balbynians to identify with the French Communist party.

Popular Culture in Bobigny: Balkanization and Isolation

In describing popular culture in twentieth-century Bobigny, we must first look at a central institution of modern France, the nuclear family. It prevailed in Bobigny households and was a crucial component of local working-class culture. In addition, the family in Bobigny was characterized by what historian James McMillan has called the "doctrine of separate spheres." Men and women had distinct roles in the family and in local life as a whole.[2] As in the rest of France, however, they shared a preference for marriage over the single life.[3] Nearly 70 percent of all adults in the community aged twenty and over were married—72 percent of all men and 66 percent of all women. A majority of the unmarried adults were over fifty years of age; many were widowers and, especially, widows living alone or with married children. There was no important sector of unmarried young and middle-aged adults, no "singles" culture.[4] Few Balbynians chose to live together without marriage; in 1927, 90 percent of all couples living together were married. Like unmarried individuals, unmarried cohabiting couples were generally over fifty, much older than the average married couple.[5]

Bobigny's character as a commuter suburb contributed to the strength of marriage and the nuclear family there. Many people moved to suburbs like Bobigny for a better, less-crowded environment for their children or those they planned to have. The advertising posters put up by allotment developers in the Paris area often emphasized how family life would benefit from individual home ownership; one such poster featured two smiling crows happily installed in a tree over a caption calling on prospective lot buyers to come furnish their nests.[6] In the early 1920s Auguste Lallet decided to move out of Belleville to buy a lot in Bobigny; his foreman at work had just done so and advised Lallet to move his young family there.[7] Bobigny's abbé Ferret described a typical working-class family deciding whether to buy a lot in the community:

> The father and mother, followed by their children, after many trips to Bobigny, finally decide where they will set up their new home. . . . They think it over for a long time. . . . "What do you think, dear, should we buy? You know, it's for you and the children that I want to do this; all I'll get out of it is fatigue from the long journey that I will have to make to and from work every morning and night."[8]

Since the people of Bobigny, especially the working class and lower middle class in allotments, chose to settle there because they cherished domesticity, their attitudes toward family life were not necessarily typical French ones. They represented the direction in which France was headed, however. Bobigny was an extreme example of the geographical and cultural separation between the workplace and the home that had been increasing in France since the late nineteenth century. In the allotments, one consequence of this growing separation was a greater emphasis on family life.[9]

Another, more direct, consequence of the separation between work and home was that between men's and women's work. Fewer married women were employed outside the home, and their husbands faced a long journey to and from work. In spite of the contemporary myth of the new working woman after World War I, the percentage of married women working in nonagricultural jobs declined slightly from 1906 to 1936. Following patterns similar to those throughout France, in 1921 71 percent of all married working-class women in Bobigny were housewives. As adolescents and young adults, working-class women often had jobs. Once they married, however, they usually shifted from the paid to the non-paid sector, from workplace to household.[10]

While most working-class wives worked at home, most husbands commuted to work. As the Parisian father noted above, this could be a lengthy journey. Commuting usually took at least thirty minutes each way and often much more. French workers had won the eight-hour day in 1919, but in the interwar period the majority of factories in the Paris area did not apply this standard. As a result, male workers in Bobigny were often absent from home for twelve hours or more, Monday through Saturday.[11]

The lives of adult women and men thus differed sharply, that of men dominated by their jobs, generally in Paris or another suburb, and by the long commute there and back. For them, changes in the workplace —such as increasing mechanization and greater control by employers over production—shaped daily life.[12] For housewives in modern France, there has unfortunately been little scholarly investigation. Joan Scott and Louise Tilly have noted that as married women worked less outside the home, their housekeeping duties became more demanding and required more time. Bobigny's households in the 1920s and 1930s still had few modern conveniences, largely because of the community's poor facilities. The absence of water mains meant that housewives had to go to water pumps in the street; the few stores made shopping for food and other necessities a time-consuming task; and the generally unsanitary conditions in the town made keeping a clean household a continual chore. Working-class housewives in Bobigny faced these tasks alone since their husbands were absent much of the time.[13]

Yet this division of domestic labor did not diminish the significance of family relations in couples' lives. Marriage remained popular, and if the miserable living conditions during the interwar period made life harder for housewives, they also meant that husbands took a larger role in the household. Many men living in allotments built their own houses, for example; repairing the defective allotments often led them to invest time in community affairs. The difficulties that working-class Balbynians faced in creating a home, and the fact that they did, show that both men and women had a strong commitment to the household.[14]

The demands of working-class life in Bobigny left little time for leisure activities.[15] Yet people did manage to make time for recreation. Popular entertainment in early twentieth-century Bobigny was halfway between the traditional festivities uniting workplace and community and the post-1945 commercialized mass recreation. The absence of commercial leisure facilities in Bobigny has already been noted. Although movies were increasingly popular, Bobigny's workers had few opportunities to avail themselves of this entertainment, since the city had only two theaters, opened in the late 1920s.[16] Music was a more popular (and available) recreational activity. There were orchestras and other types of musical groups in Bobigny throughout the early twentieth century, usually sponsored by the municipality. Music classes, especially violin lessons, were also popular. In 1939 a resident of the Pont de Bondy noted the existence of three separate music societies in his neighborhood.[17]

In the early nineteenth-century suburban areas outside Paris, many cafés and dance halls furnished cheap entertainment to Parisians. By the twentieth century the suburbs no longer had this function; few city dwellers thought of going there to have a good time. Yet Bobigny did have a few *guinguettes,* or taverns featuring musical entertainment. Many Balbynians were hostile to such places and sometimes tried to close them down.

> For a while now, residents of the Pont de Bondy, and particularly of the rue de Drancy, have been complaining that their neighborhood has been greatly disturbed since the opening of the Zappoli dance hall in Drancy on the border of Bobigny. Because local hoodlums of both sexes congregate there, not a week passes without brawls, quarrels, and exchanges of gunfire between rivals and antagonists, horrifying the peaceful families of this isolated neighborhood.[18]

This was not the attitude of all Balbynians; but dance and music halls were not a central part of popular entertainment in Bobigny. Unlike Saint-Denis, the community seems to have been too family-oriented to have provided much business for them.[19]

Sports in Bobigny at the time also spanned traditional and mass popular culture. Richard Holt has noted that in interwar France, team sports were often polarized by the conflicts between capital and labor. This was the case in Bobigny: during the 1930s the Communists sponsored a local branch of the Union sportive ouvrière, and at least one factory, the Gérard hatmaking plant, maintained its own sporting club. These groups, and team sports in general, however, do not seem to have attracted much interest in the community.[20] Traditional individual sports retained the loyalty of many Balbynians; the most popular were fishing and *pétanque.* Fishing did serve to supplement poorer Balbynians' food supply, but it was also a means of relaxation and sociability; at least two fishing societies in the city sponsored contests with prizes along the canal de l'Ourcq. *Pétanque,* a form of *boules,* was very popular with male Balbynians, as were card games like *belote.*[21]

During the interwar period many workers in Paris spent their Sundays or weekends with friends in the suburbs, the closest they could get to the countryside. Many Balbynians had moved to Bobigny precisely to take advantage of pastoral pursuits and occupied much of their leisure time in the small gardens adjoining their homes in the allotments. Promenades were also popular, especially along the canal de l'Ourcq, not quite the industrial sewer it is today. On the whole, working-class leisure time in early twentieth-century Bobigny was peaceful, family-oriented, and largely noncommercial.[22]

Cafés had an important place in popular culture in Bobigny. Here men usually met to play cards and to organize games of *pétanque*. More than the rest of the commercial sector, the growth of Bobigny's cafés matched that of the population; by 1939 the town had 81 cafés, or one for every 215 residents. They were simple places where local residents could sit, talk, and drink. By contrast to cafés in urban communities before World War I, Bobigny's cafés did not function as hiring halls for workers. Still, they were the most popular public space in a community where much of life centered on the household.[23]

In many ways, working-class popular culture in Bobigny was respectable and prosaic, contrary to contemporary bourgeois expectations for a community that regularly voted Communist. One aspect of local life that significantly deviated from this bourgeois pattern was religious practice. Like other Paris suburbs at this time, Bobigny was well on the way to secularization. When the abbé Canet arrived in 1923 to take over from the retiring priest, Jules Ferret, the church could claim only 150 practicing Catholics out of a population of roughly 7,000.[24] Even for working-class areas around Paris this figure was extraordinary; it explains the interest of Catholic evangelists in spreading the gospel in Bobigny. In France even nonpracticing Catholics will often have their children baptized. Yet this ceremony was performed for only two-thirds of all children born in Bobigny in 1931. The church was even less successful with marriages: in 1921 fewer than half of the city's newlyweds had religious weddings.[25] For most of this period, Bobigny had only one church; like everything else in the community, religious life was affected by the gap between the growth of the population and urban facilities. Yet this factor had minor importance. Bobigny mirrored the alienation from the church characteristic of urban workers in twentieth-century France.[26]

Isolated from religion, workers in Bobigny also experienced a sharp division between production and consumption, between work and home. The symbol and immediate cause of this split was the tramway, which at the same time unified the Paris area and reinforced subdivisions within it. The division of male and female life into separate spheres was an important consequence of the geographical separation of work and home, this balkanization of daily life. Off the job, few Balbynians had much contact with Paris or the leisure opportunities it offered. Working-class culture was thus not mass culture in early twentieth-century Bobigny because workers had little contact with cinemas, department stores, or other such institutions.[27]

More important was their social isolation within Bobigny. The allotments were populated mostly by workers and members of the lower middle class; the community as a whole had few bourgeois residents. Furthermore, the social segregation of the Paris area was replicated within the community; except for the employés, other groups such as shopkeepers and market gardeners lived in the center of town, away from the working-class allotments. Workers had little daily contact with members of other social groups. More than their cultural isolation from catholicism, their social isolation affected people's views of life in general. Like the workers of late nineteenth-century Britain studied by Gareth Stedman Jones, those of early twentieth-century Bobigny lived in a world apart.[28]

The Culture of Communism in Bobigny

In analyzing the political culture developed by the French Communists in Bobigny, we would be wrong to refer simply to the ideas propagated by the national leaders. Although local Communists did follow the general PCF policy, they also simplified and adapted it to correspond to the experiences of the local population. They were certainly not successful in making this connection all the time, but in some ways local Communist political culture had affinities with the attitudes described above.[29] It centered on a few themes. The most basic was class conflict, the oppression of the working people of Bobigny by the French bourgeoisie. In a resolution voted by the city council on the fiftieth anniversary of the 1884 municipal law, this point of view was clearly expressed:

> [The city council] decides . . . to pursue ceaselessly, at the head of the laboring population of Bobigny that elected it, the task of education and combat to substitute for false bourgeois democracy the true democracy of the people against its profiteers.
>
> [We oppose] to the general interests of capital the interests of the workers against those of their exploiters.[30]

The theme was especially popular during election campaigns, when Clamamus and other Party politicians portrayed the electoral battles between the Communist party and its opponents as symbols of the class struggle.[31]

Implicit in the concept of class conflict was that of class solidarity; in order to fight capitalism the working class would have to unite. In Bobigny class solidarity had two dimensions, according to the PCF: support for the struggles of workers in other parts of France and abroad, above all in the Soviet Union; unity of the working people of Bobigny. The former dimension prompted the various symbolic city council resolutions discussed in the fifth chapter, and was also expressed by constant propaganda praising the achievements of the Bolsheviks and calling for the defense of the Russian revolution.[32]

Bobigny's Communists tended to express the theme of class solidarity in terms of concrete mutual aid rather than of political principles. Their activities in helping the elderly, the unemployed, and other needy Balbynians they characterized not as charity but as working-class unity. During the June 1936 sitdown strikes the local PCF made sure to call attention to the municipality's efforts for the strikers.

> During all of these [strike] movements, the municipality and working-class organizations, as well as the entire population, gave important assistance to the workers and their families.
>
> Kitchens in the factories and in the center and Pont de Bondy schools furnished copious meals. Benevolent comrades ran the kitchens. In the midst of it all, the wife of comrade Clamamus worked from morning until night.[33]

A third element in the political culture of Communists was the view of their community as the possession and citadel of the working class—symbolized, of course, by the town's PCF municipality, whose achievements were portrayed as examples of what the working class was capable of doing to lift itself up by its own efforts. The frequent use of this theme by Bobigny's Communists was an attempt to fuse class consciousness with local pride and enlist both in support of the local PCF.[34] They found many vehicles: city council resolutions, newspaper articles, demonstrations by local PCF organizations, and symbolic activities. These last were especially important; they had a more direct and general impact than speeches or written propaganda and showed local communism at its most creative. Prominent examples of such activities included renaming city streets after heroes of the Communist movement and the French Left as well as public demonstrations.

Demonstrations certainly did not occur every day; they seem to have been no more frequent in Bobigny than in other Paris suburbs, regardless of their political coloration. Political demonstrations were usually held on national holidays or to celebrate major local events, such as the completion of important municipal projects. Armistice Day commemorations gave Bobigny's Communists an opportunity to combine the traditional observance of this date with protests by local politicians against war and militarism.

> In Bobigny, the local Communist section organized . . . a meeting attended by 150 people. At the end of the meeting . . . about sixty of them, led by Clamamus, marched, singing the "Internationale" and crying "Down with war," to the place de la Mairie, where a Communist orator harangued them.[35]

Bobigny's Communists strongly protested against war, expressed in a context of class conflict, not simple pacifism. War was characterized as victimizing poor workers from all countries to benefit capitalists and generals.[36] Class struggle was usually a central theme of these demonstrations. By contrast, festivities held to celebrate local events tended to stress the importance of working-class solidarity and civic pride in a workers' community. Such celebrations were held to open a new city facility—the new school group in the Pont de Bondy or the *maison du peuple*.[37]

Communist demonstrations in Bobigny were often very colorful affairs. They usually started off with parades; participants marched under the banners of the various PCF organizations to which they belonged. After arriving at their destination, the marchers listened to speeches by various Communist dignitaries, local, regional, or national. Mayor Clamamus was the most frequent orator. Then came cultural activities: singing groups, dancers, and skits, usually political. Accounts of such demonstrations suggest that pageantry and performance took up much more time than speechmaking. All were political, but Bobigny's Communists evidently felt that their ideological medicine would go down easier if administered in solution.[38]

Probably the most spectacular public events staged by the PCF in Bobigny were the famous (or notorious) "red baptisms," rituals that were only the most dramatic symbol of a bitter conflict between the Communists and the Catholic church in the 1920s and early 1930s. At its root lay the church's rather belated recognition of its weakness in Bobigny and other working-class Parisian suburbs. Under the impetus of aggressive evangelists like Pierre Lhande, in the 1920s the church began a major effort to reconvert the suburban workers to Christianity. Bobigny was chosen as a key target for this campaign because of its reputation as a red citadel, and because secularization was so far advanced there. As Denis Brogan has phrased it, "In the red zone around Paris he [the French priest] had to start almost at the beginning. . . . The old rural Bobigny had gone, and the new Bobigny had to be treated like a mission field."[39]

Given the abysmal character of the relations between the church and the PCF until the Popular Front of 1936, it is not surprising that Bobigny's Communists, including members of the city government, fought tooth and nail against the attempt to reconvert their community. The red baptisms were one of their most imaginative means of doing so. In recounting Catholic efforts to develop a strong congregation in Nouveau Village, the city's biggest allotment, two associates of Father Lhande vividly described one of these ceremonies. The baptism, which had been widely publicized, began with a parade of the local Red Pioneers led by members of the city council along the rue de Rome. As the parade passed the church the demonstrators shouted slogans like "Priests to the lamppost" and "Death to the Christians," and sang blasphemous songs. One priest reported,

Here is an example of one of these songs, sung to the tune of "Midnight, Christians":

"Religion, daughter of Ignorance,
In centuries past, to ensure its dominance,
Martyred the masters of Science,
All thinkers, artisans of Progress.
Priest assassin, you who have soiled History
With so much blood, in the name of the Creator,
Yes, we know that, under your black robe,
Still hides the evil Inquisitor."

The red baptism ceremony began at 4:30 in a municipal field. An individual disguised as a priest mimicked religious ceremonies . . . the children's parents were given a baptismal certificate, in correct form, carrying the signatures of the father, the mother, the godfather, and godmother, with the seal of city hall and the signature of Monsieur . . . Clamamus![40]

In April 1936 the "main tendue" speech of Maurice Thorez signaled a new PCF policy of detente toward the Catholic church that brought the end of the red baptisms in Bobigny. In general, Bobigny's Communists faithfully followed the new policy on religion. In addition to terminating the red baptisms, the PCF stopped all attacks on the church in the local press. In February 1936 the municipality appointed abbé Canet vice-president of a committee to aid the unemployed, presided over by Clamamus.[41]

Like the Lenin School, the red baptisms were a popular symbol of Communist Bobigny in the interwar years, both for those who lived there and for outside observers. Their significance for Communist political culture in Bobigny goes beyond this, however. The re-Christianization campaign waged by the church in the Paris suburbs failed miserably, in part because outsiders were bringing different cultural practices to the area. The red baptisms, by contrast, involved residents defending working-class popular culture and revealed an affinity between it and Communist ideology. They demonstrated that the cultural identification of the workers with the PCF extended to the sphere of religion.[42]

Bobigny's Communists also renamed local streets in a less spectacular but more permanent attempt to make their political culture a part of daily life in the town. By 1939 it had changed the names of twelve local thoroughfares, most to those of figures of the French Left: prewar French socialists and working-class activists such as Edouard Vaillant, Pierre-Joseph Proudhon, and Louise Michel. The PCF regarded itself as the rightful successor of militants like Jaurès and Michel; the naming of streets after them can be interpreted as an attempt to reappropriate this heritage. Like the city council resolutions to honor Lafargue and Rouget de Lisle, the intention was to anchor the Bobigny PCF firmly in the traditions of the French Left.

The city government did not however neglect those who had achieved distinction within the ranks of the PCF, like Henri Barbusse and Paul Vaillant-Couturier. The municipality also commemorated working-class martyrs in renaming streets. André Sabatier, killed in Suresnes while participating in the PCF's general strike of 12 October 1925, was one; Sacco and Vanzetti, two American anarchists executed for murder in 1927, also had a street named after them.[43] In addition to the illustrious dead, other politically significant designations were applied to streets; to celebrate the world's first socialist state, streets were named after Moscow, Leningrad, and Odessa. The world Communist movement was commemorated by the rue de l'Internationale.[44]

The municipality changed street names to ensure that Communist ideals would play a major role in Bobigny's collective memory. Renaming streets was one of the most purely symbolic activities undertaken by the Communists and yet one with practical impact. The names of Bobigny's streets were the most obvious and immediate manifestation of the city's Communist political culture. Its essential goal was to create a sense of identity between the local PCF and the workers of Bobigny. Its two most important themes, class conflict and class solidarity, demonstrated this identity. Certainly not all of the Party's local propaganda addressed these themes directly, but they formed the basic underpinnings of its weltanschauung. Communist dominance of local political life showed the PCF's ability to create this consensus. Its use of the idea of working-class solidarity, not class struggle, had the greatest appeal for the workers of Bobigny and thus formed the most effective ideological link between them and the French Communist party.

Neighborhood and Community Life

The geographical and social isolation of their lives made class conflict an abstract concept for many workers. Whatever their experiences on the job, at home in Bobigny there was no bourgeois presence to lend the idea of class struggle a concrete reality. By contrast, their isolation made working-class solidarity more tangible. They experienced this solidarity not so much in political terms as in feelings of closeness to their neighbors and ease in their *quartier*. This important sentiment of local community made the Communist stress on class solidarity readily comprehensible.

In short, communism in Bobigny owed its strength partly to a strong sense of community, especially at the neighborhood level. However, community in Bobigny did not come into being automatically but formed gradually during the early twentieth century as the city grew. Local politics was instrumental in developing neighborhood life, and the PCF's role in shaping local institutions and activities was significant. Since Bobigny was undergoing rapid and far-reaching change in the early twentieth century, its community formation was not traditional but intimately connected with larger patterns of urban growth and political change affecting the Paris area as a whole.[45]

The same process that turned Bobigny into a commuters' suburb of Paris discouraged the formation of neighborhood sentiment (Map 5). There were many newcomers in the town; in 1921 only 13 percent of Bobigny's residents had been born there. Bobigny had no major ethnic groups, people who had come from the same region and could therefore reconstitute old community ties. Such ethnic concentrations have often been crucial in giving neighborhoods in modern urban areas a special character and sense of cohesiveness.[46] Bobigny's character as a commuter suburb constituted a stubborn obstacle to community conscious-

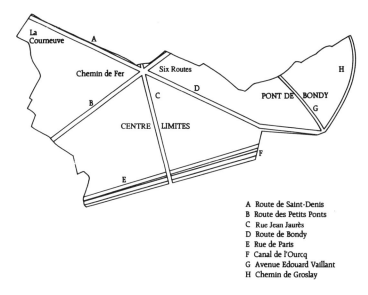

A Route de Saint-Denis
B Route des Petits Ponts
C Rue Jean Jaurès
D Route de Bondy
E Rue de Paris
F Canal de l'Ourcq
G Avenue Edouard Vaillant
H Chemin de Groslay

Map 5. Bobigny neighborhoods in 1920.

ness. The absence of much of the population during the day made Bobigny a fragmentary, bedroom community; as studies of similar commuter villages have shown, neighborhood loyalty and identification are often quite weak in such places.[47] The physical character of the town reinforced its fragmentary identity. Aside from a canal along its southern boundary, there were no landmarks to distinguish Bobigny from other similar suburbs surrounding it. A town that is merely one part of a larger suburban sprawl is less likely to inspire local pride than one that is distinct and self-contained.

Given these factors, it would seem that residents of Bobigny in the early twentieth century were doomed to live in self-contained households without ever getting to know their neighbors. Yet certain structural characteristics of the town's development promoted neighborhood sociability and therefore counteracted the factors described above. Most important was the sociological homogeneity of the local population. Close to three-fourths of Bobigny's residents were individuals, working class or lower middle class, with roughly similar incomes and life-styles. As several studies have shown, neighborhoods with a homogeneous population are more likely to have strong community life than are more diverse areas.[48]

The structure of transportation facilities in Bobigny provided an important spur to neighborhood sociability. One cause of Bobigny's suburbanization was the working-class tram system, with low fees on certain tramcars during commuting hours. This meant that Bobigny residents taking the tram in off-hours to visit friends or relatives elsewhere in the Paris area paid full fare for inconvenient tram travel at night; it limited the mobility of Bobigny's workers and made spending their social time within walking distance of their homes more likely.[49]

The large number of cafés in Bobigny also helped promote workers' sociability. The contribution of cafés to local leisure and urban life has already been noted. Their distribution was unlike that of most businesses in Bobigny, which were clustered around the old town center. The cafés were to be found in all areas, both downtown and in the peripheral neighborhoods. Therefore, they provided an institutional framework to develop local sociability. But they not only fostered neighborhood sentiment; they showed it already existed. Another measure of the strength or weakness of neighborly feeling is the records of local marriages. By calculating what percentage of brides, grooms, and marriage witnesses lived in the same neighborhoods, we can discover to what extent people in Bobigny formed close relationships based on where they lived.[50]

An analysis of Bobigny's marriage records during the 1920s and 1930s shows that general neighborhood sentiment was a significant component of local sociability but by no means the dominant one. Of newlyweds in Bobigny, 35 percent were couples who lived in the same neighborhoods, whereas 56 percent included a spouse from outside Bobigny. Gaston Laroche and Sylvie Marchal, unskilled laborers, were living a few blocks from each other, on the avenue Jean Jaurès and the allée de la Madeleine, respectively, before they married.[51] The pattern is similar for witnesses; 40 percent lived in the bride's or the groom's neighborhood, and 56 percent lived outside Bobigny. In both cases the highest levels of neighborhood sociability occurred at the beginning of the period we study; in 1923, 39 percent of new spouses and 49 percent of witnesses came from the same neighborhoods. In general, however, the data do not reveal any clear trends during the interwar period.[52]

If neighborhood relations did not dominate local sociability, occupational or workplace sociability was even less important. Of all newlyweds in Bobigny during this period, only 14 percent married spouses employed in the same occupation. Again, the statistics for witnesses are similar; only 16 percent of witnesses belonged to the same occupation as either the bride or the groom. The marriage records are an imperfect guide to workplace sociability, since they do not indicate the actual firms in which people were employed; many workplaces employed people from different occupations. Still, they indicate that workplace relations were not a major factor in local social life. Given the separation between workplace and residence so characteristic of life in Bobigny, this is not surprising.[53]

If neither residential nor occupational closeness determined the social lives of Bobigny residents during the 1920s and 1930s, what were their primary social networks? The data available do not give us a definitive or statistical answer, yet they show that family relationships, and networks formed in the places of origin of new Bobigny residents, were consequential. Family ties usually constitute a primary form of sociability for the urban working class in France and other industrial societies. Although the Bobigny marriage records did not always indicate whether witnesses were related to the newlywed pair, a large number of them seem to have been. In 1911 two-thirds of the marriage witnesses (91 out of 141) were relatives, especially brothers, brothers-in-law, and uncles; one-third of these relatives lived in the same neighborhood as either bride or groom. Of the four witnesses present at the wedding of Etienne Faurisson and Marie Chardon in 1911, three were brothers and the fourth was a sister-in-law; one brother lived in the same Bobigny neighborhood as the newlywed pair, and the other witnesses lived elsewhere in the Paris area.[54] As for networks from the "old country," there were many examples of brides and grooms who came from the same region in the provinces, or whose parents lived in the same area.[55]

The crucial lesson to be drawn from this analysis of Bobigny's marriage records is that the majority of people's close relationships did not result from where they lived, but that neighborhood life was still an important factor in their networks of sociability. It probably had an even greater role in casual friendships. One overriding reason for the strength of neighborhood sociability in Bobigny was the condition of the neighborhoods. The need to get streets paved, streetlights put up, and water service established brought neighbors together. Consequently, people developed the habit of looking out for those who lived around them.

> Among these . . . *mal-lotis* who all have the same problems, there exists a certain solidarity that most often reveals itself by collections taken up haphazardly, according to whether the immediate neighbors organize it. One will give fifty centimes, another five francs—there is no guarantee of equality of sacrifice. Then this collection is given, almost like charity, to a comrade afflicted by adversity. . . . We have been able to affirm that occasionally two, even three collections were taken up in our allotment during the same week.[56]

Taken from a local Communist newspaper, this description of mutual aid shows not only its importance to the workers of Bobigny but also how the PCF attempted to organize such practices and give them an ideological cast.[57]

Local solidarity arose both from neighbors' need to deal with inadequate living conditions and from their voluntary organization. Urban sociologists have proposed a theory, the "phase hypothesis of community development," which has relevance to Bobigny. This hypothesis contends that heightened community and neighborhood sociability are characteristic of new housing estates during the first phase of their existence, as people get to know one another and have to deal with common problems involved in settling into a new place. Once this initial phase is completed, however, community sociability tends to decline. In Bobigny this phase of intense neighborliness was prolonged because of the crisis of the allotments and the underdevelopment of the urban facilities in general.[58]

One form of local activity that helped generate local sociability was the petition drive. Although Balbynians expected the city government to improve living conditions in their areas, they did not simply wait for this to happen but put pressure on the municipality to follow through on its promises. Petitions were a favorite means of doing so. At most of its meetings during the 1920s and 1930s the Bobigny city council had to deal with petitions from its constituents requesting various improvements in city services and facilities. These petitions came from all over Bobigny, especially from the allotment neighborhoods, and usually involved residents of a few adjacent streets. Working on petitions made people aware of their neighbors and of the problems they shared with them.[59]

Community activism in Bobigny went beyond petitions, however; it also had an important organizational side. One organization that played a significant role in local life was the local interest committee (LIC), or *amicale*. During the interwar period there were five of these groups in Bobigny; the oldest, that of the Pont de Bondy, was founded in 1913. The LICs were active in organizing petition drives and other campaigns to upgrade the quality of life in their neighborhoods. The following report from a Nouveau Village LIC meeting gives a good overview of the work done by the LICs. These activities may seem mundane, given the reputation of red Bobigny, but they mattered to the residents of the city's working-class neighborhoods.

> Our comrade Pesch presented a summary of the activity of the group since our last assembly. All questions of interest to the population of our *quartier* were dealt with: street repairs, public lighting, paving streets and sidewalks, sewer cleaning, and so on. All these have been or are about to be dealt with by our municipality. Then, our children's festival was decided upon. . . .[60]

Elected leaders did the bulk of the work of the LICs, and most members looked on. The committees nonetheless provided a forum to discuss local concerns and come up with ways to deal with them. As such, they helped bring neighbors together to develop a concrete sense of community.

Also working on common neighborhood matters were the allotment-based associations syndicales, or lot owners' associations. There were sixteen of them, and they were founded in the 1920s as part of the national effort to make the defective allotments more habitable. Unlike the local interest committees, the associations were less voluntaristic; any allotment dweller who wanted paved streets or other improvements had to join the local association. The two types of organizations were concerned with similar problems and often worked closely together.[61] Their presence and a more general community consciousness helped the PCF succeed in Bobigny. No political force could have assembled the kind of strength the Communists had in interwar Bobigny without at least some presence in the neighborhoods, and the PCF made itself a part of grassroots politics.

For one thing, Communists led many if not most of the local interest committees and associations syndicales. At least three of the five LICs were headed by PCF city councillors, and much of the leadership of the associations was also Communist. Furthermore, the city council and especially Mayor Clamamus worked to establish virtually all the associations syndicales. The two community organizations were not simply PCF fronts; sometimes even their Communist leaders came into conflict with the municipality, as is shown by the following letter from Adrien Dumontier, PCF city councillor and secretary of Les Vignes' LIC, to Mayor Clamamus:

> Comrade,
>   In accord with the general discontent of the residents of the Les Vignes allotment concerning the repair of the roads of this allotment, I remind you that Chemin, a secretary at city hall, has held up these works for at least eighteen months, if not two years. . . . I have no intention of covering up with my silence the incompetence of certain city hall employees. I will come by city hall on Sunday . . . to ask you about the specific reasons for this delay. . . .
>   The bureau of the local interest committee will be informed of this situation; the small property owners of the allotment will be convoked for a special meeting.[62]

Other conflicts did occur, but none serious enough to break the close relations between the LICS, the associations, and the PCF. These community organizations established a strong Communist presence at the neighborhood level; they would probably have existed even had the PCF played little or no role in Bobigny's political life, yet the Party gave them vigor and manpower.

In their functioning and their ties with Bobigny's city council, these neighborhood organizations suggest parallels with American urban political machines. The LICs represented an unofficial yet effective way for ordinary Balbynians to attract the municipality's attention to local problems. These parallels go only so far, however: Bobigny's PCF politicians had no patronage jobs like shoveling snow to offer constituents in exchange for votes, and in general French municipalities had much less power than their American counterparts.[63]

The setup of Bobigny's community organizations demonstrated an important, if unspoken, aspect of Communist political culture in Bobigny: the split between a few active leaders and a largely passive following. Much of this stemmed from the difficulties of getting people to devote time to such work. However, the Communists were not especially interested in developing a more democratic and participatory style of local politics. The hierarchical nature of the LICs and associations mirrored that of Bobigny's Communist political culture, in which a few Party activists and politicians made most important decisions; for the great majority of citizens political decision making began and ended at the ballot box. There were many more PCF voters than there were Party members; in 1925, for example, while the Communists won over a thousand votes in the municipal elections, there were only sixty-two militants in the local section.[64]

In any case, neighborhood sociability and identity were important to the workers of Bobigny, and the Communists were adept both in maintaining these sentiments and in channeling them toward their own goals. The question remains: to what extent did community solidarity equal class solidarity in interwar Bobigny? The two concepts were not equivalent; a woman who brought over food or cleaned house for her neighbor whose husband was sick hardly interpreted her actions in terms of abstract class solidarity. Yet the isolation of Bobigny workers in their own communities was significant. To a large extent workers lived next to, socialized with, and married other workers. Thus in emphasizing the importance of class loyalty, the Communists of Bobigny were simply trying to give explicit expression to values already implicit in local working-class popular culture.[65]

Communist Cultural Activities in Bobigny

In their efforts to build a mass base for themselves in the community, Bobigny's Communists devoted much energy to organizing cultural events. Such functions had greater potential to reach out to citizens who were apathetic toward or at best only somewhat interested in politics; the average individual, even in interwar Bobigny, would probably rather attend a block party or a film than a factual political lecture or demonstration. Even committed Party militants must have fun sometimes.

Another reason for the PCF's emphasis on this activity was the notable lack of cultural resources in Bobigny. Although unfortunate for the residents, the situation was in some ways advantageous for the PCF; if it could establish a strong cultural sphere in the community, it would not have to worry about competition from non-Communist sources. Both the PCF and the Communist municipality did have a large part in cultural activities in Bobigny between the wars, and we must note this impact in assessing the Party's strength.

The simplest and most common cultural activities organized by Bobigny's Communists were neighborhood festivals; nearly every local group sponsored them at one time or another. Although the municipality did not officially organize festivals, Clamamus and other members of the city council often attended, and the city government frequently gave subsidies to neighborhood groups to defray the festivals' costs.[66] Usually these festivals had a political theme. For example, in 1935 the Maurice Bureau quarter held a children's festival to honor its namesake, one of the Communist martyrs killed during the riots of 9 February 1934. On Bastille Day in 1930 the municipality sponsored "red balls" throughout the city. Yet these festivals were genuine parties, with music, dancing, games, and sometimes performers; unlike demonstrations, they rarely featured marches or political speeches.[67]

In contrast, those entertainments sponsored by the PCF itself, not by its "front" groups or affiliated organizations, generally gave politics pride of place. A 1926 fundraiser for the PCF's twenty-first regional district (*rayon*) began with a concert. During the intermission a representative from the PCF's Paris regional federation spoke, praising the Communists of Bobigny and accusing the Socialists of betraying the working class. The concert was followed by a one-act play, "The Idea," depicting the betrayal of strikers by a fellow worker.[68] Such arid ideological performances were at least as much propaganda as entertainment. They were to be found in Bobigny throughout the interwar period, but it is difficult to believe that they attracted more than the Party faithful.

In the field of music we find a similar distinction between political groups and groups that were also political. Before the PCF won control of the city government in 1920 the city had a municipal music society. The Communists continued this tradition, founding the Harmonie de Bobigny, which played at local functions like the inauguration of new city buildings, graduation ceremonies, and so forth. The Harmonie had more political uses, however; from time to time it also played at PCF rallies and demonstrations in the Paris area. In addition to this official organization, Bobigny's Communists were active in several nonmunicipal music groups in the city, such as the Aube artistique balbynienne.[69] In contrast to the Harmonie de Bobigny was the local music and drama group known as the Blue Blouses of Bobigny. This PCF organization, associated with the Young Communists, was modeled after similar, cabaret-style performing groups organized by German Communists in the 1920s. It specialized in singing Communist songs at political events. A correspondent for the *Journal de Saint-Denis* described his impressions of the group's performance at an electoral rally for Clamamus:

Clamamus then offered a presentation of "speaking choruses" by the Blue Blouses of Bobigny. It is truly inadmissible to hear children from twelve to fifteen years of age pronounce words of hatred, chanting slogans like "The Red Front is on the march," "Dynamite is what we are acting," and "The republic deserves to be swept away with a broom." Then the same young boys and girls, carrying wooden rifles and gunbelts, sang a march, that of the future Red Army: "Forward," they sang, "toward the civil war."[70]

Other Communist cultural activities in Bobigny included sports and, at least during the Popular Front, film. The Workers' Sports Union of Bobigny organized instruction, teams, and competitions in various sports; in 1930, for example, it was given three hundred francs by the municipality to organize bicycle and foot races for the city's annual festival. The films shown by PCF and neighborhood organizations were generally either from the Soviet Union or dealt with the Spanish civil war. There was a short-lived Soviet film society in Bobigny during the 1930s; the Friends of the Soviet Union and other local groups also sponsored showings from time to time. Films sometimes figured as part of the entertainment at festivals; for example, as part of the city's celebration of the sesquicentennial of the French Revolution in 1939, the municipality sponsored a viewing of Jean Renoir's film *La Marseillaise*.[71]

Finally, the PCF contributed to local entertainment by maintaining several Communist cafés in Bobigny. The most famous and important of these was the maison Pesch, owned by Deputy Mayor Léon Pesch, in the Pont de Bondy. The Pont de Bondy local interest committee usually met here, as well as several other local PCF organizations. These cafés were important centers of Communist political culture in Bobigny, serving as neighborhood meeting halls, distribution points for the Party press, and places for activists to socialize. For example, one got a glass of red wine by ordering a Clamamus.[72]

We can divide the cultural activities of the Bobigny PCF into two main categories: the more overtly political ones that most often provided entertainment at Party rallies, and those in which political themes were present but not dominant. Although the former occurred more frequently in the city, the latter, especially the neighborhood festivals, probably did more to involve average Balbynians in Communist culture. Except for these festivals, it is doubtful that Communist cultural activities had an impact on the leisure of the people of Bobigny. For one thing, such activities were not frequent, rarely occurring more than once a month even during the Popular Front. When people did take part, they often remembered the entertainment but not the politics.[73] The PCF was often the only source of such cultural activities in Bobigny, but the overtly political types of cultural expression offered by the Communists seem not to have become an integral part of local popular culture.[74]

The culture of communism in interwar Bobigny was built on a distinctive working-class consciousness produced both by suburban development and Communist activism. At the base of structural conditions shaping this consciousness lay the division between home and work, which increased the segregation of classes in the Paris area. The split between job and home gave rise to overrapid development of the allotments in Bobigny; as residential issues became more distinct, they assumed an importance of their own. Working-class consciousness in Bobigny was to a large extent *mal-loti* consciousness; workers in allotments put a lot of effort into making their homes and communities decent places to live and considered the struggle to accomplish this goal vital to their lives.

The workers' social segregation also played a key role. One central characteristic of working-class life in Bobigny was isolation from other social groups, and from bourgeois society as a whole. The radical base of Bobigny's electoral support for the PCF was both a product and a symbol of the physical, sociological, and cultural separation of the community's workers from the dominant culture of early twentieth-century France. This social isolation also strongly colored community activities. For various reasons, especially the substandard local living conditions, neighborhood life was very important in Bobigny. Because of the town's segregated population, local solidarity was in effect identical to working-class solidarity, since a worker's neighbors were almost always other workers or employés.

The result in Bobigny was a working-class consciousness that emphasized class solidarity and unity over the class struggle. With no local bourgeoisie to struggle against, class struggle was an abstract concept; one could easily see the need for workers to help each other. The Communists emphasized both. Whereas Balbynian workers were certainly not hostile to struggle, class solidarity more closely fit their own experiences. The most concrete manifestation of this spirit was community activism. The well-developed network of community institutions in Bobigny demonstrated the importance of community issues in the city's political life. No correspondingly large and active group of institutions was set up to deal with workplace problems. Bobigny did have local unions, but they were small and had less place in local life than did, say, the local interest committees.[75] The PCF's influence in them helped solidify its electoral hold over the community. But this influence worked two ways: the concerns of Bobigny's community groups also tended to reinforce the PCF's interest in community issues. The PCF's major role in daily life in Bobigny served to integrate it into local popular beliefs and practices. Though this political culture did have political utility, on the whole the culture of communism was more a product of the PCF's political strength than a reason for it. More than anything else, it used symbolic acts like renaming streets and various cultural activities, specifically Communist symbols, to distinguish life in Bobigny from that in other, non-Communist Paris suburbs.

There was an interesting tension in Bobigny's Communist culture between the desire to challenge capitalist society and the wish to present an alternative to it. The PCF itself strongly favored the former option, which goes far to explain its essentially nondemocratic political practices. Yet in developing this culture the Party was implicitly advocating an alternative to bourgeois culture and to bourgeois society as a whole. This vision of an alternative, more than the emphasis on class conflict, was key in continuing Communist power in Bobigny after 1945 down to the present day. Otherwise, French Communism's unrevolutionary partial integration into mainstream French politics would have reduced its appeal to Balbynians. It is still said today that in the suburbs of Paris one is born, not made, a Communist. The example of the culture of communism developed in Bobigny between the world wars shows how this could be so.

Conclusion

In late nineteenth-century France certain social theorists, concerned with what they saw as a morally and politically degenerate working class, advocated removing workers from the noxious Parisian slums and resettling them outside the city. By isolating them from cafés and other evil urban influences and by making them property owners these theorists believed they could move the workers of Paris toward bourgeois respectability and political reliability.

By the early twentieth century this vision had been largely achieved, not by the recipes of social theorists, but as a consequence of the patterns of capitalist urbanization. The increasing price of land in the capital, its growing specialization of function, and the resultant crisis of working-class housing made Paris inhospitable to most workers after 1900. The development of industry in the suburbs and connection of that area to the city through mass transit facilities made suburban working-class habitation more feasible. The rise of the allotments converted a strong possibility into an overwhelming reality.

Yet the political consequences of this evolution sharply contradicted the hopes of many middle-class observers. Allotment life turned out to be a vicious parody of the dream of home ownership, with the result that by the mid-1920s the anger of the *mal-lotis* had become a crucial political issue. In Bobigny and many other suburban communities the French Communists rode this issue to political dominance. The political history of the Paris suburbs thus seemed to rest on a profound paradox: instead of "moralizing" the working class, suburbanization created the

169

Red Belt, menacingly encircling the city that no longer had room for its working-class inhabitants.

By the mid-1920s the PCF had a dominant position in the political life of Bobigny that has remained little contested. As such, Bobigny is a fitting symbol of the Red Belt that French Communists created in the Paris suburbs during the interwar years. However, the PCF's easy success in Bobigny was not representative of its electoral history in the region. During the 1920s it faced sharp competition from the Socialist party and the Radicals for suburban votes, only emerging as the predominant political force in the heady years of the Popular Front. It was this "springtime of the French Left," from 1935 to 1938, that made the Red Belt an enduring part of the national political landscape.

Although the French Communist party did not immediately take control of the Paris suburbs, it was from the beginning proportionately much stronger in the Department of the Seine than in the nation as a whole (Table 20).

In the Paris suburbs, the PCF received a percentage three times its national vote during the interwar period; the suburban population was strongly working class, which helps to explain this roughly constant differential. As Bobigny demonstrated, workers were more likely to vote Communist. PCF vote totals in the suburbs of the Seine, however, unlike those in Bobigny, did vary significantly, mirroring the shifts of the Party's national vote totals. Communist strength in the area was responsive to changes in the Party line.

TABLE 20

THE PCF'S PERCENTAGE OF THE VOTE
IN FRENCH LEGISLATIVE ELECTIONS

	Seine–Suburbs	France
1924	26	10
1928	26	11
1932	24	8
1936	39	15

SOURCES: Peter Campbell, *French Electoral Systems and Elections since 1789* (London, 1958), pp. 97–101; François Goguel, "Géographie des élections françaises sous la Troisième et la Quatrième République," *Cahiers de la Fondation nationale des sciences politiques* 159 (1970): 78–97; Annie Fourcaut, "Bobigny, banlieue rouge," *Communisme* 3 (1983): 11.

Another indicator of Communist influence in the Paris suburbs was the number of municipal governments it controlled. At its birth in 1920 the PCF was the dominant political force in sixteen municipalities out of a total of seventy-nine in the suburban Department of the Seine. By the eve of the 1925 municipal elections a number of suburban administrations had defected, and the French Communists controlled only four city halls in the suburbs of the Seine. The 1925 elections doubled the number of their suburban municipalities to eight, and the next set of elections further increased the score to ten. In municipal as in legislative elections, the Popular Front caused the real breakthrough. In the municipal elections of 1935 the PCF finally surpassed the number of suburban city halls it had begun with, winning control of twenty-seven, more than any other political party.[1]

An electoral map shows us the PCF's three geographical strongholds in the Department of the Seine in the 1920s and 1930s: the suburbs directly to the north of Paris, those to the northeast, and those located south-southeast of the capital. To the north, Saint-Denis, Clichy, Gennevilliers, Epinay, Villetaneuse, Pierrefitte, and Stains all had Communist municipalities for at least part of this period. To the northeast, the PCF controlled Bobigny's city hall; the canton of Noisy-le-Sec regularly sent Mayor Clamamus to the Chamber of Deputies. South of Paris, Ivry, Vitry, Villejuif, Choisy-le-Roi, and Alfortville were communities where the PCF was especially strong in the interwar years.[2]

There were also suburban zones in the Department of the Seine where the PCF was extremely weak. The French Communists never made much headway in the highly industrialized working-class suburbs of Suresnes, Boulogne-Billancourt, and Puteaux directly to the west of Paris; these communities remained bastions of the Socialists throughout the 1920s and 1930s. Similarly, the PCF was weak in Antony, Rungis, Creteil, Saint-Maur-des-Fossés, and Bry-sur-Marne, along the southern and eastern peripheries of the Department. These areas generally voted for the Radicals or the Right in municipal elections.

Without completely altering this general pattern, the Popular Front did raise the French Communist party from a strong presence to the dominant political force in the suburbs of the Department of the Seine. The political breakthrough in the municipal elections of 1935 and the legislative elections of 1936 was the fruition of years of organizing by Communist militants; it also vindicated certain changes in PCF electoral tactics. The PCF allied with the SFIO in 1934, ending the years of internecine quarrels that had severely weakened the French Left. During the 1929 municipal elections the PCF lost contests in Arcueil, Montreuil, and Clamart that it would probably have won if the SFIO had instructed its voters to support the Communists on the second round. The electoral alliance of 1934 meant that in 1935 Socialists and Communists did support each other on the second round of the elections, thus winning several municipalities that had been held by the Right.[3] The Party also attracted new members because it turned greater attention to organizing neighborhoods. It adopted a less antagonistic stance toward non-Communists, halting the often bitter conflicts between itself and evangelistic Catholics and appealing more to social groups, like shopkeepers, that it had previously neglected. Finally, the new nationalism of the French Communists was clearly manifested in the suburbs, as PCF municipalities began naming streets after national heroes like Rouget de Lisle and sponsoring city festivals in honor of Bastille Day.[4]

These changes in PCF orientation produced impressive results in the Paris suburbs. In the Popular Front elections of 1935 and 1936 the Red Belt assumed the form it would have ten years later: in the first postwar legislative elections of 1946 the PCF won almost exactly the same percentage of the vote. Moreover, in the 1935 municipal elections the Communists took power for the first time in several suburbs—such as Drancy, Montreuil, Orly, and Nanterre—that they have controlled ever since. The Red Belt evolved from a symbol of the PCF's isolation from French politics to one of its partial integration into the national political culture.

I have argued throughout that the PCF owed its success in Bobigny and the Red Belt more to community concerns than to workplace conflicts. Yet the workers of Bobigny did spend much of their lives on the job. Therefore, to test the validity of my conclusions I briefly review the conditions they encountered in the workplace, and the political ramifications of their reactions to those conditions. Given the vast diversity of industry in the Paris area during the early twentieth century, I can sketch only a general portrait, but even this should help us understand the political choices made by Bobigny's workers.[5]

Both contemporary observers and historians of French working-class labor in the early twentieth century have emphasized challenges to skill levels and workplace control posed by changes in the production process and by the rise of a new population of semiskilled machine operatives, the *ouvriers spécialisés*.[6] Even before 1900 many commentators and union leaders warned against the dangers of increasing mechanization and the degradation of skills; such complaints increased in the years before 1914.[7] But in this regard as in so many others, the First World War provided a turning point. Facing a shortage of skilled laborers, many employers hired unskilled women and foreigners and adopted new machines and Taylorist practices—all expedients that threatened traditions of workplace control.[8]

Such changes characterized much wartime industrial production in the Paris area and had the greatest impact in the large metallurgical plants on the periphery of the city. Above all, automobile factories like Renault and Citroën became symbols of modern industry in the wartime and interwar years. From his studies of the working-class experience at Renault, Alain Touraine argues that French industry entered what he terms "Phase B," which introduced large numbers of semiskilled workers and mass production techniques such as the assembly line.[9]

Semiskilled workers and assembly lines alike were evident in large metropolitan factories like Renault and Citroën. In the late 1920s Renault and Citroën began to reorganize production along more "scientific" lines, in a process referred to as rationalization that increased mechanization, made wider use of timeclocks, and broke tasks into simpler components, to increase both employees' output and employers' control on the shop floor.[10] Rationalization, especially its greater mechanization, required more semiskilled workers, who now became a significant proportion of the industrial labor force. In 1925, for example, 46.3 percent of Renault's workers were skilled, versus 53.7 percent semi- and unskilled; by 1939 their respective proportions were 31.8 percent and 68.2 percent.[11]

The scope and impact of these changes were often less than contemporary observers hoped or feared. The growth of the labor force and longer hours of work often related more to heightened wartime output than rationalization; many wartime innovations failed to survive after 1918. During the 1920s and 1930s even the modernizing plans of André Citroën, the prototypical American-style entrepreneur, remained only on paper; many new workplace conditions did not mature until after 1945. Yet the growth of the population of semiskilled workers was real and important. If their experience did not resemble the vision of Fritz Lang in his 1926 film, *Metropolis*, it differed significantly from that of prewar skilled and unskilled workers.[12]

What was life on the job like for these new proletarians? First, we must note that a large majority were from the provinces, unused to large factories.[13] They had to adapt rapidly to a strange new environment that was noisy, dirty, and full of big machines—and also highly controlled. The use of the timeclock and other methods to eliminate unproductive time were widespread in large Parisian factories. The jobs of semiskilled workers were usually not physically taxing. But most who described such jobs in the interwar years emphasized their boring, repetitive character.[14] For both semiskilled and unskilled workers the basic fact of life in plants like Renault and Citroën was a lack of control over their workplace. Not only was there little autonomy in the production process, but large factories maintained networks of spies to prevent working-class discontent from getting out of hand. Discontent was expressed in passive, individualistic ways, such as very high turnover rates.[15] Moreover, many workers accepted or at least resigned themselves to conditions as they were, in the absence of realistic prospects for change.[16]

It has become a truism of French social history that skilled workers are more likely to become involved in union and radical political activity than those with little or no training.[17] This is borne out by the experience of French workers between the wars. Except for the years immediately after World War I, French unions before 1936 were small and weak, rarely winning the adhesion of more than one-tenth of the labor force. Their members tended to be either skilled workers or government employees; the overwhelming numbers of semiskilled and unskilled workers remained indifferent. Given this situation, strike activity in these years was anemic at best. Citroën experienced only three significant strikes between 1920 and 1935, all of them failures. Until the massive upheavals of the Popular Front, most semiskilled and unskilled workers remained firmly outside the French labor movement.[18]

Renault, Citroën, and other large suburban factories were not typical of the average workplace, which provided no refuge from the changes they symbolized.[19] Smaller workshops in the 1920s and 1930s had fewer machines, and rationalization was a vague rumor rather than a concrete threat. Yet semiskilled and unskilled labor was widely used in the Paris region; even outside the giant industrial fortresses workers had little interest in or control over their jobs. Arnold Brémond, a Protestant theology student who worked in several factories in Ivry during the mid-1920s, noted that whereas skilled workers loved to talk about their jobs, others preferred to talk about sex. Henri Vielledent describes in his memoirs the frustration of having been trained as a skilled metalworker only to end up trapped in a semiskilled job.

These were the conditions that Bobigny's workers, who were mostly semiskilled and unskilled, faced on the job. They had little opportunity to exercise control over jobs that often had no intrinsic interest. Moreover, the expression of radical political views was strongly discouraged by employers and by fellow workers as well.[20] Therefore the average workplace provided only meager opportunity to develop union or political consciousness, let alone activism, before 1936. Given this situation, it is not surprising that their residential problems gave the workers of Bobigny a focus for their energies that also helped form a Communist political consensus there.

Clearly, Bobigny was not an exception as much as an advanced example of the widespread influence French Communism enjoyed in the Paris suburbs during the interwar years. We can now answer the question why Bobigny strongly and consistently supported the PCF. To sum up the arguments I advance here, Communist strength in the community derived from four specific considerations.

First, the conditions of urban growth in the Paris area in the late nineteenth and the early twentieth century set the stage. Increased residential segregation created working-class ghettoes like Bobigny, whose social composition differed radically from that of other French communities at large. The general tendency of French workers to vote for the Left was accentuated in Bobigny by the absence of elite populations that could have exercised a countervailing political influence. The disastrous, chaotic suburban growth contributed to the problems and changed many hopeful homeowners into embittered *mal-lotis*, whose resentment was to have profound political implications.[21]

Second, the ability of Bobigny's Communists to deal with the manifold problems of their community was crucial. The crisis in the allotments was the largest challenge. The PCF alone did not lift Bobigny's *mal-lotis* out of the mud—the national Sarraut Law was instrumental in this effort—still the municipality worked to resolve the problem. It also made major efforts to provide urban facilities, like schools, utilities, and marketplaces, commensurate with the size of Bobigny's population.

Third, the strong community networks and their support for the PCF facilitated its political dominance. The local interest committees and the associations syndicales gave an institutional framework to the Communist presence in Bobigny's neighborhoods. Strong, general working-class solidarity made Balbynians receptive to the PCF's ideology and to its view of red Bobigny as a working-class citadel.

Fourth, Mayor Clamamus's dynamism and determination deserved much of the credit for the PCF's success in Bobigny during the interwar years. Although structural factors like the local population's social composition figured in the political life of the Paris suburbs, individual personalities also exercised a significant impact on community politics. Mayors often dominated their cities in this period. Clamamus was such a strong mayor, the symbol and to a large extent the architect of red Bobigny. His greatest contribution to the people who continually reelected him was in dealing with the allotments, both as mayor and as a member of the Chamber of Deputies. In many other ways, Clamamus worked to build a resilient political culture in Bobigny and place the community prominently on the map of French communism.

Underlying these four factors in the PCF's political strength in Bobigny was a distinct working-class consciousness. Throughout the period local workers voted predominantly for the Left, first the Socialists and after 1920 the Communists. The PCF municipality's handling of urban problems during the 1920s strengthened this tradition but did not create it; Bobigny's workers voted Socialist even before the SFIO had any such accomplishments to its credit. The similarly successful reconstruction of the Communist polity in Bobigny after 1944 in spite of Clamamus's treason resulted from the resilient working-class identification with the Left.

This identification was not unique to the workers of Bobigny in twentieth-century France, but local conditions reinforced their class consciousness. Bobigny's workers lived in a monochrome world, where their neighbors and acquaintances were almost all from their own social class. Moreover, if working-class Balbynians were unlikely to meet many members of another class, they were still less likely to join another class: the majority came from working-class backgrounds that made upward mobility an elusive option.

A striking paradox of Bobigny's political history is that Communists achieved strength in a community composed for the most part of property owners. In fact, owning property in Bobigny strengthened class consciousness. It forced working-class neighbors to depend on one another for immediate mutual aid and for a long-term political solution to their common problems. The bitterness of the *mal-lotis* stemmed largely from the belief that once again the workers had been cheated out of their due. The crisis of the allotments hammered home the lesson that workers could better themselves only through class action, not through individual self-reliance.

This working-class community consciousness was the basis of PCF strength in Bobigny, and local Communists willingly cultivated and politicized it. It was in this context that symbolic activities like red baptisms and the renaming of streets had significance. The PCF gave Bobigny its definition and identity; Bobigny was a *commune ouvrière*, something to be proud of, not a miserable slum. Yet the activities of the PCF did not foster working-class consciousness but rather reflected its political importance. Bobigny's workers voted for the Communist party as part of their class identification and took pride in the achievements of the PCF municipality as in something they themselves had accomplished.[22]

This study of Bobigny has focused on two major forces in twentieth-century France, the working class and the French Communist party, and on the relation between them. For historians of the PCF the story of Bobigny offers two interesting paradoxes. Despite its constant stress on the workplace as the main locus of proletarian politicization, the PCF put most of its efforts in Bobigny into residential issues. In the late 1930s Communists emphasized the urgency of local workplace conflicts but subordinated such conflicts to consumer issues like housing, schools, and utilities.

From this flows the other observation, that communism in Bobigny was not simply a miniature version of the national PCF ideology. The traditional view of French communism in the 1920s and 1930s has been of a tightly centralized organization in which all ideas came from the top and originally from Moscow. Bobigny's Communists did respond to major shifts in the Party line, as the community's experience of the Popular Front demonstrates. Yet local concerns always strongly conditioned their responses. For example, the red baptisms were more a reaction to local evangelism than to official Communist pronouncements on religion. Moreover, the Party's attempts to reshape its local structure were often unsuccessful; Bobigny's PCF militants remained subordinated to its city councillors. In light of these experiences we observe that French communism was a product of Party ideology and of local problems.

As for the history of modern French workers, the rise of the Red Belt in the Paris suburbs suggests that students of working-class politicization after 1914—especially of unskilled and semiskilled workers —might well complement their emphasis on the workplace with greater attention to the residential sphere. Historians of nineteenth-century French social history have demonstrated the value in studying the workplace of artisans and skilled workers. The efforts of these groups to hold on to control of their workplace and to resist de-skilling did much to shape the history of working-class politics.

By the interwar years, however, the battle for control of the productive process was a lost one, as far as many workers were concerned. This situation and the increasing distance between workplace and residence have led twentieth-century workers to favor their homes over their jobs. Workers in Bobigny could do little to improve their wages or working conditions during the 1920s and 1930s, but they could vote for a municipality that would deal with the allotments. Paved streets may not have brought the revolution nearer, but they made life easier and gave Bobigny's workers a sense of empowerment in the present and feelings of hope for the future.[23]

Finally, the experience of Bobigny in the early twentieth century offers insights on the urban dimension of both class and politics in modern France. Social class was extremely important in Bobigny, but it was perceived more as a function of urban structure than of workplace stratification. This suggests that although class structure's objective cause may be the system of production, people's actions follow subjective perceptions that we in turn must consider in studying class consciousness and its political consequences.

The history of Bobigny also furnishes valuable lessons on urban politics, both its potential and its limitations. Urban politics enabled the Communists to put together an almost unshakable alliance of workers and employés in Bobigny and to lay the foundations for the Red Belt. Thus as an *electoral* device it proved to be of great value. But politics, especially revolutionary politics, consists of more than elections. Electorally useful, urban politics in the Paris suburbs failed to provide the direct challenge to capitalism that supposedly formed the PCF's raison d'être. This experience does not mean that urban politics necessarily lacks revolutionary content or significance, just that French communism in the Red Belt evolved more as an electoral formation than as a social movement during the early twentieth century.[24]

Consequently, the rise of the Paris Red Belt during this period stands out as a graphic example both of working-class political radicalism and of the political impact of French capitalism. The fact that so many suburban workers voted Communist, especially during the Party's lean and hungry years, illustrated the workers' desire for urban amenities, and the depth of their alienation from bourgeois society. Yet capitalist urban development shaped this alienation. Both the PCF's ideological emphasis on the factory, and its practical concern with neighborhood problems, reflected the balkanization of working-class life into separate spheres of home and work that was so much a product of capitalist urbanization. The Communists' grafting of revolutionary phraseology onto matter-of-fact urban administration ultimately could not substitute for policies to heal this split and challenge the forces that created places like Bobigny. The Communists' achievements in improving the quality of life in the Paris suburbs were real and important; but they could not alter the urban evolution of the Paris metropolitan area. The Red Belt was certainly a working-class fortress, but it was also a working-class prison. The keys to its gates remained as always within the city.

Appendix

JEAN-MARIE CLAMAMUS, BOBIGNY'S RED PATRIARCH

Any history of Bobigny in the early twentieth century is incomplete without a look at its perennial mayor, Jean-Marie Clamamus. No one did more to bring about the PCF's political dominance in local politics or to deal with the considerable urban problems that confronted the community in the 1920s and 1930s. The fact that a glass of red wine was often called a Clamamus in Balbynian cafés during this period testifies to his wide influence and popularity.

Jean-Marie Clamamus was born in the Department of the Nièvre on 27 July 1879, into an upwardly mobile working-class family: his father was first a miner, then a railroad employé. After completing secondary school Jean-Marie studied commercial law, and became an expert accountant. By the turn of the century Clamamus had married and the couple lived with his wife's parents in Paris. In 1907 or 1908 he and his wife moved with their infant son to Bobigny, where they bought land in the Union de Bobigny allotment. Like his neighbors, therefore, Clamamus became a *mal-loti*. He soon became active in Socialist politics in the eastern suburbs of Paris and first ran for office in Bobigny in 1912. Clamamus lost that race but was elected to Bobigny's city council in July 1914, just before the war broke out.[1]

World War I strengthened not only Bobigny's Socialist party but also Clamamus's political position. His military duty included serving in auxiliary functions and on the front lines in 1914 and 1915. He suffered a gas attack on the Champagne front in March 1915, was retired from active duty, and spent the rest of the war in Bobigny.

Resuming his duties as a city councillor, Clamamus soon took the lead in dealing with food shortages. In March 1916 he submitted a long, detailed report to the council noting how the city's population struggled with high prices

181

and proposing to establish a municipal butchershop to stockpile frozen meat and sell it to residents at low prices. The majority of the Bobigny city council expressed doubts about the practicality of Clamamus's idea. He pushed hard on this issue, however, and made it his most important concern and achievement as a city councillor during the war years; he eventually persuaded the council to work out a scheme whereby it turned a local food cooperative into a temporary municipal butchershop to store frozen meat. Clamamus's success on this question, with his work on other problems for Bobigny's working-class population, helped propel him to the leadership of the SFIO in Bobigny.[2]

In November 1919 Clamamus was reelected to the Bobigny city council which came under the control of the SFIO for the first time. His colleagues expressed their confidence in him by electing him mayor, a position he held for twenty-five years. One of his first tasks was to guide Bobigny's Left past the perils of the Congress of Tours and the split between Socialists and Communists. At the Congress of Tours, Clamamus had been a delegate of the Federation of the Seine and had voted for adhesion to the Third International. Appointed to an administrative position in the fledgling PCF, Clamamus persuaded many sections of the old SFIO to join the new Party. Locally, his strong leadership helped make Bobigny one of the few Communist municipalities that remained consistently loyal to the Party during the 1920s.[3]

Like some other suburban Communist mayors, Clamamus achieved a position in national politics as well. He was first elected to the Chamber of Deputies as a PCF representative in May 1924, and was reelected in 1928 and 1932. In the chamber Clamamus proved to be an active legislator, working on several different commissions and sponsoring numerous bills. The issue of allotments remained the most dear to his heart; he presented his own proposals and worked with other representatives to deal with the situation. Yet Clamamus dealt with other important issues, notably unemployment, reproductive rights (attempting to legalize contraception and abortion), and aid to women and children.[4]

In 1935 Clamamus decided to stand for election to the Senate from the northeastern suburbs of Paris. He lost this race by a slim margin but did manage the following year to win election to a Senate seat vacated by Pierre Laval. As was the case in the Chamber of Deputies, in the Senate Clamamus showed himself to be a capable legislator, interested in many different issues and able to work well with non-Communists and Communists alike.[5]

Clamamus valued his role as a national political leader, yet it seems that his work in Bobigny was even more important to him; above all, he was a city mayor. Clamamus was extremely popular. In the personality contests offered by legislative elections, Bobigny's PCF consistently scored higher than in municipal elections, demonstrating Clamamus's individual appeal. His popularity was well deserved, for Clamamus was an activist mayor, implementing most of the Communist municipality's improvements in urban facilities. The problems of the *mal-lotis* were Clamamus's major political concern; his attempts to aid them were not limited to trying to enact national legislation. Even though he and the PCF had opposed the Sarraut Law, Clamamus played a key role in making it work for his constituents. He was at the center of negotiations between the associations syndicales, the allotment developers, construction companies, and the prefecture concerning allotment repairs.

Perhaps most important of all, Jean-Marie Clamamus was a very visible mayor; like the classic American city politician, he knew how to get out and press the flesh. Judging from local accounts, Clamamus made an appearance at virtually every meeting, demonstration, or ceremony of any size in Bobigny. He gave speeches at rallies on May Day, Bastille Day, and other annual occasions; he marched in picket lines at local strikes; he appeared at soup kitchens and neighborhood celebrations; he visited Bobigny's summer camps and talked to the children there; he presided over inaugurations of new municipal facilities; and he even played the "priest" during the red baptisms. During the 1920s and 1930s Clamamus was the flesh-and-blood symbol of red Bobigny, a manifestation of evil incarnate to the Right, a fatherly representative of working-class solidarity to his constituents.

Given his central place in interwar Bobigny, Clamamus's subsequent history is paradoxical and tragic. In September 1939 the PCF was banned and all Communist municipalities in France were officially dissolved. As a result, Clamamus was relieved of his duties as mayor of Bobigny. In the same month he resigned from the PCF, a decision he made public on 12 October 1939. Bobigny's red patriarch had stepped down, draining to bitter dregs his glass of red wine.[6]

What explains this shift? The Nazi-Soviet Pact was at least partially responsible. Fellow Balbynian Communists noted that he seemed profoundly disturbed during the 26 August meeting of the local Party section that discussed the pact. Without access to Clamamus's personal papers we cannot give a definitive answer; but he was first and foremost a city politician. It must have been exceedingly difficult for him to give up a position that he had held for twenty years; his immense personal prestige had incalculable value for the PCF in Bobigny (despite the PCF's condemnation of electoralism). Yet his position created ties that went beyond the bounds of Party doctrine. Confronted with a choice between his traditional position in Bobigny and the PCF, Clamamus chose the former.[7]

After his split with the Communists in September 1939, Clamamus turned to full-scale collaboration. In December, having retained his seat in the Chamber of Deputies, he helped form a group of ex-Communist parliamentarians. On 10 July 1940 Clamamus voted in favor of granting emergency powers to Marshall Pétain and later that year joined a small collaborators' party led by a fellow ex-Communist, Marcel Gitton. In February 1942 he was restored to his position as mayor of Bobigny, where he worked with the German authorities until the end of the occupation. After the liberation Clamamus was arrested, then set free in August 1945. He moved to Paris and broke all ties with Bobigny, returning only at times to visit the grave of his son.[8]

The path taken by Jean-Marie Clamamus during World War II provides a striking parallel with that of Jacques Doriot, former Communist mayor of Saint-Denis and leading French Fascist during the occupation. Both men were prominent PCF politicians in the Paris suburbs in the 1920s and 1930s who ended up leaving the Party and collaborating with the Germans. The parallel is not complete: Doriot was a far more powerful PCF leader than Clamamus and became a full-fledged Fascist (indeed, a sort of French Mussolini), whereas Clamamus became a collaborator in the more usual sense of the term. Yet the similarities suggest that if a revolutionary party allows individuals to build up local bases of power, it may find that these individuals become more interested in their power than in the revolution.[9]

Jean-Marie Clamamus's long life ended obscurely in Paris in February 1973. It is an ironic footnote to the history of Communism in Bobigny that the man who did so much to make it a presence now has no place in the city's collective memory; there are no statues to Clamamus, no streets or buildings named after him. His ultimate legacy, Balbynian communism, has endured long after 1945. But in betraying the cause he championed for so long, Clamamus forfeited the right to claim credit for it.

Notes

All translations from the French are those of the author.

Introduction

1. T. J. Clark, *The Painting of Modern Life: Paris in the Art of Manet and His Followers* (New York, 1985), chap. 3.

2. There are no precise figures on the composition of classes in Parisian suburbs in the early twentieth century. My research suggests that, although figures vary widely from one suburb to another, workers and their families constituted roughly one-third of the suburban population. On this point, cf. Jean Bastié, *La Croissance de la banlieue parisienne* (Paris, 1964); and Michel Mollat, ed., *Histoire de l'Ile-de-France et de Paris* (Toulouse, 1971).

3. On this point see Edouard Blanc, *La Ceinture rouge* (Paris, 1927); Pierre (Père) Lhande, *Le Christ dans la banlieue* (Paris, 1927); and the works of Jacques Valdour, such as *Ateliers et taudis de la banlieue de Paris* (Paris, 1923) and *Ouvriers parisiens d'après-guerre* (Paris, 1921).

4. Rémy Butler and Patrice Noisette, *Le logement social en France, 1815–1981: de la cité ouvrière au grand ensemble* (Paris, 1982), p. 63.

5. Interview with Florence Aumont on 7 January 1985, Foyer Gaston Monmousseau, Bobigny.

6. One of the few major studies on French communism to focus on Party membership is Annie Kriegel, *The French Communists: Portrait of a People* (Chicago, 1972). See also Philippe Robrieux, *Histoire intérieure du parti communiste* (Paris, 1980–83); Annie Kriegel, *Aux origines du communisme français*, 2 vols. (Paris, 1969); Daniel Brower, *The New Jacobins* (Ithaca, 1968); Jean-Paul Brunet, *Saint-Denis, la ville rouge* (Paris, 1980).

7. The literature on French social history in the nineteenth century is vast and still growing. Important works in this field include Rolande Trempé, *Les*

185

Mineurs de Carmaux, 2 vols. (Paris, 1971); Michelle Perrot, *Les Ouvriers en grève*, 2 vols. (Paris, 1974); Yves Lequin, *Les Ouvriers de la région lyonnaise, 1814–1914*, 2 vols. (Lyon, 1977); Joan Scott, *The Glassworkers of Carmaux* (Cambridge, Mass., 1974); Michael Hanagan, *The Logic of Solidarity* (Urbana, 1980); Ron Aminzade, *Class, Politics, and Early Industrial Capitalism* (Albany, 1981); and John Merriman, *The Red City* (Oxford, 1985). For a critique of this approach, see Tony Judt, *Marxism and the French Left* (Oxford, 1986).

Chapter 1

1. Many Parisians came to Bobigny during summer weekends, giving local shopkeepers important business. The city festival in May drew especially large numbers of visitors. Registres des débats du conseil municipal, Bobigny, 1900–1939 (hereafter RDCM), 18 February 1901, and ·12 March 1901; *Journal de Saint-Denis*, 23 May 1901, p. 3. See also Clark, chap. 3, and Maurice Agulhon, ed. *Histoire de la France urbaine*, vol. 4 (Paris, 1983), on the Paris suburbs as nineteenth-century weekend recreational retreats.

2. Lhande, *Le Christ dans la banlieue*, p. 57; Conseil général de la Seine, *Etat des communes de la Seine à la fin du 19e siècle: Bobigny* (Paris, 1899), pp. 25–26. On late nineteenth-century Bobigny see also Abbé Masson, *Bobigny-lez-Paris* (Paris, 1887).

3. A realization of this trend suffuses the last few pages of Masson's book (*Bobigny-lez-Paris*). See also Maurice Agulhon, "L'opinion politique dans une commune de banlieue sous la Troisième République. Bobigny de 1850 à 1914," in *Etudes sur la banlieue de Paris*, ed. Pierre George (Paris 1950), p. 30; Michel Phlipponneau, *La Vie rurale de la banlieue parisienne* (Paris, 1956), pp. 398–405; Jules Ferret, *Bobigny, ses maraîchers, ses nouveaux-venus, les Parisiens* (Paris, 1910), pp. 36–37.

4. The highest point in Bobigny was 55 meters; the lowest, 40 meters (Conseil général de la Seine, p. 28). To the north of Bobigny lay Drancy and La Courneuve; to the east was Bondy, and to the west, Aubervilliers and Pantin.

5. Conseil général de la Seine, pp. 25–26, 28–31. In 1900 Bobigny had one butchershop, two bakeries, two grocery stores, and ten cafés (Archives nationales, Paris: Annuaire de commerce—Didot Bottin [hereafter Didot Bottin], 1900, p. 3317). For descriptions of small-town life near Paris at the turn of the century, see Mollat; and Evelyn Ackerman, *Village on the Seine* (Ithaca, 1978).

6. Lhande, *Le Christ dans la banlieue*, p. 57; Agulhon, "L'opinion politique," pp. 36–37; Ferret, pp. 36–37; Phlipponneau, p. 245–57; René-Charles Plancke, *La Vie rurale en Seine-et-Marne de 1853 à 1953* (Paris, 1984).

7. "Les quartiers de Bobigny," dossier in Bobigny City Archives, p. 4; Bastié, *Croissance*, pp. 27–28; Louis Chevalier, "La formation de la population parisienne au 19e siècle," *Cahiers de l'Institut national des études démographiques* 10 (1950): 131; Pierre Sorlin, *La Société française*, vol. 1 (Paris, 1969), pp. 112–18.

8. National Route no. 3 from Paris to Metz, the largest road in Bobigny, bordered the canal de l'Ourcq; between it and the canal were several industries (Conseil général de la Seine, pp. 42, 57; Didot Bottin, 1900, p. 3317; Agulhon, "L'opinion politique," p. 42).

9. Pierre Dupé and Pierre Thivollier, *Ferment chrétien dans une terre sans Dieu* (Paris, 1948), pp. 9–16; Lhande, *Le Christ dans la banlieue,* p. 60; Pierre Lhande, *Le Dieu qui bouge* (Paris, 1930).

10. Listes nominatives du recensement, Bobigny (hereafter LN), 1896; Didot Bottin, 1902, p. 3860; Agulhon, "L'opinion politique," p. 29; Etat civil, Bobigny (Actes de naissances, décès, et mariages) for 1900.

11. Agulhon, "L'opinion politique," p. 38; Phlipponneau, pp. 401–5. See also Bastié, *Croissance,* and Jean Bastié, *Géographie du grand Paris* (Paris, 1984), p. 35; Roger Price, *The Modernization of Rural France* (New York, 1984); Plancke.

12. Agulhon, "L'opinion politique," pp. 33–34; Phlipponneau, pp. 68–71; Bastié, *Géographie,* p. 35; Mollat, pp. 133–39.

13. The Blancmesnil family, the traditional *seigneurs* of Bobigny, owned land in the southwestern part of town, hence the name of the Blanc-mesnil quarter (Phlipponneau, pp. 400–402; Masson).

14. Dupé and Thivollier, p. 15; Masson.

15. From 1870 until the early twentieth century, Bobigny's farmers often supported the conservative Republicans led by Adolphe Thiers, whereas the market gardeners usually favored the left-wing Republican opposition. Bobigny's conservatives wanted to maintain public order and private property, while the Radicals were anti-clerical and defended the small producer. Neither side had developed a political program, however, and election results often revealed group identification more than ideology. On this point see chapter 4. See also Agulhon, "L'opinion politique," pp. 36, 50–51; Phlipponneau, p. 401.

16. Phlipponneau, pp. 357–62; Bastié, *Croissance*; Plancke.

17. Lhande, *Le Christ dans la banlieue,* p. 55; Ferret, pp. 37–38. The Grande Ceinture railroad completely encircled Paris (Conseil général de la Seine, pp. 48–49). On mass transit between Paris and its suburbs, see Pierre Merlin, *Les Transports parisiens. Etude de géographie économique et sociale* (Paris, 1967); and Jean Robert, *Les Tramways parisiens* (Paris, 1959).

18. Jean Robert, pp. 41, 49–58. See also Charles Rearick, *Pleasures of the Belle Epoque: Entertainment and Festivity in Turn-of-the-Century France* (New Haven, 1985); Ackerman; Gérard Jacquemet, *Belleville au XIXe siècle* (Paris, 1984), pp. 141–42.

19. Jacquemet, *Belleville,* pp. 45–51. One market gardener asked, "What's the use of laying pipes for drinking water here? We market gardeners each have our own wells, and therefore as much water as we need" (Ferret, p. 38).

20. On the growth of Paris in the nineteenth century, see Chevalier, "La formation"; Bastié, *Croissance* and *Géographie*; Philippe Ariès, *Histoire des populations françaises* (Paris, 1948); Jeanne Gaillard, *Paris, la ville, 1852–1870* (Paris, 1976).

21. Susanna Magri, *Politique du logement et besoins en main-d'œuvre* (Paris, 1972), p. 49; Ariès, pp. 386–417; Chevalier, "La formation." On low natality in nineteenth-century France, see Francis Ronsin, *La Grève des ventres* (Paris, 1980).

22. David Pinkney, *Napoleon III and the Rebuilding of Paris* (Princeton, 1958), p. 156; Chevalier, "La formation," pp. 164–70, 209–13. The rural population fell about 9 percent from 1875 to 1906. J. H. Clapham, *The*

Economic Development of France and Germany, 1815–1914 (Cambridge, 1951), pp. 158–70; Sorlin, pp. 45–73.

23. Chevalier, "La formation," p. 281.

24. Part of the increase in working-class population came from the inner suburbs annexed in 1860; their industrial structure, distinct from that of central Paris, used more unskilled labor. Magri, pp. 70–72; Chevalier, "La formation," pp. 119–48; Anne-Louise Shapiro, *Housing the Poor of Paris* (Madison, 1984), p. 55; Jacquemet, *Belleville*, pp. 281–84. Lenard Berlanstein discusses historians' overestimate of the bourgeoisie in late nineteenth-century Paris, in *The Working People of Paris* (Baltimore, 1984), pp. 5–9.

25. Pierre George and Pierre Randet, *La Région parisienne* (Paris, 1959), p. 29; Pinkney, *Napoleon III*, pp. 151–73; Chevalier, "La formation," pp. 104–9, 120–30; Magri, pp. 56–59, 65; Berlanstein, *Working People*; Maurice Daumas and Jacques Payen, eds., *Evolution de la géographie industrielle de Paris et sa proche banlieue au XIXe siècle*, vol. 2 (Paris, 1976), pp. 339–449.

26. On transportation and industrial development in Paris see especially René Clozier, *La Gare du Nord* (Paris, 1940); Chevalier, "La formation," pp. 119–48; Magri, pp. 59–60; Daumas, vol. 1, pp. 318–35. David Harvey emphasizes the point in *Consciousness and the Urban Experience* (Baltimore, 1985).

27. George and Randet, pp. 29–30; Chevalier, "La formation," pp. 119–48; Magri, pp. 59, 72. The lessening of skills involved the decline of *compagnonnages*, associations of skilled workers that trained apprentices and sent journeymen throughout France to perfect their skills; see Jean-Pierre Bayard, *Le Compagnonnage en France* (Paris, 1978).

28. In addition to Pinkney's classic study, see more recent works by Pierre Lavedan, *Histoire de l'urbanisme à Paris* (Paris, 1975); Gaillard; Harvey; Anthony Sutcliffe, *The Autumn of Central Paris* (Montreal, 1971); Louis Girard, *La Nouvelle Histoire de Paris: Paris, la Deuxième République et le Second Empire* (Paris, 1981).

29. Residential segregation by class existed earlier in Paris, but Haussmann's renovations increased it significantly (Pinkney, *Napoleon III*, pp. 9–12; Chevalier, "La formation," pp. 241–49; Magri, p. 59).

30. Norma Evenson, *Paris: A Century of Change, 1878–1978* (New Haven, 1979), pp. 203–5; Roger H. Guerrand, *Les Origines du logement social en France* (Paris, 1967), pp. 202–21; Shapiro, pp. 56, 75–76; Octave DuMesnil and Charles Mangenot, *Enquête sur les logements, professions, salaires, et budgets* (Paris, 1899).

31. DuMesnil, p. 55; see also the article by Gérard Jacquemet, "Belleville aux XIXe et XXe siècles," *Annales—Economies, Sociétés, Civilisations* 30, no. 4 (July–August 1975).

32. Shapiro, p. 60; on government urban development policies and land prices in Paris, see Maurice Halbwachs, *Les Expropriations et le prix des terrains à Paris* (Paris, 1901); Sutcliffe; Evenson.

33. Jules Siegfried expressed this point of view in advocating working-class housing: "Shall we create people who are at the same time happy, and true conservatives; shall we combat at the same time poverty and the errors of

socialism; shall we increase the guarantees of order, of morality, of political and social moderation? Then let us create working-class housing developments!" (quoted in Guerrand, *Les Origines*, p. 283).

34. The Villard Commission's report to the Paris city council in 1883 reflected this bias against governmental involvement beyond the construction of model low-rent buldings to stimulate private construction. The commission feared that more low-rent housing would increase the flow of poor provincials to the capital (Shapiro, pp. 118–19).

35. Shapiro, pp. 127, 99–101. A similar lack of low-cost housing for the poor of London is described by Gareth Stedman Jones in *Outcast London* (London, 1971).

36. Guerrand, *Les Origines*, pp. 280–310; Shapiro, p. 102. On the history of the HBM, see Sanford Elwitt, "Social Reform and Social Order in Late Nineteenth-Century France: The Musée Social and its Friends," *French Historical Studies* 11, no. 3 (Spring 1980): 431–51; Lucien Lambeau, *Ville de Paris. Monographies. Les logements à bon marché. Recueil annoté des discussions, délibérations et rapports du conseil municipal de Paris* (Paris, 1897).

37. On disease and public health in late nineteenth-century Paris, see Jacques Bertillon, *De la fréquence des principales causes de décès à Paris* (Paris, 1906); Bertillon, *De la fréquence des principales maladies à Paris pendant la période 1865–1891* (Paris, 1894); Gustave Lagneau, *Rapport sur les maladies épidémiques observées en 1890 dans le département de la Seine* (Paris, 1891).

38. Lagneau, pp. 62–64, 78–83; Guerrand, *Les Origines*, pp. 202–14; Evenson, pp. 203–12; Magri, p. 94. See also Louis Landouzy, "La mortalité parisienne par tuberculose il y a vingt ans," *Congrès international de la tuberculose* (Paris, 1906), vol. 2, pp. 696–706; Charles Leroux, "Enquête sur la descendance de 442 familles ouvrières tuberculeuses," *Revue de médecine* 32 (1912); Henri Dehau and René Ledroux-Lebard, *La Lutte antituberculeuse en France* (Paris, 1906); Selman Waksman, *The Conquest of Tuberculosis* (Berkeley, 1964).

39. Guerrand, *Les Origines*, p. 235; he quotes another similar song (pp. 235–36):

> The landlord is a disgusting fellow,
> One always has to give him money,
> He ruins the people, the poor proletarian,
> Yes, the landlords are dirty guys.

40. On the working-class left and the Paris housing question, see Shapiro; Guerrand, *Les Origines*. An imaginative, if short-term, solution to the problem was *déménagement à la cloche de bois* (midnight flight), in which (often organized) groups of workers moved a working-class family's furniture out of the apartment in the middle of the night to avoid its confiscation for nonpayment of rent (Jacques Borge and Nicolas Viasnoff, *Archives de Paris* [Paris, 1981], pp. 130–33).

41. Jacques Bertillon, *Essai de statistique comparée du surpeuplement des habitations à Paris et dans les capitales européennes* (Paris, 1894); Octave DuMesnil, *L'Hygiène à Paris* (Paris, 1890); DuMesnil and Mangenot, *Enquête*.

42. On the growth of the Paris suburbs in the late nineteenth century, see Bastié, *Croissance* and *Géographie*; Mollat; Albert Demangeon, *Paris, la ville et sa banlieue* (Paris, 1936); Sorlin, pp. 112–18.

43. George and Randet, pp. 52–54; René Clozier, "Essai sur la banlieue," *La Pensée* 2, no. 4 (July–September 1945): 53–54.

44. Chevalier, "La formation," pp. 130–48; Magri, pp. 59–67, 73–75; Jean-Paul Brunet, "L'industrialisation de la région de Saint-Denis," *Acta Geographica* 4 (October 1970): 231–40; Bastié, *Croissance*, pp. 107–22.

45. Sam Bass Warner, *Streetcar Suburbs* (Cambridge, 1978). For a critique of transportation in suburbanization, see F. M. L. Turner, *The Rise of Suburbia* (Leicester, 1982); and Robert Fishman, *Bourgeois Utopias* (New Brunswick, 1987).

46. Brunet, "L'industrialisation," pp. 231–41; Bastié, *Croissance*, pp. 107–34; Magri, p. 60; Chevalier, "La formation," p. 133.

47. Chevalier, "La formation," pp. 130–44; Magri, pp. 59–64; Bastié, *Croissance*, pp. 137–60.

48. Chevalier, "La formation," pp. 131–33; Brunet, "L'industrialisation," p. 247; Magri, p. 56.

49. Magri, pp. 130–44; Daumas and Payen, pp. 77–83. See also Louis Bergeron, *L'Industrialisation de la France au XIXe siècle* (Paris, 1979).

50. Chevalier, "La formation," p. 131.

51. Chevalier, "La formation," pp. 104–44; Magri, pp. 55–67; Daumas and Payen, pp. 77–83, 257–84. During the nineteenth century the southern suburbs industrialized less and later than those to the north, because industrial transport facilities were concentrated north of the Seine, closest to the most industrialized parts of France (and Europe), and because most Parisian workers lived on the Right Bank (except for the thirteenth arrondissment).

52. On suburban factories in the late nineteenth century, Daumas and Payen, pp. 449–517; Berlanstein, *Working People*, pp. 92–107. Large suburban plants existed in other European countries as well; scc Donald Howard Bell, *Sesto San Giovanni* (New Brunswick, 1986).

53. Bell, pp. 58–65. Chevalier explains, "The French government's decree of 13 September 1810 ordained that henceforth the suburbs would house 'cemeteries that diffuse cadaverous odors in the center of the capital, incommodious or malodorous workshops or manufactures' " ("La formation," p. 131). For discussion of production in these new industries in the late nineteenth century, see David Landes, *The Unbound Prometheus* (Cambridge, 1972), pp. 249–76.

54. Brunet, "L'industrialisation," pp. 232–33; Chevalier, "La formation," pp. 250–62. In the southern suburbs, however, immigration and population growth may have depended less on industrialization; see Bastié, *Croissance*, pp. 213–17.

55. Bastié, *Croissance*, pp. 222–23; Chevalier, "La formation," pp. 250, 257.

56. Chevalier, "La formation," pp. 161, 251; Magri, p. 73; Sorlin, p. 117; Brunet, "L'industrialisation"; Berlanstein, *Working People*, pp. 92–107.

57. Berlanstein, *Working People*, pp. 55–59, 70–72, 74–121; Chevalier, "La formation," pp. 120–30, 238–48; George and Randet, pp. 29–36; Daumas and Payen; Peter Stearns, *Lives of Labor: Work in a Maturing Industrial Society* (New York, 1975).

58. John McKay, *Tramways and Trolleys: The Rise of Urban Mass Transport in Europe* (Princeton, 1976), pp. 14–15, 40–41; Warner; Fishman. On the history of tramways in Paris, see Merlin; Jean Robert; L. Lagarrigue, *Cent ans de transports en commun dans la région parisienne* (Paris, 1956).

59. Evenson, pp. 80–85. The failure of the suburban tramlines owed much to their arrangement with the General Omnibus Company (GOC), which had a monopoly over lines in Paris and kept the most profitable routes for itself. Tramways North and Tramways South were forced to pay GOC a large indemnity for the privilege of running their suburban lines into the capital.

60. Guerrand, *Les Origines*, pp. 271–90; Shapiro. On Le Play see Paul Leroy-Beaulieu, *La Question ouvrière au XIXe siècle* (Paris, 1899); Elwitt, "Social Reform"; Catherine Bodard Silver, ed., *Frédéric Le Play: On Family, Work, and Social Change* (Chicago, 1982).

61. Quoted in Evenson, pp. 209–10.

62. Shapiro, pp. 120–21. In "The Question of Working-Class Housing in Paris and London," George Picot studied a model working-class housing project near the British capital: "For all these constructions outside London, the most important question is the price of transport. The establishment of inexpensive commuter trains to the outskirts of town that enable the voyager to travel sixteen kilometers at an average cost of twenty centimes has ensured the success of these habitations" (*La Réforme sociale* 14 [15 September 1885]: 258). On inexpensive mass transit in suburban London, see H. J. Dyos, *Victorian Suburb* (Leicester, 1961), pp. 74–77; Turner.

63. McKay, p. 161.

64. As McKay explains, "the goal was extremely cheap fares which would allow the worker to save his energy at the least, and facilitate his quest for better, more distant housing at best" (McKay, p. 117; pp. 149–50).

65. The tramways business was dominated by two firms, Thomson-Houston and the General Traction Company. Thomson-Houston, a former American subsidiary founded in 1893 and the first investor in tramways, owned the General Omnibus Company; the General Traction Company began in 1896 and owned most of the suburban lines created after 1900. The newer General Traction Company expanded more aggressively and set lower fares; those policies, and the overvaluation of its shares on the stock market, brought the Paris tramways as a whole to the brink of disaster after 1900 (McKay, pp. 125–62; Jean Robert, pp. 48–49).

66. Government concessions to the tramway companies were handled by several government agencies: some were granted by the city of Paris, some by the Department of the Seine, some even by individual suburban municipalities; contractual obligations varied from company to company. A poorly coordinated tramway system resulted, as governmental officials tried to break the near-monopoly of the General Omnibus Company in the 1890s without direct governmental regulation. McKay, pp. 146–47; Jean Robert, pp. 47–64.

67. McKay, pp. 159–60; Jean Robert, pp. 13–14.

68. Again, on governmental liberalism in urban development and poverty, the comparison with the British case is instructive; cf. Jones, Turner, and Fishman.

69. Jean Robert, p. 60.

70. Mollat, pp. 524–37; Bastié, *Croissance* and *Géographie*; Evenson, p. 221; Gérard Noiriel, *Les Ouvriers dans la société française* (Paris, 1986), pp. 120–52. The mass migration to the suburbs, and the consequent housing crisis there, became the subject of numerous newspaper articles: see *L'Information sociale*, 2 September 1926 and 9 December 1926; *Le Populaire*, 29 October 1923 and 18 December 1927; *L'Humanité*, 19 September 1925 and 11 February 1928.

71. Bastié, *Croissance*, p. 226; Arthur Fontaine, *French Industry during the War* (New Haven, 1926); Jean-Jacques Becker, *Les Français dans la grande guerre* (Paris, 1980); Patrick Fridenson, ed., *1914–1918: l'autre front* (Paris, 1977).

72. Arthur Fontaine, p. 192; Bastié, *Croissance*, p. 225; Ariès, pp. 295–344.

73. M. Bonnefond, "Les colonies de bicoques de la région parisienne," part 1, *La Vie urbaine* 25 (1925): 542–45. On the Paris housing crisis during World War I, see also Sutcliffe, pp. 256–57; Evenson, pp. 212–13; Nils Hammarstrand, "The Housing Problem in Paris," *Journal of the American Institute of Architects* (February 1920); Tyler Stovall, "Sous les toits de Paris: The Working Class and the Paris Housing Crisis, 1914–1924," *Proceedings of the Annual Meeting of the Western Society for French History* 14 (1987).

74. Stovall, "Sous les toits," p. 544; Bastié, *Croissance*, pp. 233–34. Often ignorant of rent control laws and moving more often, working-class Parisians benefited less from rent control than those with greater incomes.

75. Bastié, *Croissance*, pp. 233–34; Magri, pp. 83–92; Bonnefond, pp. 532–33; Anita Hirsch, "Le logement," in *Histoire économique de la France entre les deux guerres*, ed. Albert Sauvy, vol. 3 (Paris, 1972).

76. On the eight-hour day see Gary Cross, "Les Trois Huits: Labor Movements, International Reform, and the Origins of the Eight-Hour Day, 1914–1924," *French Historical Studies* 14, no. 2 (Fall 1985): 240–68; Cross, "The Quest for Leisure: Reassessing the Eight-Hour Day in France," *Journal of Social History* 18, no. 2 (Winter 1984): 195–216; Jean-Luc Bodiguel, *La Réduction du temps de travail* (Paris, 1969).

77. Bonnefond, pp. 545–46.

78. Jacques Valdour, *Le Désordre ouvrier* (Paris, 1937), p. 35.

79. Butler and Noisette, p. 63. On the allotments crisis, see Bastié, *Croissance*; Lhande, *Le Christ dans la banlieue* and *Le Dieu qui bouge*; Roger Guerrand, *Le Logement populaire en France* (Paris, 1979), p. 160; Wladimir d'Ormesson, *Le Problème des lotissements* (Paris, 1928); Charles Collin, *Silhouettes de lotissements* (Paris, 1931); René Bouffet, *Un Problème d'urbanisme: l'aménagement des lotissements défectueux* (Paris, 1930); Maurice Polti, *Etude théorique et pratique sur les lotissements* (Paris, 1926); Pierre Combe, *Les Lotissements* (Lyon, 1933).

Chapter 2

1. Charles Videcoq, *Les Aspects permanents de la crise du logement dans la région parisienne* (Paris, 1932), pp. 38–45, 70–71. The Department of the Seine was divided into the northern arrondissement of Saint-Denis with thirteen cantons (including Noisy-le-Sec), and the southern arrondissement of Sceaux with nine cantons. The canton of Noisy-le-Sec included the suburbs of Bobigny, Bondy, Drancy, Noisy-le-Sec, Pavillon-sous-Bois, Romainville, Rosny-sous-Bois, and Villemomble. On the northeastern suburbs in this period see Louis Cheronnet, *Paris extra muros* (Paris, 1929); Georges Poisson, *Evocation du grand Paris,* vol. 3, *La Banlieue nord-est* (Paris, 1961); Louis Thomas, *Le Grand Paris* (Paris, 1941).

2. Phlipponnneau, pp. 399–405; Bastié, *Croissance,* p. 254; Jean Robert, pp. 45–47; Demangeon; Mollat; Georges Archer, *De Terentiacum à Drancy. Histoire d'une commune de la Seine* (Montpellier, 1964); Jean-Marie Bontemps and Jacques Jolinon, "La municipalité de Montreuil-sous-Bois, 1900–1939," mémoire de maîtrise, Université de Paris–1, 1971.

3. For a broader discussion of rapid urbanization, see Rosemary Righter and Peter Wilsher, *The Exploding Cities* (London, 1975); and Manuel Castells, *The City and the Grassroots* (Berkeley, 1983). The experience of the Paris suburbs in this period bears some similarity to the frenetic growth experienced by contemporary Third World cities; on this point see Bryan Roberts, *Cities of Peasants* (London, 1978); Bernard Granotier, *La Planète des bidonvilles: perspectives de l'explosion urbaine dans le tiers monde* (Paris, 1980); Janice Perlman, *The Myth of Marginality* (Berkeley, 1976).

4. Rates of growth in other Paris suburbs from 1896 to 1931 include Saint-Denis, 151 percent; Aubervilliers, 204 percent; Asnières, 262 percent; Romainville, 766 percent; and Drancy, which mushroomed, 4,668 percent (*Annuaire statistique de la ville de Paris et des communes suburbaines, 1929–1931* [Paris, 1932]).

5. Videcoq, p. 38; RDCM, 23 March 1923; Permis de construire, 1926. Since only cities with more than 10,000 inhabitants were required to keep construction permit records, 1926 was the first year in which Bobigny did so.

6. Budgets et comptes de la ville de Bobigny, 1900, 1915. On French municipal budgets in this period see Eugène Raiga and Maurice Félix, *Le Régime administratif et financier du département de la Seine et de la ville de Paris,* 2 vols. (Paris, 1935); Jean-Paul Brunet, *Un Demi-siècle d'action municipale à Saint-Denis la rouge* (Paris, 1982).

7. LN, 1896–1936. On housing densities in the Paris suburbs in this period cf. also Videcoq; Henri Sellier, *La Crise du logement et l'intervention publique* (Paris, 1921); Valdour, *Ateliers et taudis.*

8. This typical pattern of suburban growth turned isolated villages into the centers of large new residential areas. The old villages did not function as municipal centers and had little to do with the allotment areas (see Dupé and Thivollier, pp. 15–17).

9. On public transportation and life in the Paris suburbs, see Henri Bunle, "L'agglomération parisienne et ses migrations alternantes en 1936," *Bulletin de*

la Statistique générale de la France (October–December 1938); Jean-Paul Brunet, "Constitution d'un espace urbain: Paris et sa banlieue de la fin du XIXe siècle à 1940," *Annales—Economies, Sociétés, Civilisations* 40, no. 3 (May–June 1985).

10. Ferret, p. 46. Tramway service led to the suburbanization of Bobigny, as the town's rates of population growth demonstrate. If the growing population had attracted the tramway, then the rate of growth from 1896 to 1901 should have been spectacular; in fact, it hardly exceeded that of the late nineteenth century. In the 1906 census the rate soared; on this point see Fishman.

11. In *Paris-Est* articles from 1902 on 11 January and 25 January; 15 February; 31 May; 28 June; 5 July and 12 July; and 16 August.

12. *Paris-Est*, 12 August 1902. See also Ferret, pp. 42–50; Agulhon, "L'opinion politique," pp. 44–45. Many open-field farmers favored the tramway and the land speculation, hoping to profit from selling their land to the developers.

13. RDCM, 24 July 1902; *Paris-Est*, 20 September and 27 September 1902; *Journal de Saint-Denis*, 18 September 1902.

14. *Paris-Est*, 7 March 1903; 25 March 1911; 1 April and 22 April 1911; 21 October 1911; 25 January 1913; 10 December 1921; *Journal de Saint-Denis*, 4 July 1915; 17 September 1921; RDCM, 10 February 1911.

15. RDCM, 7 September 1906; 18 December 1906; 21 March 1908; 9 October 1908; 23 July 1909; 10 February 1911; *Paris-Est*, 12 January 1907, 4 July 1908; *Journal de Saint-Denis*, 18 November 1906, 6 December 1906.

16. *Paris-Est*, 4 August 1906, 12 April 1913, and 12 July 1913; *Journal de Saint-Denis*, 9 August 1906; RDCM, 18 December 1909, 12 April 1922, and 18 February 1924; *Le Prolétaire de Bobigny*, 20 April 1929. There were also complaints about trams arriving too early.

17. RDCM, 23 April 1921, 21 October 1922, 15 December 1923, 1 August 1925, 27 April 1931.

18. RDCM, 26 June 1908, 15 December 1923, 18 February 1924, 1 August 1925; *L'Aube sociale*, 2 January 1926, 27 March 1926, 24 July 1926; *Emancipation nationale*, 26 November 1937.

19. Didot Bottin, 1927, pp. 1771–73; 1937, pp. 1950–54. The STCRP began to replace major tramlines with buses in 1930; most were closed by 1935, and the last tram disappeared from the Paris region in 1938 (Jean Robert, p. 15).

20. *Workers* include all those gainfully employed. Of the censuses I consulted, only that of 1931 listed workplaces, but data were spotty and incomplete—in many cases giving only the location without the name of the workplace. Since by the 1930s Bobigny had developed an industrial sector, the percentage of commuters was probably less in 1931 than in the previous decades.

21. RDCM, 12 April 1922. Before its reduction to eight hours, the average working day in France was ten hours long. On commuting, see Brunet, "Constitution"; Bunle.

22. Workers often ate lunch in inexpensive restaurants near their places of employment (Valdour, *Ateliers et taudis; Ouvriers parisiens*; Arnold Bremond, *Une Explication du monde ouvrier* [Alençon, 1927]; Simone Weil, *La Condition ouvrière* [Paris, 1951]; *Emancipation nationale*, 26 November 1937).

23. For example, in *J'avais vingt ans* (Paris, 1967) René Michaud describes how as a young man in Paris he would look for work by simply walking the thirteenth district from one neighborhood workshop to the next—a less fruitful prospect in Bobigny. On life and work in this Parisian setting, see also Jacques Valdour, *De la Popinqu'à Menilmuch'* (Paris, 1924); Jean Bailhache, *Monographie d'une famille d'ouvriers parisiens* (Paris, 1905); Jacques Destray-Caroux, *Un Couple ouvrier traditionnel* (Paris, 1974).

24. Areas undergoing rapid urbanization often develop such a gap between the population's size and adequate physical, social, and cultural structures; cf. Jean-Jacques Peru, "Du village à la cité ouvrière, Drancy 1896–1936," mémoire de maîtrise, Université de Paris–1, 1977–1978; Righter and Wilsher, pp. 115–25; Castells, *City and the Grassroots*, pp. 185–90.

25. The best overview of the allotments is that of Bastié in *Croissance*, pp. 229–331.

26. Bastié, *Croissance*, pp. 241–63, 278–300.

27. Ferret, p. 43; see also Agulhon, "L'opinion politique," p. 44.

28. Bobigny, Archives communales, dossier on the city's allotments, 1900–1945; Bobigny, Associations syndicales (hereafter cited as AS), dossiers of allotments: La Bergère; Les Vignes; La Courneuve; Le Nouveau Village; André Jaouen; La Conscience; La Renaissance; Le Parc; Le Chemin de Fer; rues Herzog, Perron, and Perrusset; La Grande Denise.

29. Ferret, pp. 43–52; *Paris-Est*, 8 August 1908; AS dossier on Nouveau Village; Bastié, *Croissance*, pp. 250–54.

30. LN, 1911, 1921, 1931. Neither census nor other sources show clearly who lived in Bobigny's allotments. I arrived at these approximate figures by counting how many people lived on streets that belonged to allotments, but some streets belonged to them only in part.

31. Dupé and Thivollier, pp. 15–16. The authors' population figures for Nouveau Village and Village parisien are wildly inflated; the former had little more than one thousand residents in the 1920s.

32. LN, 1896, 1911; Conseil général de la Seine; J. F. Mangin, "Les transformations de structure d'une commune en banlieue: Bobigny, 1871–1970" (mémoire de maîtrise, Université de Paris–1, 1971–1972). The third largest group was agricultural workers. In studying the population of a suburban allotment in 1931, Jean Bastié found that 78 percent were workers and employés (*Croissance*, p. 254).

33. Ferret, pp. 55–56. Outsiders describing the Paris suburbs in the interwar years noted not just their anarchic squalor but also their sharp contrast to the rational beauty of Paris (Cheronnet; Alain Meyer and Christine Moissinac, *Représentations sociales et littéraires: centre et périphérie, Paris 1908–1939* [Paris, 1979], pp. 157–83).

34. AS dossier on Bobigny's allotments.

35. On this point see Bastié, *Croissance*, pp. 252–54; Guy Caplat, *Le Problème des lotissements* (Dijon, 1951); d'Ormesson; Polti.

36. RDCM, 31 January 1913; 25 January 1920; 10 September 1922; *L'Aube sociale*, 13 November 1926 (an article, "To get out of the mud"); 15 January 1927; AS dossier Les Vignes, 11 February 1923; AS dossier rue Perron, 25 August 1924.

37. Paris-Bobigny AS dossier, "Rapport de l'agent-voyer communal," 8 March 1926.

38. The eighth district was one of the wealthiest in Paris, and the twentieth one of the poorest. On health conditions in the Paris suburbs, see Anne Fontaine et al., *Antony. Du petit village à la grande cité de banlieue* (Antony, 1980); Henri Sellier, *Les Banlieues urbaines* (Paris, 1920); Evenson, pp. 220–21.

39. In 1911, for example, housing for a majority of Balbynians was less than one room per person (Sellier, *La crise du logement,* p. 84).

40. Bastié, *Croissance,* pp. 265–66; Evenson, p. 231; Bonnefond, pp. 552–54; Hazemann, R., "Les lotissements dans la banlieue de Paris et leur répercussion sur la santé publique (à Vitry et à Ivry)," *Revue d'hygiène et médecine préventive* (1928).

41. Didot Bottin for Bobigny, 1910–1939; see also Catherine Rodier and Fathi Bentabet, "L'immigration Algérienne et l'hôpital franco-musulman, dans la région parisienne, entre les deux guerres (1915–1947)," mémoire de maîtrise, Université de Paris–1, 1980–1981.

42. The classic study of life in a commuter suburb remains Herbert Gans, *The Levittowners* (New York, 1967); see also Claude Cornau, ed., *L'Attraction de Paris sur sa banlieue* (Paris, 1965); Scott Donaldson, *The Suburban Myth* (New York, 1969); Kenneth Jackson, *Crabgrass Frontier* (New York, 1985); Fishman; Warner.

43. The figures given in pp. 54–57 are taken from Didot Bottin.

44. Didot Bottin, 1901, 1911, 1921, 1931, 1939. On commerce in the Paris suburbs, see Alain Metton, *Le Commerce et la ville en banlieue parisienne* (Paris, 1980).

45. Metton; Didot Bottin, 1911, 1921, 1931, 1939.

46. Berlanstein, *Working People,* pp. 127–37; Michael Marrus, "Social Drinking in the Belle Epoque," *Journal of Social History* 7, no. 2 (Winter 1974): 115–42.

47. On French artisans, see Lee Shai Weissbach, "Artisanal Response to Artistic Decline: The Cabinetmakers of Paris in the Era of Industrialization," *Journal of Social History* 16 (1982); Michael Hanagan, *The Logic of Solidarity* (Urbana, 1980); Steven Zdatny, "The Artisanat in France: An Economic Portrait, 1900–1956," *French Historical Studies* 13, no. 3 (Spring 1984): 415–40.

48. In distinguishing artisan workshops from small industries, I followed the classification of Didot Bottin, listing as factories establishments labeled *entreprises.*

49. Before and after the Communists took over in 1920, the Bobigny municipality protested against the siting of chemical plants in the area (RDCM, 12 March 1901; 11 May 1907; 12 April 1922).

50. On the metals industry see Berlanstein, *Working People,* pp. 75–107; Brunet, *Saint-Denis,* pp. 201–2; Patrick Fridenson, *Histoire des usines Renault* (Paris, 1972); Sylvie Schweitzer, *Des engrenages à la chaîne* (Lyon, 1982); Gilbert Hatry, *Renault, usine de guerre* (Paris, 1978); Bertrand Gille, *Histoire*

de la métallurgie (Paris, 1966); Paul de Rousiers, *Les Grandes Industries modernes,* vol. 2, *La Métallurgie* (Paris, 1927); Nicholas Papayanis, "Alphonse Merrheim and Revolutionary Syndicalism, 1871–1917," Ph.D. diss., University of Wisconsin, Madison, 1969.

51. Bastié, *Croissance,* pp. 332–36; Brunet, *Saint-Denis,* pp. 201–6.

52. See *L'Humanité,* 23 July 1933, for an article by Bobigny's Communist mayor Clamamus on problems posed by the city's low tax base; on this point see also Graham Taylor, *Satellite Cities: A Study of Industrial Suburbs* (New York, 1915); Harlan Paul Douglass, *The Suburban Trend* (New York, 1925); Brunet, *Un Demi-siècle.*

53. *Paris-Est,* 10 February 1912; see also RDCM, 25 January 1920.

54. RDCM, 3 July 1900; 2 February 1904; 16 October 1906; 23 July 1909; *Journal de Saint-Denis,* 10 November 1920.

55. RDCM, 15 January and 20 August 1903; 19 February 1904; 4 May 1906; 26 February 1907; and 2 August 1912.

56. *Journal de Saint-Denis,* 25 October 1903; *Paris-Est,* 26 December 1903; RDCM, 26 November 1904; 12 July 1907; 25 December 1917.

57. LN, 1896, 1911, 1921; RDCM, 21 November 1913; 6 April 1919; 17 September 1920. On French schools in the early twentieth century see Maurice Crubellier, *L'Enfance et la jeunesse dans la société française, 1800–1950* (Paris, 1979); F. Pisani-Ferry, *Monsieur l'instituteur* (Paris, 1981); Antoine Prost, *Histoire de l'enseignement en France, 1800–1967,* 2d ed. (Paris, 1977).

58. RDCM, 18 February 1905; 2 July and 18 November 1906; 23 November 1907; *Journal de Saint-Denis,* 30 April 1921.

59. Cheronnet; Meyer and Moissinac; Bonnefond.

60. Radical municipalities in this period stressed fiscal restraint and often charged that Socialist and Communist municipalities levied high taxes. "A policy of careful and strict use of the public funds by both the state and municipalities is also a condition of national security. The Democratic Alliance is justified in warning against the demogogues, against the flatterers of the electoral clientele. . . . Taxes are heavy; any errors in municipal policy will only further burden the taxpayers, and for a long time to come" (electoral manifesto of the Democratic Republican Alliance, *Le Temps,* 1 May 1935, p. 1).

61. The relation between allotments like the Pont de Bondy and the center approximated in miniature that between Paris and its suburbs. Bobigny's center, however, was less urban than residential, with a population that included many of Bobigny's remaining market gardeners; few Balbynians from other parts of the community worked there.

62. Henri Lefebvre discusses this issue in *Le Droit à la ville* (Paris, 1972) and *La Révolution urbaine* (Paris, 1970), as does Harvey. I think Lefebvre's thesis useful, if we acknowledge that the development Paris underwent in the late nineteenth century stripped local workers of the power to impose a "right to the city." If living in Paris meant inhabiting tiny rooms without light or air, many workers in the early twentieth century preferred to leave.

63. Bastié, pp. 275–77.

64. d'Ormesson, pp. 2–3; see also Collin.

Chapter 3

1. Bobigny LN, 1921, 1926, 1931; Etat civil, Bobigny: Actes de mariages 1919.

2. On the demography of the Paris area in the early twentieth century, see Ariès; Michel Huber, *La Population de la France* (Paris, 1937); Magri; Bastié, *Croissance* and *Géographie.*

3. Ariès, p. 294. The Department of the Seine increased its population by 79 percent over the same period.

4. Huber, pp. 66, 135, 169; Magri, p. 51; Ariès, p. 332. In 1931 the Department of the Seine had the second lowest birthrate of any department in France. On early twentieth-century urbanization, see Agulhon, *Histoire*; Lequin, *Ouvriers*; Leslie Page Moch, *Paths to the City* (Beverly Hills, 1983).

5. Moch. On the ages of urban populations, see E. A. Wrigley, *Industrial Growth and Population Change* (Cambridge, 1961); Adna Weber, *The Growth of Cities in the Nineteenth Century* (New York, 1899).

6. Huber, pp. 41–42; Ariès, pp. 293–94.

7. On the lower middle class and politics, see Arno Mayer, "The Lower Middle Class as a Historical Problem," *Journal of Modern History* 47 (1975); Pierre Delon, *Les Employés. Un siècle de lutte* (Paris, 1969).

8. Magri, pp. 48–51. There is no general description of the class structure of the Paris suburbs in the interwar period; most of the communities I have read about were strongly working class or lower middle class. See the studies in Pierre George, ed., *Etudes sur la banlieue de Paris* (Paris, 1950); Jacques Girault, ed., *Sur l'implantation du parti communiste français dans l'entre-deux-guerres* (Paris, 1977); several works by Valdour (*Ateliers et taudis; Le Désordre ouvrier; Popinqu'à Menilmuch'; Ouvriers parisien*); Archer; Anne Fontaine; Jean-Emile Denis, *Puteaux. Chroniques du temps des puits* (Puteaux, 1969); Roger Pourteau, *Pantin. Deux mille ans d'histoire* (Paris, 1982); Bontemps and Jolinon.

9. Sellier, *La Crise du logement*. For purposes of comparison, in 1931 the natality rate in the Department of the Seine was 1.27 percent, the mortality rate 1.40 percent (Huber, pp. 135, 169).

10. On urbanization and natality in modern France, see Agulhon, *Histoire*, vol. 4, pp. 31–59; Ronsin; Moch; Ariès; Huber.

11. Evenson, p. 231; Bastié, *Croissance*, pp. 265–66; Hazemann.

12. By 1931 at least six major allotments (Paris-Bobigny, Le Parc, rues Perron and Perrusset, l'Avenir de Bobigny, André Jaouen, and Les Vignes) had been provided with sewers and sidewalks (AS dossiers).

13. Unfortunately, the 1896 census records did not give places of birth. In Saint-Denis, by contrast, one out of every four local residents was born in that suburb (Brunet, *Saint-Denis*, p. 206).

14. On this point, see Moch; Stephen Thernstrom and Ralph Sennett, eds., *Nineteenth-Century Cities* (New Haven, 1969); Stephen Thernstrom, *The Other Bostonians* (Cambridge, Mass., 1973); David Crew, *Town in the Ruhr* (New York, 1979); Lequin, *Ouvriers*.

15. In 1896, 69 percent of the people of Bobigny were born in the French provinces. By contrast, the steadily rising percentage of Balbynians born in Paris—probably related to the improved mass transit—suggests that Bobigny was becoming a more classic suburb (Brunet, *Saint-Denis*, p. 206; Ariès; Noiriel).

16. The metropolitan region as defined here includes the Departments of the Seine, Seine-et-Oise, and Seine-et-Marne; large parts of the latter two departments were still rural. However, most Balbynians listed in Table 10 as from the Paris area came from the Department of the Seine (Demangeon; Mollat).

17. Etat civil, Bobigny: Actes de mariages 1921. For memoirs of workers from the Paris area in these years, see Michaud; Henri Vielledent, *Souvenirs d'un travailleur manuel syndicaliste* (Paris, 1978); Lucien Monjauvis, *Jean-Pierre Timbaud* (Paris, 1971).

18. Extended family networks were less disrupted than in a more distant move (Moch; David Pinkney, "Migrations to Paris during the Second Empire," *Journal of Modern History* 25, no. 1 [1953]: 1–12; Chevalier, *Laboring Classes;* Lynn Hollen Lees, *Exiles of Erin. Irish Migrants in Victorian London* [Manchester, 1979]).

19. Both before and after World War I parties of the French Left were generally stronger in the Paris area than elsewhere (François Goguel, *Géographie des élections françaises sous la Troisième et la Quatrième République* [Paris, 1968], pp. 60–97). See also Berlanstein, *Working People*, chap. 5; Kriegel, *Aux origines*; Brower.

20. People born in the French provinces composed 47.1 percent of Bobigny's population in 1921 and 43.5 percent in 1931 (LN, 1921, 1931). Bobigny contrasts with Belleville, which also voted massively for the Left but contained mostly native-born artisans and craftworkers (Berlanstein, *Working People*, p. 164; Jacquemet, *Belleville*).

21. Ariès, pp. 315–27; Chevalier, "La formation," and *Laboring Classes*; Pinkney, "Migrations to Paris."

22. On communities of provincial immigrants in Paris, see Chevalier, "La formation"; Agulhon, *Histoire*, pp. 383–85; Berlanstein, *Working People*, p. 166; Françoise Raison-Jourde, *La Colonie auvergnate de Paris au XIXe siècle* (Paris, 1976); Valdour, *Ateliers et taudis*.

23. I found no evidence in Bobigny of social, political, or other organizations for people who came from the provinces; on this point see Etienne François, ed., *Immigration et société urbaine en Europe occidentale, XVIe–XXe siècles* (Paris, 1985).

24. André Armengaud, *La Population française au XXe siècle* (Paris, 1973), p. 48; Odile Rabut, "Les étrangers en France," *Population*, special issue ed. Roland Pressat (June 1974): 150. See also Gary Cross, *Immigrant Workers in Industrial France* (Philadelphia, 1983).

25. Few foreigners in Bobigny lived in allotments but rather in the few multifamily dwellings (LN, 1921, 1931).

26. LN, 1921. One group, the Italians, lived in various neighborhoods but preserved some sense of community and identity, since many worked in

construction. Apparently many were antifascist refugees from Mussolini's Italy, which led Communists to honor them as examples of international proletarian solidarity.

27. Of 67 Balbynians of foreign origin whose occupations were given in the 1931 census, 44 were unskilled workers and 19 were skilled; of the latter, 10 were Italian masons.

28. They were typical of populations in allotment communities (Bastié, *Croissance*, pp. 272–73; Noiriel; Archer; Bontemps and Jolinon; Peru).

29. Possible exceptions were many new Balbynians born in Paris who came from areas like Belleville, with strong local traditions of voting for the Left, which may have figured in their willingness to vote Communist in Bobigny (Berlanstein, *Working People*, pp. 159–64; Brunet, *Saint-Denis*, pp. 34–37).

30. Huber, p. 46.

31. Moch, pp. 123–67; Chevalier, "La formation"; Pinkney. Domenico Mastrangelo notes in his dissertation ("Bologna, 1889–1914" [University of Wisconsin, Madison, 1977], p. 105) that over 80 percent of the migrants into Bologna were under forty.

32. Public concern in France over the aging of the population preceded the First World War, but France's great losses gave the issue renewed immediacy after the war (Dyer, pp. 64–67; Ariès; Joseph Spengler, *France Faces Depopulation* [Durham, 1938]).

33. Stearns, *Lives of Labor*, p. 245; James F. McMillan, *Housewife or Harlot: The Place of Women in French Society, 1870–1940* (New York, 1981), p. 40. On social class and fertility, see Michael Haines, *Fertility and Occupation: Population Patterns in Industrialization* (New York, 1979).

34. Abbé Ferret reported a woman's plea to him for aid in finding housing in Bobigny: "Monsieur l'abbé, monsieur l'abbé . . . help me find even a simple room. . . . I am fleeing Paris, where I just lost my son, a boy of sixteen years, my dear child. The doctor told me my daughters needed open air, so I left immediately" (Ferret, p. 42).

35. Households and families are not equivalent; however, given the difficulties of tracing families (including that of family members not living at home), it seemed reasonable to analyze household structure instead. See Michael Anderson, "Household Structure and the Industrial Revolution," in *Household and Family in Past Time*, ed. Peter Laslett (Cambridge, 1972).

36. LN, 1896, 1911, 1921, 1931. In 1931, for example, census figures listed 73.7 percent of market gardening households with four or more members; but these data sometimes included hired hands who were not members of the extended family.

37. The rich literature on nuclear and extended families includes Edward Shorter, *The Making of the Modern Family* (New York, 1975); Michael Katz, *The People of Hamilton, Canada West* (Cambridge, Mass., 1975).

38. LN, 1896, 1911, 1921, 1931. On French women widowed in World War I see Alain Decaux, *Histoire des Françaises*, vol. 2 (Paris, 1972), pp. 1002–13; Geneviève Gennari, *Le Dossier de la femme* (Paris, 1965), pp. 180–275; McMillan.

39. LN, 1896, 1911, 1921, 1931; Colin Dyer, *Population and Society in Twentieth-Century France* (New York, 1978), pp. 64–65; Decaux; Gennari; McMillan.

40. During the First World War 211 men from Bobigny died in combat (Annie Fourcaut and Jacques Girault, "Les counseillers municipaux d'une commune ouvrière et communiste," *Cahiers d'histoire de l'Institut Maurice Thorez* 10, no. 1 [1976]: 64). On the effects of the war on French society, see especially Antoine Prost, *Les Anciens Combattants et la société française, 1914–1939*, 3 vols. (Paris, 1977).

41. For example, in 1931 58.3 percent of all adolescents in Bobigny lived with adult relatives, and 74.0 percent of them were employed (LN, 1931). On working-class youth see Berlanstein, *Working People*, pp. 144–47; Moch, pp. 129–42; Michael Anderson, *Family Structure in Nineteenth-Century Lancashire* (Cambridge, 1971); John R. Gillis, *Youth and History* (New York, 1974).

42. This trend was general among the French working class; see Jean and Françoise Fourastié, "Le genre de vie," and Evelyne Sullerot, "Conditions de la femme," both in *Histoire économique de la France entre les deux guerres*, ed. Albert Sauvy, vol. 3 (Paris, 1972), pp. 418–53; McMillan; Joan Scott and Louise Tilly, *Women, Work, and Family* (New York, 1978); Stearns, *Lives of Labor*, pp. 245–46; Shorter, *Modern Family*.

43. Conversely, a working class can establish its independent life-style and remain dependent on bourgeois ideology; Eric Hobsbawm discusses this point and the British working class in *Industry and Empire* (Penguin, 1968), pp. 287–91.

44. On working-class culture in the Paris suburbs after World War II, see Cornau; Pierre Chombart de Lauwe, *Paris et l'agglomération parisienne* (Paris, 1952); Fernand Dupuy, *Etre maire communiste* (Paris, 1975); Maurice Roncayolo, ed., *Histoire de la France urbaine*, vol. 5 (Paris, 1985), pp. 616–27; Raymond Pronier, *Les Municipalités communistes, bilan de trente années de gestion* (Paris, 1983).

45. Etat civil, Bobigny: Actes de mariages 1911, 1921, 1931. Although the majority of shopkeepers in Bobigny opposed the PCF, several shopkeepers were Communist or sympathetic to its positions, such as café owner Léon Pesch, the deputy mayor of Bobigny.

46. Metton; Berlanstein, *Working People*, pp. 47–52.

47. LN, 1921, 1926, 1931, 1936. On shopkeepers in the Paris area, see Philip Nord, *Paris Shopkeepers and the Politics of Resentment* (Princeton, 1986).

48. Even in the nineteenth century, the community's *grand seigneur*, the count of Blancmesnil, did not live in Bobigny (Agulhon, "L'opinion politique," p. 32). On the aversion of middle- and upper-class Parisians to suburban life, see Fishman, pp. 107–16.

49. On the growth of the tertiary sector in Paris cf. Claudie Lesselier, "Employeés de grands magasins à Paris avant 1914," *Le Mouvement social* 105 (1978); Theresa McBride, "A Woman's World: Department Stores and the Evolution of Women's Employment, 1870–1920," *French Historical Studies* 10 (1978).

50. Ariès, pp. 293–95; Louise-Marie Ferré, *Les Classes sociales dans la France contemporaine* (Paris, 1936), p. 190; Berlanstein, *Working People*, pp. 30–35, 65–73, 188– 97; Mayer; Delon.

51. In fact, many employés were militant at work. I uncovered a reference to one functioning Communist workplace cell in the Bobigny area before the Popular Front of 1936; it involved railway employés in Le Bourget and Drancy (Archives nationales, Paris [hereafter cited as AN], series F7 13097, police report of 1 February 1925).

52. Theresa McBride, *The Domestic Revolution. The Modernization of Household Service in England and France, 1820–1920* (London, 1976); Bonnie Smith, *Confessions of a Concierge* (New Haven, 1985).

53. LN, 1896, 1911, 1921, 1931; Scott and Tilly; McMillan.

54. Theodore Zeldin, *France, 1848–1945: Ambition and Love* (Oxford, 1979), p. 351.

55. On women's occupations in interwar France see McMillan, pp. 157–62; Sullerot; Fourastié; Scott and Tilly; Lesselier; McBride, "A Woman's World."

56. LN, 1921, 1926, 1931; Scott and Tilly.

57. Table 18 measures intergenerational mobility of brides and bridegrooms but not shifts from agricultural to industrial occupations. Information I was able to glean from the actes de mariages suggests that most children of agricultural families who left the farm became artisans or shopkeepers, not industrial workers. Mobility, both upward and downward, most commonly involved transitions between the working class and employés—the daughter of a day laborer, for example, becoming an office worker. Social divisions between the two groups, though real, were more permeable than those between these groups and others in the community, thus these groups made more political alliances.

58. Low levels of social mobility have been seen as promoting radicalism in contemporary societies; see Seymour Martin Lipset and Reinhard Bendix, *Social Mobility in Industrial Society* (Berkeley, 1967), pp. 3–4; William H. Sewell, Jr., "Social Mobility in a Nineteenth-Century European City," in *Industrialization and Urbanization*, ed. Theodore Rabb and Robert Rotberg (Princeton, 1981).

59. For a detailed analysis of metallurgy, see Philippe d'Hugues and Michel Peslier, "Les professions en France," *Institut national d'études démographiques* 51 (1969): 75–103; Fridenson, *Histoire*; Schweitzer; Gille; Papayanis.

60. On unskilled labor in twentieth-century France, see Michel Collinet, *Essai sur la condition ouvrière* (Paris, 1951); Noiriel; Weil.

61. On the chemicals industry, see Chevalier, "La formation"; Arthur Fontaine.

62. On the occupations and skill levels of French workers between the wars, see Ferré, pp. 195–215; Collinet. Students of the French working class have underscored the radicalism of skilled workers, in contrast to unskilled and semiskilled factory workers (Bernard Moss, *The Origins of the French Labor Movement: The Socialism of Skilled Workers* [Berkeley, 1976]). Yet Lenard Berlanstein notes that in industrial suburbs at the turn of the century such

workers voted Socialist as often as more skilled workers in Parisian neighbor-hoods like Belleville (*Working People*, pp. 159–64).

63. Commentators have noted that the skilled metalworkers' traditional radicalism continued into the twentieth century, figuring in the Communists' success in the Paris suburbs (James Cronin and Carmen Sirianni, eds., *Work, Community, and Power* [Philadelphia, 1983]; Noiriel; Kathryn Amdur, *Syndicalist Legacy* [Urbana, 1986]). Several of Bobigny's Communist city councillors were skilled metalworkers.

64. I found no indication that specific working-class occupations clustered in any Bobigny neighborhoods.

65. The argument about the absence of local elites is similar to the "isolated mass" hypothesis of sociologists Clark Kerr and Abraham Siegel, who argue that individuals like miners and sailors, who work in isolated conditions, are more apt to strike than workers more integrated into general society. Bobigny, an isolated working-class community, exemplifies this argument to an extent (Clark Kerr and Abraham Siegel, "The Interindustry Propensity to Strike," in *Industrial Conflict*, ed. Arnold Kornhauser [New York, 1954], pp. 189–212). See the rebuttal to this thesis in Edward Shorter and Charles Tilly (*Strikes in France* [Cambridge, Mass., 1974], pp. 287–95). Though agreeing with aspects of Shorter and Tilly's critique, I feel that Kerr and Siegel's thesis has more relevance to electoral activity than to strikes.

66. AS dossier La Favorite, letter from Louis Raymond to Mayor Clamamus, 17 September 1925. Wladimir d'Ormesson suggests that the contrast between the luxuries of Paris and the squalor of the suburbs, evident to workers who commuted into the city every day, would increase their resentment of the upper classes (d'Ormesson, pp. 7–8).

67. On this point see Stearns, p. 326; Guenther Roth, *The Social Democrats in Imperial Germany* (Totowa, N.J., 1963).

Chapter 4

1. Neighboring Drancy, which grew even faster, was controlled by the SFIO; Aubervilliers, also a working-class suburb, was dominated by Pierre Laval and the Radicals (Peru; Archer; Jean Jolly, *Dictionnaire des parlementaires français*, vol. 6 [Paris, 1970], pp. 2161–65).

2. Agulhon, "L'opinion politique," pp. 50–51; Phlipponneau, p. 401.

3. On the early years of the Third Republic and its fight for stability see Sanford Elwitt, *The Making of the Third Republic* (Baton Rouge, 1975); Adolphe Thiers, *Notes et souvenirs, 1870–1873* (Paris, 1903); Daniel Halévy, *La Fin des notables* (Paris, 1930); Maurice Réclus, *L'Avènement de la Troisième République, 1871–1875* (Paris, 1900).

4. Agulhon, "L'opinion politique"; Phlipponneau, p. 401; Conseil général de la Seine, p. 15.

5. On late nineteenth-century French party politics, see François Goguel, *La Politique des partis sous la Troisième République* (Paris, 1958), pp. 33–109; David Thomson, *Democracy in France since 1870* (London, 1969); Emanuel Beau de Lomenie, *Les Responsabilités des dynasties bourgeoises*, 3 vols. (Paris,

1943–1954); Sanford Elwitt, *The Third Republic Defended* (Baton Rouge, 1986); Denis Brogan, *The Development of Modern France, 1870–1939*, 2 vols. (Gloucester, Mass., 1970); Léon Jacques, *Les Partis politiques sous la Troisième République* (Paris, 1913); Robert de Jouvenel, *La République des camarades* (Paris, 1934); Peter Campbell, *French Electoral Systems and Elections, 1789–1957* (New York, 1958).

6. See Agulhon, "L'opinion politique," p. 52; also Masson. On class and politics in the Third Republic, see Thomson, pp. 39–74.

7. Goguel, *La Politique*, pp. 110–50; Brogan, vol. 1, pp. 357–87. On the Dreyfus affair, see Douglas Johnson, *France and the Dreyfus Affair* (London, 1966); on late nineteenth-century French socialism, see Harvey Goldberg, *The Life of Jean Jaurès* (Madison, 1962); Claude Willard, *Le Mouvement socialiste en France. Les Guesdistes* (Paris, 1965); Georges LeFranc, *Le Mouvement socialiste sous la Troisième République* (Paris, 1963); Patrick Hutton, *The Cult of the Revolutionary Tradition: The Blanquists in French Politics, 1864–1893* (Berkeley, 1981).

8. Ferret. The conservative *Journal de Saint-Denis*, which supported the municipal administration, attacked its more liberal opponents, charging that "the republic, for many of them . . . is a regime of bureaucrats, budget busters, wasters of finances, or of men thirsty for honors and for profits" (*Journal de Saint-Denis*, 23 August 1903).

9. *Paris-Est*, 29 November 1902, p. 3. See other issues of *Paris-Est*: 6 September, p. 3, and 8 November 1902, p. 3; 18 April 1903, p. 3; also Agulhon. On radicalism in 1900, see Jean-Thomas Nordmann, *Histoire des radicaux, 1820–1973* (Paris, 1974), pp. 115–45; Goldberg, pp. 235–92; Georges LeFranc, *Les Gauches en France, 1789–1972* (Paris, 1973), pp. 158–68; Madeleine Rébérioux, *La République radicale? 1898–1914* (Paris, 1975).

10. *Paris-Est*, 9 November 1901, p. 3.

11. Since problems in the allotments were just surfacing, the progressive Radicals did not address them then or develop any later expertise in dealing with them, judging from their propaganda. This failing was crucial, because allotments loomed large in Bobigny politics and because employés living in allotments should have been the Radicals' natural constituency. Paul Peysson was an employé d'administration; several of his followers were market gardeners (*Paris-Est*, 23 April 1904, p. 3).

12. *Paris-Est*, 28 December 1901, p. 3. Some problems also arose from personality conflicts (*Paris-Est*, 19 April 1902, p. 3; 30 May 1903, p. 3; 6 June 1903, p. 3).

13. *Paris-Est*, 12 April 1902, p. 3. Adrien Veber was a Republican Radical Socialist; in 1905 he took part in forming the SFIO, which expelled him in 1918 for his pro-war stance. In 1919 he ran against the Socialists for reelection to the legislature and was defeated (Jolly, vol. 8, pp. 3162–63).

14. *Paris-Est*, 17 May 1902, p. 3. See other comments in *Paris-Est*, 19 April 1902, p. 3; *Journal de Saint-Denis*, 27 April 1902, p. 3.

15. *Paris-Est*, 26 March 1904, p. 3; 7 May 1904, p. 2; *Journal de Saint-Denis*, 19 May 1904, p. 1; 14 August 1904, p. 4.

16. *Paris-Est*, 17 May 1902, p. 3; 30 May 1903, p. 3; 6 June 1903, p. 3; 26 March 1904, p. 3; 23 April 1904, p. 3. The members of the Republican Committee were its electoral candidates; most opposing candidates were market gardeners.

17. In March 1904, for example, Peysson wrote a long article in *Paris-Est* detailing how the growth would benefit groups in the community. It would increase the value of farmers' and market gardeners' land and reduce the amount of agricultural produce, thus lessening competition. More people would buy shopkeepers' wares; a larger city would be richer and could provide better services for workers. Some of Peysson's reasoning was tortuous, but for the leftist Radicals, growth and urbanization equaled progress, which was good for everyone (*Paris-Est*, 19 March 1904, p. 3).

18. *Journal de Saint-Denis*, 16 August 1903, p. 3; 24 December 1903, p. 3.

19. *Journal de Saint-Denis*, 17 December 1903, p. 3; 30 August 1903, p. 3; 4 October 1903, p. 2. They labeled Peysson a follower of Marx and Jaurès, wanting to collectivize everything in sight, and an opportunist for allying with Veber and the socialists.

20. In the 1905 election for arrondissement council, and usually in elections for national office, the traditional Radicals backed Nationalist candidates (*Journal de Saint-Denis*, 22 June 1905, p. 1; 29 June 1905, p. 1; *Paris-Est*, 1 July 1905, pp. 1, 3).

21. *Paris-Est*, 1 July 1905, p. 3.

22. *Paris-Est*, 18 January 1902, p. 1; 26 April 1902, p. 3. On relations between the Republican Left and the Socialists before 1905 see Goldberg, especially pp. 293–357; Nordmann, pp. 119–54; Willard.

23. In 1905, the Second Internationale's condemnation of Socialist participation in bourgeois governments led the new SFIO to withdraw its support from the governing Republican coalition (Goguel, *La Politique*, p. 122; Goldberg, pp. 322–57).

24. *Paris-Est*, 31 March 1906, p. 3; 7 April 1906, p. 3; 26 May 1906, p. 1; Agulhon, "L'opinion politique," p. 53.

25. *Paris-Est*, 20 October 1906, p. 3; 2 May 1908, p. 3; 4 April 1908, p. 3; 9 May 1908, p. 3; 14 May 1910, p. 1.

26. *Paris-Est*, 20 April 1912, p. 3; Nordmann, pp. 182–85.

27. *Paris-Est*, 30 December 1911, p. 4; 20 April 1912, p. 3; 4 May 1912, p. 3; Agulhon, "L'opinion politique," pp. 53–54.

28. *Paris-Est*, 8 May 1912, p. 3; *Journal de Saint-Denis*, 28 April 1912, p. 4. Montigny was elected mayor by the city council in December 1910, after Mayor Jacquelot resigned. I found little information about the Republican Socialist list, probably of remaining leftist Radicals; it opposed the city council on gas service for Bobigny.

29. *Paris-Est*, 25 May 1912, p. 3; see also *Journal de Saint-Denis*, 28 April 1912, p. 4.

30. On the Republican Left before 1914, see Jacques, pp. 223–66, 351–67; Nordmann, pp. 119–188; Rébérioux.

31. *Journal de Saint-Denis*, 10 April 1904, p. 1. On socialism in France before 1905 see, among others, Goldberg; Willard; Hutton; Moss; Hanagan;

Scott, *Glassworkers*; Jolyon Howorth, *Edouard Vaillant* (Paris, 1982); Trempé; Alexandre Zevaes, *Le Socialisme en France depuis 1871* (Paris, 1908).

32. *Paris-Est*, 1 July 1905, p. 1; Roger Price, *A Social History of Nineteenth-Century France* (London, 1987), pp. 255–57; Berlanstein, pp. 167–68; Henri Leyret, *En plein faubourg* (Paris, 1895). On politically conservative workers in the early twentieth century, see Robert Roberts, *The Classic Slum* (Manchester, 1971); Robert Tressell, *The Ragged-Trousered Philanthropists* (London, 1971).

33. Another example is city councillor Vernet, of working-class origin, who was elected as a traditional Radical but resigned in 1906 to join the SFIO (*Paris-Est*, 2 June 1906, p. 3).

34. Peru; Bontemps and Jolinon; Berlanstein, *Working People*, pp. 156–68; Brunet, *Saint-Denis*, pp. 34–168; Price, *Social History*, pp. 257–58.

35. *Journal de Saint-Denis*, 10 May 1906, p. 2; *Paris-Est*, 12 May 1906, p. 1; 26 May 1906, p. 1; Jolly, p. 3162.

36. Nothing came of the meeting to create a People's University section. *Paris-Est*, 15 January 1910, p. 3; 29 January 1910, pp. 3, 4; *Journal de Saint-Denis*, 13 June 1912, p. 2. On the *universités populaires* see Goldberg, pp. 269–70.

37. *Paris-Est*, 28 May 1910, pp. 3, 4.

38. On the SFIO and municipal policy, see Adrien Veber, *Le Socialisme municipal* (Paris, 1908); Pierre Mimin, *Le Socialisme municipal* (Paris, 1911); M. J. McQuillen, "The Development of Municipal Socialism in France, 1880–1914," Ph.D. diss., University of Virginia, 1973; Joan Scott, "Mayors versus Police Chiefs: Socialist Municipalities Confront the French State," in *French Cities in the Nineteenth Century*, ed. John Merriman (New York, 1981).

39. RDCM, 2 August, 19 October, and 30 November 1912; 31 May 1913. In 1912 workers composed roughly 40 percent of the population of Bobigny.

40. *Paris-Est*, 18 July 1914, p. 3. The city council resignations followed that of Mayor Jacquelot, whose reasons for leaving office I could not discover.

41. On the beginnings of World War I in France see Jean-Jacques Becker, *1914: Comment les Français sont entrés dans la guerre* (Paris, 1977); Jean-Jacques Becker and Annie Kriegel, *La guerre et le mouvement ouvrier français* (Paris, 1964).

42. On wartime life in France see Becker, *Les Français*; Fridenson, *1914–1918*; Amdur, pp. 56–120; Alfred Rosmer, *Le Mouvement ouvrier pendant la guerre*, 2 vols. (Paris, 1936–1956).

43. RDCM, 8 August and 29 August 1915.

44. RDCM, 25 December 1917. Despite the Socialists' recommendation, nothing indicates that the council abolished tipping.

45. RDCM, 23 August 1914; also 13 September 1914; 21 January, 7 March, 11 April, 6 June, 18 June, and 22 June 1915; 12 March and 10 May 1916; 9 June 1918. Brunet, *Saint-Denis*, pp. 184–85; McMillan, pp. 102–3.

46. RDCM, 21 January, 19 September, and 14 November 1915; 23 January and 22 June 1916.

47. RDCM, 23 September 1916.

48. Goguel, *La Politique*, pp. 215–25; Brogan, vol. 2, pp. 556–57; Maurice Labi, *La Grande Division des travailleurs* (Paris, 1964); Jean-Louis Robert, *La Scission syndicale de 1921* (Paris, 1980); Kriegel, *Aux origines*; Robert Wohl, *French Communism in the Making, 1914–1924* (Stanford, 1966); Annie Kriegel, *La Croissance de la Confédération générale du travail 1918–1921* (Paris, 1966); Colette Chambelland and Jean Maitron, eds., *Syndicalisme révolutionnaire et communisme: les archives de Pierre Monatte, 1914–1924* (Paris, 1968); Jean Charles, ed. *Les Congrès de Tours. Texte intégral* (Paris, 1980). On the international dimension, see Cronin and Sirianni; Charles Bertrand, *Revolutionary Situations in Europe, 1917–1922* (Montreal, 1977).

49. *Paris-Est*, 22 November 1919, p. 2; Goguel, *Géographie des élections*, pp. 76–77; Wohl, pp. 148–52.

50. *Journal de Saint-Denis*, 13 November 1919, p. 1. For the first time in many years, Paul Peysson did not run for office.

51. Pronier, p. 21; see also Raymond Leslie Buell, *Contemporary French Politics* (New York, 1920), pp. 152–69.

52. On the SFIO and the 1919 elections, see Kriegel, *Aux origines*, pp. 423–39; Wohl, pp. 148–52.

53. The census figures bear out this shift (LN, 1911, 1921).

54. The independent Socialists changed their slates from election to election and never put out election manifestos; their lack of wartime representation on the city council was a great handicap.

55. Brunet, *Saint-Denis*, p. 236; see chapter 1, which discusses this combined development.

56. On social class, the Left, and politics in modern France, see Thomson, pp. 39–74; Kriegel, *The French Communists*; Judt, *Marxism*; Richard F. Hamilton, *Affluence and the French Worker in the Fourth Republic* (Princeton, 1967); Richard DeAngelis, *Blue-Collar Workers and Politics: A French Paradox* (London, 1982); Maurice Duverger, ed., *Partis politiques et classes sociales* (Paris, 1955).

57. *Paris-Est*, 27 December 1919, p. 1. The Socialists, of course, would have said they made a greater effort to keep constituents informed of city business.

58. RDCM for 1920: 6 August, 25 January, 18 November, 17 September, and 25 January.

59. Pronier, p. 22; Girault, *Sur l'implantation*; Brunet, *Saint-Denis*, pp. 241–45; François Platone, "L'implantation municipale du parti communiste français dans la Seine et sa conception de l'administration communale," mémoire de maîtrise, Fondation nationale des sciences politiques, 1967.

60. *Le Populaire*, 24 October 1922, pp. 1, 2; Brunet, *Saint-Denis*, p. 267; Girault, *Sur l'implantation*.

61. Brunet, *Saint-Denis*, pp. 245–68.

62. RDCM, 23 October 1931.

63. RDCM, 23 March 1923. After Clamamus said he had verified the membership of La Prolétarienne in the PCF's Labor Sports Federation, the city council approved the endorsement over Vasseur's dissenting vote.

64. *Paris-Est,* 6 December 1919, p. 2; RDCM, 17 May 1925.

65. Brunet, *Saint-Denis,* p. 236; Girault, *Sur l'implantation,* pp. 108–17.

66. Denis; Bontemps and Jolinon; Peru.

67. On Bobigny's municipal elections in the 1920s and 1930s, see *L'Humanité* and the *Journal de Saint-Denis* for May 1925, May 1929, and May 1935. In 1928 the prefect of the Seine annulled the results of the regular legislative election in Clamamus's district because of suspected voting irregularities; Clamamus easily won the special election held in October 1928, in spite of vigorous campaigns by both the SFIO and the Right (AN, series F7 13112, police reports of 7 July, 20 September, 15 October 1928; F7 13017, police reports of 4 October, 6 October, 9 October, and 11 October 1928; F7 13260, police reports of 5 October and 13 October 1928).

68. The legend of the Red Belt has obscured the SFIO's presence in the Paris suburbs between the wars, running the city halls of Suresnes, Champigny, Puteaux, and Boulogne-Billancourt, the largest suburb and site of the giant Renault plant (Archer; René Sordes, *Histoire de Suresnes* [Suresnes, 1965]; Denis; Pourteau).

69. Bernard Chambaz, "L'implantation du parti communiste français a Ivry," in *Sur l'implantatation du parti communiste français dans l'entre-deux-guerres,* ed. Jacques Girault (Paris, 1977), pp. 156, 158; Brunet, *Saint-Denis,* pp. 245–60.

70. Bobigny, Archives communales, PCF electoral manifesto for 1929 municipal elections.

71. Fourcaut and Girault, p. 70.

72. Bobigny, Archives communales, PCF 1935 electoral manifesto.

73. "La ruine de la petite commerce" (Bobigny, Archives communales, PCF pamphlet, 1935).

Chapter 5

1. For a detailed analysis of this law, see Léon Morgand, *La Loi municipale* (Paris, 1923).

2. William Munro, *The Government of European Cities* (New York, 1927), pp. 230–34. The prefect of the Seine was not a complete autocrat, however; he worked with the Conseil général de la Seine, whose members were elected by the public. On the council's deliberations, see its *Procès-verbaux,* 1900–1939.

3. "It is well known that those passions which incline either toward a surprise *coup* against the established government . . . or toward a new distribution of wealth by pillage and by ferment in large cities . . . form a powerful base of support on which revolutionaries know they can always rely. The state itself is therefore singularly interested in watching over everything that happens in a city like Paris" (Albert Lavallée, *Le Régime administratif du département de la Seine et de la ville de Paris* [Paris, 1901], pp. 1–2). On the special legislation governing the Department of the Seine, see also Raiga and Félix.

4. On conflicts between municipalities and the national government, see Berlanstein, *Working People*, pp. 159–64; Brunet, *Saint-Denis* and *Un Demi-siècle;* Scott, "Mayors versus Police Chiefs." Brunet asserts that, at least in the Paris area, conflicts between leftist mayors and the prefecture were sharper before World War I than in the 1920s and 1930s.

5. Scott, "Mayors versus Police Chiefs," pp. 233–34; Willard, pp. 181–97; McQuillen. During an electoral campaign in Lille, Guesde informed a crowd of listening workers that, whereas they could take city hall by ballots, they could take the prefecture only by gunfire (quoted by Albert Treint, "Les élections municipales," *Cahiers de bolchévisme*, February 1925, p. 787).

6. "Le parti communiste et le parlementarisme," *Thèses, manifestes et résolutions adoptés par les Ier, IIe, IIIe, et IVe congrès de l'Internationale communiste*, p. 68. On the beginning of the Communist International, see Helmut Gruber, ed., *International Communism in the Era of Lenin* (New York, 1972); Jane Degras, ed., *The Communist International, 1919–1943* (London, 1971); Dominique Desanti, *L'Internationale communiste* (Paris, 1970); Fernando Claudin, *The Communist Movement: From Comintern to Cominform* (New York, 1975).

7. Although brief, this Comintern statement had a major impact upon the PCF's position in the 1920s and 1930s. I came across paraphrasings of it in many articles in the PCF press: for example, in *Cahiers de bolchévisme*, February 1925, pp. 785–90; 15 May 1925, pp. 1187–95. Cf. a series of articles on municipal policy in *L'Humanité*, April 1929.

8. "Quatre ans de réalisations ouvrières à Clichy," *L'Humanité*, 18 April 1929, p. 2 (original author's emphasis). This article was part of a series that *L'Humanité* ran in April 1929 on Communist municipalities in the Paris suburbs, to impress their accomplishments on working-class voters before the municipal elections of May 1929.

9. That this was no idle fear is shown by the career of Jacques Doriot; he used his position as longtime mayor of Saint-Denis to lay the base for a fascist political party after his expulsion from the PCF in 1934 (Brunet, *Saint-Denis*, pp. 363–435). On PCF dissidents in the 1920s and 1930s see Girault, *Sur l'implantation*, pp. 108–17.

10. Pierre Semard and Victor Cat, "Circulaire sur le contrôle de l'action municipale," *Cahiers de bolchévisme*, February 1926, p. 385.

11. The 1925 PCF Congress decreed that in areas with Communist municipalities, local Party organizations should set up municipal commissions to advise city politicians. These commissions were to be directed by the Central Municipal Commission, under Victor Cat; the CMC set up a National Union of Communist Municipalities to coordinate the work of PCF city governments, especially in the Paris area (Victor Cat, "Fonctionnement de l'union nationale des municipalités communistes," AN, series F7 13092, undated police report).

12. Cf. on this point jederman, *La «Bolchévisation» du parti communiste français* (Paris, 1971), pp. 37–64; Philippe Robrieux, *Histoire intérieure du parti communiste*, vol. 1 (Paris, 1980), pp. 225–69. Bolchévisation restructured the PCF's organization, away from that of the old SFIO in particular and of

traditional French political parties in general, and toward that of the Communist party in the Soviet Union.

13. The Central Municipal Commission drew up municipal election campaign programs and submitted them to the national PCF Congress for approval before their use in individual municipalities; the Party wanted uniform municipal campaigns without personality contests between PCF candidates (*Cahiers de bolchévisme*, April 1925, p. 1116).

14. Among those expelled were six Paris city councillors and the majority of the Clichy city council (Pierre Semard, "Le tournant décisif dans notre politique municipale," *Cahiers de bolchévisme*, April 1930, p. 356).

15. In January 1937 the PCF was able to pressure Léon Blum's Popular Front government into investigating corruption in the Saint-Denis city hall; it uncovered significant irregularities, prompting Doriot's resignation and his crushing defeat by the PCF in a special election in June 1937 (Brunet, *Un Demi-siècle*, pp. 190–202).

16. AN, series F7 13131, police report of 17 March 1933; Girault, *Sur l'implantation*, p. 117.

17. Jean Garchery, "Programme municipal préparé pour le congrès de Lyon en 1924," *Cahiers d'histoire de l'Institut Maurice Thorez* 36, no. 2 (1980): 89; Danielle Tartakowsky, "Ecoles et éditions communistes, 1921–1933," doctorat du troisième cycle, Université de Paris–8, 1977. Giving Party militants jobs as city workers also funded PCF activism, since they often did Party tasks on the job.

18. Victor Cat, "Thèse sur l'application du mot d'ordre du 'Bloc ouvrier et paysan' à l'action municipale," *Cahiers de bolchévisme*, December 1924, pp. 256–57 (original author's emphasis); see also *Cahiers de bolchévisme*, March 1926, pp. 660–63; 1 February 1927, pp. 118–20.

19. "Rapport auto-critique sur le 1er aôut," *Cahiers de bolchévisme*, January 1930, pp. 60–67.

20. Jacques Girault makes this point in his chapter on "L'Implantation du parti communiste français dans la région parisienne," in Girault, *Sur l'implantation*, pp. 110–17; see also Jerome Milch, "The PCF and Local Government," in *Communism in Italy and France*, ed. Donald Blackmer and Sidney Tarrow (Princeton, 1975), pp. 343–44.

21. *L'Humanité*, April 1929; Brunet, *Un Demi-siècle*, pp. 115–81; Girault, *Sur l'implantation*, pp. 113–16.

22. *Cahiers de bolchévisme*, April 1930, p. 360; February 1927, pp. 118–20; *Cahiers de bolchévisme*, August 1930, pp. 836–40.

23. *La Voix de l'Est*, 19 June 1936, p. 4; Victor Cat, "Les municipalités communistes et le chômage," *Cahiers de bolchévisme*, February 1927, pp. 118–20; *L'Humanité*, 8 February 1933, p. 2.

24. On this point see Tony Judt, "Une historiographie pas comme les autres: the French Communists and their history," *European Studies Review* 12, no. 4 (1982): 465. For a different viewpoint, cf. the preface by Aristide R. Zolberg to Kriegel, *The French Communists*, pp. xvi–xvii.

25. AN, series F7 13112, police report of 12 May 1928. The *Journal de Saint-Denis* charged that the Bobigny municipality used a city truck to drive

Clamamus's son to school in Paris (6 April 1929, p. 5); printed PCF leaflets in city hall (27 December 1930, p. 3); dismissed non-Communists from unemployment relief (17 March 1934, p. 6).

26. Jean Maitron, ed., *Dictionnaire biographique du mouvement ouvrier français, 1914–1939* (Paris, 1982–1984), vol. 22, pp. 325–29.

27. Roland Gaucher obtained this information from his interview with Clamamus (*Histoire secrète du parti communiste français* [Paris, 1974], p. 6). See also Jules Humbert-Droz, *L'Œil de Moscou sur Paris* (Paris, 1964); Jules Humbert-Droz, *Les Partis communistes des pays latins et l'Internationale communiste dans les années 1923–1927* (Boston, 1981); Jenny Humbert-Droz, *Une pensée, une conscience, un combat: la carrière politique de Jules Humbert-Droz* (Neuchâtel, 1976).

28. The account of this event indicated the interpenetration of Bobigny's municipality with the local PCF section; "the municipality and the secretariat of the section, represented by Pesch, Duval, Menou, Langlois, took the first honor guard"—all four were city councillors (*La Voix de l'Est*, 27 November 1936, p. 1; 14 May 1938, p. 4; 7 October 1938, p. 1; 20 January 1939, p. 4).

29. *Journal de Saint-Denis*, 17 February 1934, p. 3; *L'Humanité* printed the full text of the prefectural order (24 October 1925, p. 2). On the strike see Ronald Tiersky, *French Communism 1920–1972* (New York, 1974), pp. 42–44.

30. *L'Humanité*, 13 November 1925, p. 1 (emphasis in original). Clamamus's claim that municipal employees were acting on their own was inaccurate.

31. Fernand Grenier, *Ce Bonheur-là* (Paris, 1974). Cf. also jederman; A. Bernard, "L'école de Bobigny," *Cahiers de bolchévisme*, October 1925, pp. 1961–67.

32. "L'école de Bobigny," *Cahiers de bolchévisme*, October 1925; Tartakowsky; Grenier.

33. Jacques Duclos, *Mémoires*, vol. 1: 1896–1934 (Paris, 1968), p. 174. See also Grenier, who remembers Duclos as the school's star pupil.

34. Quoted in Gaucher, p. 174.

35. *L'Humanité*, 7 December 1924, p. 1; 10 December 1924, pp. 1, 2.

36. *L'Humanité*, 8 December 1924, p. 1; AN, series F7 13188, police report from 1924.

37. One exception was the city council's endorsement of a resolution by the Communist municipality of Ivry to liberate Henri Dumoulin, a mutineer in the Black Sea fleet revolt; Dumoulin was elected to the Ivry city council in a June 1927 byelection (RDCM, 3 August 1927). On the fleet revolt, see Jacques Raphael-Leygues, *Les Mutins de la mer Noire* (Paris, 1981).

38. RDCM, 1 September 1921; 26 May 1936; 5 June 1937. Most of these grants were for very little money, and therefore had symbolic importance only. For a comparison with prewar Socialist municipalities, see Berlanstein, *Working People*, p. 160.

39. Many grants were made during the Popular Front, which explains why a PCF municipality would honor the author of the French national anthem (on this point see Brower).

40. RDCM, 7 October 1925.

41. RDCM, 11 March 1930.
42. RDCM, 22 June 1931; 18 June 1926.
43. RDCM, 1 August 1925.
44. Perhaps the city council did not have much money for political causes; it rarely voted political motions without some subsidy.
45. *La Banlieue rouge*, 28 January 1922, p. 3; 25 February 1922, p. 3.
46. AN, series F22 224, report of 14 June 1932.
47. *La Voix de l'Est*, 19 June 1936, p. 4; 26 June 1936, p. 4; 15 January 1937, p. 4; 20 January 1939, p. 4; 24 February 1939, p. 4.
48. During my conversations with Christine Mercier, Mathilde Lacroix, and Jean Cortot, they all emphasized the urban reforms as the reason for the Communists' strength in Bobigny (interviews conducted 7 January 1985, Foyer Gaston Monmousseau, Bobigny).
49. For a detailed example of budgetary analysis, see Brunet, *Un Demi-siècle*. The actual work of drawing up the budgets was done by the city tax inspector (*receveur municipal*), an official appointed by the president of the republic and subject to the Ministry of Finance. This system made city budgets one of the aspects of municipal administration least subject to mismanagement, since a municipality could not easily falsify its budget without higher authorities taking notice (Brunet, *Un Demi-siècle*, pp. 127–28).
50. Archives de la Seine, Budgets et Comptes, Bobigny (hereafter cited as BC). The system of budget keeping that prevailed among French municipalities in the interwar period was complex. All budgets were divided into receipts and expenditures; each of these two sections was divided into three parts: ordinary, extraordinary, and supplemental. Moreover, a city government drew up two budgets each year: one, the *budget primitif*, estimated receipts and expenditures for the coming fiscal year and was submitted to the prefect for his approval; the other, the *compte administratif*, stated the amounts the municipality actually collected and spent during the year. In analyzing the four city budgets, I used the comptes administratifs.
51. The centimes additionnels were based on four national taxes: on land, on movable property, on doors and windows, and on commercial licenses (*patentes*). The national government limited the number of centimes additionnels to prevent local governments from exhausting their tax bases (which would endanger the national government's source of funds) (Brunet, *Un Demi-siècle*, p. 137).
52. For the PCF, see *Cahiers de bolchévisme*, April 1925, p. 1049; for the SFIO, see *Le Populaire*, 23 November 1927, p. 1; see also Brunet, *Un Demi-siècle*.
53. See Bobigny, Archives communales, for the PCF section's program for the 1935 municipal elections.
54. For example, few Bobigny taxpayers were affected by the *patente*, one of the four national taxes (see note 51, above).
55. BC; *L'Humanité*, 8 February 1933, p. 2.
56. BC. By contrast, in other suburbs in the 1920s and 1930s public assistance constituted 27 to 30 percent of the budget in Saint-Denis, 21 to 27 percent in Boulogne, and 20 to 25 percent of the budget in Levallois-Perret. In

1930 and 1931 education was 9 percent of expenses in Neuilly, 13 percent in Boulogne, and 16 percent in Saint-Denis (Brunet, *Un Demi-siècle*, pp. 151, 158).

57. BC, 1936. RDCM for 1931: 2 March, 22 June, 29 July, and 28 October; for 1932: 7 June, 1 August, 21 October, and 29 December; 15 December 1933; for 1934: 13 March and 31 July; 13 July 1935; 29 December 1936.

58. *La Voix de l'Est*, 31 January 1936, p. 3.

59. BC, 1931.

60. On the laws concerning allotments in this period, see Geo Minvielle, *Traité pratique des lotissements* (Paris, 1936); J. Cazenavette, *Extension des villes et lotissements* (Paris, 1936); Pierre Bénoist d'Etiveaud, *Le Régime juridique des lotissements* (Paris, 1939); d'Ormesson; Bouffet; Polti.

61. RDCM, 23 October 1921; 18 November 1920; 19 December 1921; 18 February 1924.

62. RDCM, 8 November 1924; 18 February 1924. The report does not mention what percentage of the sewer's cost the developer was asked to pay, or if the developer did pay it.

63. RDCM, 1 August 1925. See also RDCM for 1924: 31 May, 22 August, and 6 December; for 1925: 14 February and especially the session of 19 April, during which the council ruled on six allotments.

64. RDCM, 14 February 1925.

65. RDCM, 3 April and 13 October 1926. This money was taken from the funds for the maintenance of the local road network.

66. The full text of the 1924 law is reprinted in Paul Rouilly, *Les Lotissements: droits et obligations des acquéreurs et des vendeurs* (Paris, 1925), pp. 83–100; see also Bénoist d'Etiveaud; Polti; Minvielle, *Traité pratique*.

67. The municipality won the case, winning significant damages of over 4,000 francs (*L'Aube sociale*, 31 July 1926).

68. RDCM, 18 February 1924. Other municipalities also took on the *lotisseurs*; in Antony Mayor Mounié had posters put up and leaflets distributed at city expense, warning potential buyers of the risks involved in buying land in an allotment (Anne Fontaine, p. 63).

69. In legislative elections, Bobigny also gave him the largest percentage of votes in the district; on the Noisy-le-Sec area see Thomas, pp. 158–61.

70. *L'Humanité*, 19 September 1925, p. 2; 7 February 1926, p. 2; 15 March 1926, p. 2; 10 April 1926, p. 2; 11 February 1928, p. 2; 26 January 1931, p. 2; 24 April 1932, p. 2.

71. *La Banlieue rouge*, 25 February 1922, p. 2.

72. *L'Aube sociale*, 13 March 1926, p. 2; the article illustrates Clamamus's ability to blend the general lines of PCF policy on this issue with the specific needs of his city government.

73. Bouffet, pp. 23–28; the text of the proposed law is reprinted in *L'Aube sociale*, 4 September 1926, p. 2.

74. Legislators had found it difficult to separate individuals who bought a lot for their own use from small developers (Bouffet, pp. 25–28; Paul Barbier, *La Question des lotissements défectueux* [Levallois-Perret, 1931], p. 78).

75. *L'Humanité*, 7 October 1928, p. 3 (emphasis in original). For other examples of the PCF's position, see *L'Humanité*, 27 November 1927, p. 2, and 10 December 1927, p. 2. Although Clamamus's proposed law was relatively harsh on the allotment developers, it did not live up to the PCF's vow to make them pay for everything; this slogan was, not surprisingly, extremely popular among the *mal-lotis* but was unrealistic because of the terms of the allotments' contracts.

76. The PCF's poor performance in the 1928 and 1929 elections in the Paris area and elsewhere had more to do with its new ultrasectarian line than with the Sarraut Law.

77. Annie Fourcaut argues that the Sarraut Law did hurt the PCF among the *mal-lotis* in Bobigny (Annie Fourcaut, "Bobigny, banlieue rouge," *Communisme* 3 [1983]).

78. RDCM for 1928: 22 May, 19 July, and 31 October. Most often the municipality asked the Department of the Seine to come up with the money.

79. For an explanation of the 1912 law's effect on associations syndicales, see Bouffet, pp. 54–67.

80. AS dossier André Jaouen, undated letter from the Union amicale des maires de la Seine.

81. On the *mal-lotis'* reaction to the Sarraut Law, see Bastié, *Croissance*, pp. 310–11; Combe, pp. 89–90.

82. See for example AS dossiers: La Renaissance, letter of 29 January 1924; Les Vignes, letter of 12 February 1926; André Jaouen, documents dated 25 June 1925, 31 October 1926; La Bergère, document of 5 March 1931; RDCM, 23 October 1933.

83. AS dossier La Renaissance, letters of 31 July, 4 August, and 28 November 1927.

84. RDCM, 23 October 1933. See also RDCM, 31 October 1928, 27 November 1929, 2 March 1931, and 18 June 1926; AS dossiers: Les Vignes, letters of 21 November 1927 and 13 July 1929; La Bergère, letters of 20 July 1932 and 9 June 1934; Paris-Bobigny, letters of 17 February 1926, 7 August and 18 August 1927; La Favorite, letters of 19 April 1921, 17 September 1925, and 30 January 1926.

85. AS dossier rues Perron and Perrusset, letter of 25 August 1924.

86. AS dossier La Renaissance, letter of 31 December 1925.

87. On the repair of defective allotments in the Paris suburbs, see Bastié, *Croissance*, pp. 301–31; Anne Fontaine, pp. 63–64; Peru.

88. RDCM, 18 November 1920; these were peripheral areas like the Pont de Bondy and Six Routes.

89. RDCM, 6 December 1924. See also RDCM for 1926: 15 February, 3 April, 10 May, 18 June, 27 July, 2 September, and 13 October; for 1927: 10 October and 14 November; for 1928: 19 March and 22 May.

90. RDCM, 27 November 1929; Bobigny, Archives communales, PCF section's 1929 municipal election platform.

91. RDCM, 29 July 1931.

92. *La Voix de l'Est*, 9 November 1935; Bobigny, Archives communales, PCF section's 1935 municipal election platform; RDCM for 1930: 25 March,

20 May, and 30 December; 29 July 1931; for 1932: 7 June and 29 December; 16 May 1933; 26 February 1935.

93. RDCM, 23 October 1921; 21 October 1922; for 1923: 23 January and 15 February.

94. RDCM for 1924: 31 May, 22 August, and 8 November; Bobigny, Archives communales, PCF section's 1929 municipal election platform.

95. RDCM, 18 November 1920; 1 March 1925. The Suburban Gas Company, which had supplied the gas lighting, submitted a proposal in November 1920 to install electrical power in Bobigny; the proposal sat in committee for years. In 1923 the city council received a more favorable bid from the North-East Parisian Power Company and got the Suburban Gas Company to cede part of its monopoly, paying Suburban Gas a 5 percent royalty for this concession.

96. *Journal de Saint-Denis*, 21 March 1925. The contract was not officially ratified until 1927.

97. RDCM, 15 February 1926; *Le Prolétaire de Bobigny*, 20 July 1929.

98. RDCM, 20 May 1930; 21 May 1938.

99. On utilities in the interwar period, see Fourastié; Michelle Perrot, "Histoire de la condition féminine et histoire de l'électricité," in *Electricité dans l'histoire, problèmes et méthodes*. Actes du colloque de l'Association pour l'histoire de l'électricité en France (Paris, 1985); Françoise Werner, "Du ménage à l'art ménager: l'évolution du travail ménager et son écho dans la presse féminine française de 1919 à 1939," *Le Mouvement social* (October–December 1984). I am grateful to Robert Frost for his suggestions on this issue.

100. *Le Prolétaire de Bobigny*, 30 March 1929; RDCM, 25 January 1920; 17 January 1922.

101. RDCM, 12 August 1922.

102. RDCM for 1922: 3 July and 26 December; for 1923: 23 March, 7 September; 2 September 1926; 21 October 1932.

103. *La Voix de l'Est*, 1 October 1937. The city council explained its decision: the growing population of the area and traffic in local streets made the old, sidewalk marketplace more inconvenient (RDCM, 7 November 1935).

104. Parti communiste français (PCF), *Compte rendu du congrès national du parti communiste français* (Villeurbanne, 1936), pp. 253–54.

105. LN, 1911, 1921, 1931. For example, in February 1919 the council talked of establishing a summer camp for needy children; nothing came of this proposal (RDCM, 23 February 1919).

106. Many children from the Pont de Bondy were sent to Bondy's schools; for this service Bobigny paid a certain amount of money per pupil to Bondy (RDCM for 1919: 6 April and 7 June; for 1920: 28 March, 27 June, 26 August, and 17 September.

107. RDCM, 3 April 1926.

108. *La Voix de l'Est*, 23 September 1935, p. 4.

109. RDCM, 29 July 1931. Before 1931 the only nursery school in Bobigny was located downtown in the girls' school.

110. *La Voix de l'Est*, 19 May 1939. On the building of the Pont de Bondy's nursery school, see RDCM, 6 October 1930; 5 December 1930; 27

April 1931; 28 October 1931; 18 December 1931; 19 June 1934; 8 December 1936; 27 April 1937; 5 June 1937. *Voix de l'Est,* 19 May 1939.

111. RDCM, 23 July 1937; 28 February 1939.

112. RDCM, 23 February 1919; 30 June 1921; *La Voix de l'Est,* 24 July 1936. La Machine's summer camp was so inexpensive because it was not a traditional summer camp; the municipality built no facilities in La Machine but sent children from Bobigny to live with families in the area. Life with "the workers of La Machine" was not just a boarding arrangement; it was intended to be integral to a child's summer experience. The campers did have programs directed by supervisors hired by the municipality of Bobigny. In the summer of 1936 Deputy Mayor Léon Pesch was a head counselor there.

113. RDCM, 10 March 1933. The land for the Ile d'Oléron's camp cost 170,000 francs; this expense was shared by the city's school chest and the municipality.

114. RDCM, 10 April 1930; *La Voix de l'Est,* 24 July 1936; camp fees were higher for children from outside Bobigny. On the general economic situation of workers, see Sauvy, vol. 2, pp. 510–26.

115. *Le Prolétaire de Bobigny,* 4 May 1929 (emphasis in original).

116. *L'Emancipation nationale,* 27 August 1937, p. 4. Given the extreme right-wing and anti-Communist bias of this newspaper under Jacques Doriot, this citation must be accepted with some caution. Yet it reflects the general nature of life at Bobigny's summer camps. Clamamus had been elected Senator in 1936.

117. *La Voix de l'Est,* 14 February 1936; RDCM, 4 July 1929; 27 November 1929; 16 November 1937; 30 May 1920; 30 June 1921; 22 August 1924; 19 April 1925; 18 June 1926; 27 July 1926; 13 January 1927; 11 May 1927; 19 July 1928; 26 December 1928; 2 August 1929; 7 June 1932.

118. RDCM, 18 February 1924. I came across over twenty city council resolutions protesting conditions of public transit or recommending changes in service, for example those of 26 May 1921, 12 April 1922, 18 February 1924, 16 May 1933, and 21 January 1938.

119. RDCM, 21 October 1922; 1 August 1925; 15 February 1926; 25 March 1930. Intersuburban public transit is still underdeveloped in the Paris area.

120. RDCM, 3 August 1927.

121. RDCM, 11 March 1930; 2 March 1931; 28 October 1931; 1 August 1932; 21 October 1932; 15 December 1933; 31 July 1934; 13 July 1935; 29 December 1936.

122. RDCM, 25 March 1929. City councils in the first decade of the twentieth century also protested such pollution.

123. RDCM, 14 November 1921.

124. Brunet, *Saint-Denis,* p. 340; Girault, *Sur l'implantation,* pp. 61–203; Fourcaut, "Bobigny."

125. Jolly, vol. 7, p. 2531; Anne Fontaine, pp. 63–66.

126. Sordes, pp. 529–37; Evenson, 212–13, 220–25. Important works by Henri Sellier on the Paris suburbs include *Les Banlieues urbaines* and *La Crise du logement.*

127. Merriman, *The Red City*, pp. 201–10. See also Scott; McQuillen; Amdur; Trempé.

128. Brunet, *Un Demi-siècle*, pp. 143–75; Girault, *Sur l'implantation*, pp. 110–16. The issue of allotments was crucial; the Communists addressed it more thoroughly and had more consistent success with the *mal-lotis* than the Socialists had.

Chapter 6

1. Raymond Williams, *The Long Revolution* (New York, 1961), p. 41. On French working-class popular culture in the early twentieth century, see Fourastié; Zeldin; Agulhon, *Histoire*, vol. 4; pp. 434–70; the works of Valdour, like *Ateliers et taudis*, are also useful.

2. McMillan, pp. 9–16; Scott and Tilly; Tamara K. Hareven and Robert Wheaton, eds., *Family and Sexuality in French History* (Philadelphia, 1980); Zeldin, pp. 179–223.

3. The historical data on rates of marriage in France are unclear, but the percentage of couples living out of wedlock appears to have increased in the nineteenth century, whereas that of married couples increased in the early twentieth century (Scott and Tilly, pp. 91–92, 96–98).

4. LN, 1921; see also Gillis.

5. LN, 1921. For a discussion of cohabitation among nineteenth-century Parisian workers, see Michel Frey, "Du mariage et concubinage dans les classes populaires à Paris (1846–1847)," *Annales—Economies, Sociétés, Civilisations* 33, no. 4 (July–August 1978): 803–29.

6. This and other such posters are reproduced in Guerrand.

7. Interview with Jean Lallet, on 19 February 1982, Hôtel de ville, Bobigny.

8. Ferret, pp. 49–50; in the end the fictional couple decides to buy the lot.

9. Berlanstein, *Working People*, pp. 139–40; Brunet, "Constitution." On American suburbia and family life, see Fishman, pp. 150–53; Jackson, pp. 47–52.

10. LN, 1921; McMillan, pp. 157–58; Scott and Tilly.

11. "Where are the factories in Ivry where the 8-hour day is observed? Through general and unpunished violation, the $9\frac{1}{4}$-hour day, normal through the adoption of the English system, is increased to 10 hours and more" (Bremond, p. 54).

12. On workplace conditions in interwar France, see Bremond; Sauvy; Tom Kemp, *The French Economy, 1913–1939* (London, 1972); Charles Maier, *Recasting Bourgeois Europe* (Princeton, 1975); Valdour, *Ateliers et taudis, Le Désordre ouvrier, Popinqu'à Menilmuch', Ouvriers parisiens*; Fridenson, *Histoire*; Schweitzer.

13. Tilly and Scott, p. 176; Werner.

14. Bastié, *Croissance*, p. 267; Ferret.

15. Jean Cortot, one of the people I interviewed on this subject, insisted that Bobigny was a working-class community where people did not have much leisure time (interview of 7 January 1985, Foyer Gaston Monmousseau, Bobigny).

16. Berlanstein, *Working People*, pp. 127–33. Some Balbynians did frequent a movie theater in Noisy-le-Sec (Cortot interview on 7 January 1985).

17. *La Voix de l'Est*, 6 January 1939, p. 4; 17 January 1939, p. 3; RDCM, 1 September 1921.

18. RDCM, 25 January 1920. See also RDCM, 13 June 1914; *La Voix de l'Est*, 28 August 1937, p. 1.

19. Cf. Berlanstein, *Working People*, on commercial leisure facilities in Saint-Denis. Much larger than Bobigny, Saint-Denis had developed more such facilities; it was exceptional among Paris suburbs in this regard.

20. Richard Holt, *Sport and Society in Modern France* (Hamden, Conn., 1981), pp. 202–6; Didot Bottin, vol. 2, Bobigny, 1930s. The local press contained little reporting on team sports nor did the people I interviewed mention them in their comments on leisure life in Bobigny.

21. *La Voix de l'Est*, 9 April 1938, p. 4; interview with Jean Cortot. By the late 1930s Bobigny had a fishing goods store to serve local fishermen.

22. Interview with Florence Aumont on 7 January 1985, Bobigny.

23. Marrus, pp. 129–32. By contrast, Paris had one café for every eighty-seven residents in 1909.

24. Dupé and Thivollier. See also Lhande, *Le Christ dans la banlieue* and *Le Dieu qui bouge*; Pierre Pierrard, *L'Eglise et les ouvriers en France* (Paris, 1984).

25. Etat civil, Bobigny: Actes de naissances et de mariages; Paroisse de Bobigny, actes de baptêmes et de mariages.

26. Dupé and Thivollier; Agulhon, *Histoire*, pp. 448–58; Pierrard.

27. Berlanstein, *Working People*, pp. 127–34; Agulhon, *Histoire*, pp. 457–70; Joffre Dumazedier, *Vers une civilisation du loisir* (Paris, 1962).

28. Gareth Stedman Jones, *Languages of Class* (Cambridge, 1983), pp. 179–238. Isolation seems to have been a key aspect of working-class life in both Britain and France. Zeldin notes, in a poll taken among French workers in the 1960s, that many respondents felt that an inability to meet and interact comfortably with different kinds of people was one of their greatest disappointments (Zeldin, pp. 272–74).

29. On the political culture of the Red Belt, see Pronier; Dupuy; Roncayolo, pp. 616–27.

30. RDCM, 19 June 1934.

31. AN, series F7 13112, police report of 20 September 1928; 13119, police report of 28 December 1930; *Le Prolétaire de Bobigny*, 27 April 1929, p. 2; 4 May 1929, p. 1. This theme played the greatest role during the ultraleft "class against class" period from 1927 to 1934.

32. AN, series F7 13112, police report of 14 October 1927; undated police report; 13119, police report of 12 November 1929. Solidarity with Republican Spain was a very popular cause in Bobigny during the late 1930s; Communist meetings often finished with donations to help this cause (*La Voix de l'Est*, 7 August 1936, p. 4; 14 August 1936, p. 4; 28 August 1936, p. 4; 22 May 1937, p. 4; 5 February 1938, p. 4; 4 June 1938, p. 4; 10 February 1939, p. 4.

33. *La Voix de l'Est*, 26 June 1936, p. 4.

34. For example, "The direct administration of Bobigny's markets, the work of our Communist municipality, thus shows the world what the workers

can do when called to run a city government" (*Le Prolétaire de Bobigny*, 30 March 1929, p. 3).

35. AN, series F7 13017, police report of 11 November 1929.

36. A police report describing a Communist demonstration in Bobigny noted that "a militant of the Association républicaine des anciens combattants (Bobigny section) took the floor to protest against the abuse made of the victims of war by . . . nationalist ceremonies; he also attacked the capitalist regime, which contains in itself the seeds of war" (AN series F7 13017, police report of 4 September 1927).

37. *La Voix de l'Est*, 19 May 1939, p. 4; 14 February 1926, p. 4.

38. *La Voix de l'Est*, 19 February 1937; 8 May 1937; 7 May 1938; *L'Humanité*, 25 June 1934; AN, F7 13119, police report of 12 November 1929; AN, F7 13522, police report of 4 February 1927.

39. Brogan, vol. 2, p. 641; see also Lhande, *Le Christ dans la banlieue*; Pierrard, pp. 505–7. With a very different political orientation, the church reached out to the workers of the Paris suburbs in the successful "worker-priest" movement of the 1940s (Oscar Arnal, "A Missionary 'Main tendue' toward the French Communists: The 'Témoignages' of the Worker-Priests, 1943–1954," *French Historical Studies* 13, no. 4 [Fall 1984]: 529–56).

40. Dupé and Thivollier, p. 66.

41. Pierrard, pp. 534–35; *La Voix de l'Est*, 14 February 1936, p. 3.

42. Note the similarity to the socialist civil baptisms described by Scott in "Mayors versus Police Chiefs," pp. 241–43.

43. *L'Humanité*, 13 October 1925; 17–18 October 1925. The PCF held a massive funeral to honor Sabatier and made the struggle to free Sacco and Vanzetti a major Communist cause during the 1920s (Brunet, *Saint-Denis*, pp. 274–75).

44. Not all people in Bobigny were happy with these name changes. Louis Cagnani protested sharply against renaming his street rue Leningrad and submitted a petition to this effect signed by twenty-three of the street's residents to the city council (RDCM, 20 May 1930).

45. The debate over the importance of community sentiment in modern life has been especially sharp among sociologists. See, among others, Ferdinand Tönnies, *Community and Society* (New York, 1957); Shorter, *Modern Family*, pp. 227–44; Michael Young and Peter Willmott, *Family and Kinship in East London* (New York, 1958); Herbert Gans, *The Urban Villagers* (Glencoe, N.Y., 1962), and Gans, *The Levittowners*; William F. Whyte, *Streetcorner Society* (Chicago, 1955).

46. Italian immigrants were the only exception to the general absence of ethnic groups in Bobigny, but the city's Italian population was too small to dominate any one neighborhood.

47. William Dobriner, *Class in Suburbia* (Englewood Cliffs, N.J., 1963); Ruth Crichton, *Commuter's Village* (Dawlish, 1964)

48. On this point see Suzanne Keller, *The Urban Neighborhood* (New York, 1968); Young and Willmott; Gans; and Elizabeth Bott, *Family and Social Network* (London, 1957).

49. Brunet, "Constitution."

50. Using marriage records to measure community sentiment has drawbacks: the profound relationships they register may tell little about the casual sociability often found among neighbors; marriage records may also have less relevance in rapidly growing communities like Bobigny. Nonetheless, these data do indicate the relative weight of neighborhood relationships (I am grateful to Elinor Accampo for her observations on this matter).

51. Etat civil, Bobigny: Actes de mariages 1921.

52. Etat civil, Bobigny: Actes de mariages 1923, 1927, 1933, 1937.

53. On the importance of workplace friendships, see Valdour's and Brémond's works listed in the bibliography; see also Claude Fischer, *To Dwell Among Friends* (Chicago, 1982).

54. Etat civil, Bobigny: Actes de mariages 1921, 1911.

55. Gans; see also Tamara K. Hareven, ed., *Family and Kin in Urban Society* (New York, 1977); Hareven and Wheaton; Shorter, *Modern Family*.

56. *Le Prolétaire de Bobigny*, 15 June 1929, p. 2. Florence Aumont, whom I interviewed on the subject, also insisted on the prevalence and importance of mutual aid in interwar Bobigny (interview on 7 January 1985, Bobigny).

57. *Le Prolétaire de Bobigny*, 15 June 1929, p. 2; this article continues: "Several comrades from Nouveau Village, bothered by this anarchic way of practicing solidarity, thought of organizing it . . . while remaining true to the practice of solidarity with, of course, a minimum of indispensable regulation and complete honesty. A society [of mutual aid] was created a few years ago, with dues of one franc per week."

58. R. N. Morris and John Hogey, *The Sociology of Housing* (London, 1965), pp. 41–44.

59. RDCM, 1919–1939. See for example RDCM, 26 May 1936; 7 November 1935; 10 November 1936; 28 March 1920; 25 January 1920; 20 May 1930; 6 October 1930.

60. *La Voix de l'Est*, 7 May 1936, p. 4. Léon Pesch, the *premier adjoint* (deputy mayor) of Bobigny during most of the 1920s and 1930s, dominated the LIC of Nouveau Village and figured in community organizations in the Pont de Bondy. He was elected mayor of Bobigny in 1944.

61. The LICs and the associations were often very close. Many associations were founded by local LICs; in some smaller neighborhoods there was little difference between them (AS dossier Les Vignes, letter of 15 June 1927; AS dossier Le Chemin de Fer, letter of 25 October 1928; AS dossier La Renaissance, letter of 1 February 1924).

62. AS dossier Les Vignes, letter from Dumontier to Clamamus, 15 June 1927.

63. On American urban political machines, see Alexander Callow, ed., *The City Boss in America: An Interpretative Reader* (New York, 1976); John Haeger and Michael Weber, eds., *The Bosses* (St. Louis, 1974); Bruce Stave, ed., *Urban Bosses, Machines, and Progressive Reformers* (Malabar, Fla., 1984); Seymour Mandelbaum, *Boss Tweed's New York* (New York, 1965).

64. A striking characteristic of Communism in Bobigny was the contrast between the PCF's large vote totals and its few militants. Even during the Popular Front, when the PCF section was at its largest point between the wars,

the ratio was usually one militant to ten PCF voters (Fourcaut, "Bobigny, banlieue rouge").

65. Etat civil, Bobigny: Actes de mariages 1923, 1927, 1933, 1937. On urban neighborhoods and class consciousness, see James Cronin, "Rethinking the Legacy of Labor, 1890–1925," in *Work, Community, and Power*, ed. James Cronin and Carmen Sirianni (Philadelphia, 1983), pp. 35–36; Hanagan; Daniel Walkowitz, *Worker City, Company Town* (Urbana, Ill., 1978), pp. 156–70; Alan Dawley, *Class and Community* (Cambridge, Mass., 1976).

66. RDCM, 31 May 1924; 20 May 1930; 16 May 1933; *La Voix de l'Est*, 15 January 1938, p. 4; 19 March 1938, p. 4; 28 May 1938, p. 4; 10 February 1939, p. 4; 16 June 1939, p. 4.

67. *La Voix de l'Est*, 29 June 1935, p. 3; AN, series F7 13119, police reports of 13 July and 14 July 1930.

68. AN, series F7 13103, police report of 25 February 1926. The twenty-first *rayon* was a subunit of the Paris area PCF, which included Bobigny and nine other northeastern suburbs, from 1924 to 1928 (Fourcaut, "Bobigny, banlieue rouge," pp. 15–16).

69. AN, series F7 13103, police reports of 2 August 1925 and 11 July 1926; RDCM, 11 May 1927.

70. *Journal de Saint-Denis*, 2 April 1932, p. 9. One of the main organizers of the Blue Blouses was Hermann Berlinski, a German Communist refugee (and a Jew) who lived in Bobigny during the 1930s. He belonged to the French Workers' Theater Federation and gave piano lessons locally (Maitron, vol. 18, p. 425).

71. RDCM, 20 May 1930; *La Voix de l'Est*, 26 March 1938, p. 4; 13 January 1939, p. 4.

72. These cafés often advertised in the local PCF press, which frequently used them as distribution centers. Among the more important were the café Séné, 74, rue de la République; the maison Hory, 3, rue de la Courneuve; and—above all—the maison Pesch, at 78, rue Sacco-Vanzetti.

73. The people I interviewed in Bobigny all remembered various festivals and celebrations, but no one noted their political content (interviews on 7 January 1985, Foyer Gaston Monmousseau, Bobigny).

74. Joffre Dumazedier notes that whereas intellectuals tend to take leisure time as an opportunity for self-education, workers are not so willing to give their free time to such pursuits; these attitudes mirror the ones we have indicated among Bobigny's Communist activists and the local working class as a whole.

75. The activities of local unions in Bobigny were covered fully by the local Communist press, especially *Le Prolétaire de Bobigny* and *La Voix de l'Est*.

Conclusion

1. *Le Populaire*, 13 May 1935, p. 3. I connsider a political party to have control of a municipality when the mayor and a majority of the city council members belong to that party.

2. Statistics for municipal elections in this period are often fragmentary and difficult to come by; for the most part I have relied on the national press, especially *Le Temps, Le Populaire,* and *L'Humanité.*

3. *Le Populaire,* 13 May 1935, p. 3.

4. On the PCF during the Popular Front see Brower, *The New Jacobins;* Georges LeFranc, *Histoire du front populaire* (Paris, 1965).

5. On life at work in the Paris area during the early twentieth century, see Fridenson, *Histoire;* Schweitzer; Alain Touraine, *L'Evolution du travail ouvrier aux usines Renault* (Paris, 1955); Noiriel, *Les Ouvriers dans la société française;* Collinet, *Essai sur la condition ouvrière;* Jean Depretto and Sylvie Schweitzer, *Le Communisme à l'usine* (Lille, 1984); Michael Seidman, "The Birth of the Weekend and the Revolts against Work: The Workers of the Paris Region during the Popular Front," *French Historical Studies* (Fall 1982).

6. Berlanstein, *Working People;* Fridenson, *Histoire;* Touraine; Amdur, pp. 15–30.

7. Such fears were most notably voiced by Alphonse Merrheim, the leader of the French Metal Workers' Federation (Papayanis).

8. On French labor during World War I, see Amdur; Fridenson, *1914–1918;* Becker, *Les Français;* Arthur Fontaine.

9. Touraine, pp. 100–124.

10. On rationalization and French labor see Touraine; Maier; Fridenson, *Histoire;* Schweitzer; Arthur Fontaine; Collinet; Cronin and Sirianni, eds., *Work, Community, and Power.*

11. Touraine, pp. 84–86. Unfortunately, these statistics do not distinguish unskilled from semiskilled workers. Touraine and others do note that in this period semiskilled workers usually replaced unskilled, not skilled, workers.

12. For criticism of the traditional view of rationalization, see Amdur; Yves Lequin, "La rationalisation du capitalisme français: A-t-elle eu lieu dans les années vingt?" *Cahiers d'histoire de l'Institut Maurice Thorez* 16 (1976).

13. Ariès, *Histoire des populations françaises,* pp. 315–32; Noiriel, pp. 145–46.

14. Noiriel; Schweitzer; Touraine; Weil.

15. Schweitzer, pp. 79–82; Noiriel, p. 149.

16. Schweitzer, pp. 117–24; Bremond; Valdour.

17. See on this point Moss; Hanagan; Scott, *Glassworkers;* Aminzade; Maurice Agulhon, *Une Ville ouvrière au temps du socialisme utopique* (Paris, 1970); Shorter and Tilly.

18. Schweitzer, pp. 155–70; on the labor movement in interwar France see Georges LeFranc, *Le Mouvement syndical sous la Troisième République* (Paris, 1967); Chambelland and Maitron; Val Lorwin, *The French Labor Movement* (Cambridge, Mass., 1966).

19. Bremond, pp. 81–82; Vielledent; Valdour, *Ateliers et taudis.*

20. Schweitzer, pp. 118–21; Valdour.

21. The counterpart to the rise of the Left in the suburbs was the rise of the Right in Paris. Twentieth-century Paris has always given a majority of its votes to the moderate and conservative side of the political spectrum (Campbell and Goguel).

22. On class consciousness and working-class politics in twentieth-century France, see Judt, *Marxism and the French Left*; Hamilton; DeAngelis.

23. In my interview with Florence Aumont she emphasized that one of the main things women in Bobigny would talk about was their hopes for the future (interview on 7 January 1985, Bobigny).

24. On urban social movements and their political implications see especially the works of Manuel Castells: *The Urban Question* (Cambridge, 1979), pp. 324–78, 459–62; also, his *City, Class, and Power* (London, 1978), and *The City and the Grassroots* (Berkeley, 1983).

Appendix

1. Maitron, vol. 22, pp. 325–29; Jolly, vol. 3, p. 1056.

2. Maitron, pp. 325–26; RDCM, 12 March 1916; 10 May 1916; 22 June 1916; 9 June 1918. During the war Clamamus also helped set up soup kitchens and food cooperatives. On working-class life in Paris during World War I see also Brunet, *Saint-Denis*, pp. 169–209; Becker, *Les Français*.

3. Maitron; Jolly; see also Brunet, pp. 233–61; Wohl, pp. 208–354; Kriegel, *Aux origines*, pp. 757–863; Girault, *Sur l'implantation*, pp. 87–117.

4. Maitron; Jolly; on Clamamus's work for the allotments, see Barbier. Clamamus submitted his proposal to deal with defective allotments to the Chamber of Deputies on 8 July 1926. His stand on reproductive rights sharply diverged from that of the majority of French legislators who, responding to a strong pronatalist campaign in the 1920s and 1930s, enacted stiff penalties for abortion and for dissemination of birth control information (McMillan, pp. 189–90).

5. Maitron; Jolly. Clamamus worked closely with Auguste Mounié, the activist Radical senator from the allotments-plagued suburb of Antony.

6. Maitron; Jolly; on the banning of the PCF in 1939 see Robrieux, *Histoire intérieure du parti communiste*, vol. 1, pp. 494–505; Stéphane Courtois, *Le PCF dans la guerre* (Paris, 1980), pp. 41–80.

7. Maitron.

8. Maitron; Jolly; see also Robert Paxton, *Vichy France* (New York, 1972), pp. 196–97; John Sweets, *Choices in Vichy France* (Oxford, 1986); Ivan Avakoumovitch, "Le PCF vu par le commandement des troupes d'occupation allemande," *Le Mouvement Social* 113 (October–December 1980): 91–101.

9. On Jacques Doriot see Brunet, *Saint-Denis*, pp. 363–435; Gilbert Allardyce, "The Political Transition of Jacques Doriot," *Journal of Contemporary History* 1, no. 1 (1966): 56–74; Bertram Gordon, *Collaborationism in France during the Second World War* (Ithaca, 1980). In addition to Doriot and Clamamus, other suburban Communist mayors who became collaborators were Fernand Soupé of Montreuil, Albert Richard of Pierrefitte, and Marcel Marshal of Saint-Denis (David Pryce-Jones, *Paris in the Third Reich* [New York, 1981], pp. 64–66).

Bibliography

Primary Sources

ARCHIVES COMMUNALES, BOBIGNY

Listes electorales,
    1920, 1924, 1927, 1932, 1935.
Etat civil: Actes de naissances, de décès, et de mariages,
    1900, 1911, 1921, 1931.
Etat civil, City Council,
    1912, 1919, 1925, 1929, 1935.
Registres des débats du conseil municipal,
    1900–1939.
Associations syndicales de lotissements, dossiers: André Jaouen; La Bergère; Le
    Chemin de Fer; La Conscience; La Courneuve; La Grande Denise; Le
    Nouveau Village; Le Parc; Paris-Bobigny; La Renaissance; rues Herzog,
    Perron, and Perrusset; Les Vignes.

PAROISSE DE BOBIGNY

Actes de baptêmes et de mariages,
    1900, 1911, 1921, 1931.

ARCHIVES DE LA SEINE, PARIS

Listes nominatives du recensement, Bobigny,
    1896, 1911, 1921, 1931.
Maîtrise de cadastre, Bobigny, D4P4, carton 13,
    1908–1919.

Budgets et comptes, Bobigny,
1921, 1926, 1931, 1936.

ARCHIVES NATIONALES, PARIS

Annuaire de commerce—Didot Bottin, 1900–1939.

Police reports, series F7, nos. 12502, 12557, 12558, 12559, 12560, 12561, 12723, 12734, 12747, 12822, 12891, 13015, 13016, 13017, 13028, 13074, 13090, 13091, 13097, 13098, 13103, 13105, 13112, 13262, 13263, 13264, 13275, 13328, 13522, 13541, 13576; series F22, nos. 131, 174, 179, 181, 182, 185, 186, 187, 196, 204, 210, 224, 227, 232, 237.

PERIODICALS

L'Aube sociale,
1925–1927.
Banlieue rouge/Banlieue ouvrière,
January–June 1922.
Cahiers de bolchévisme,
1925–1928, 1930–1938.
Emancipation nationale,
1936–1937.
L'Humanité,
1906–1939.
L'Information sociale,
1918–1935.
Journal de Saint-Denis,
1900–1926, 1928–1937.
Paris-Est,
1901–1914, 1919–1923, 1935–1936.
Le Populaire,
1919, 1921–1939.
Le Prolétaire de Bobigny,
1929.
Le Temps,
1920–1939.
La Voix de l'Est,
1935–1939.

PERSONAL INTERVIEWS

To protect the privacy of my sources, I have changed their names in this book.

Lallet, Jean. Interview with author. Hôtel de ville, Bobigny, 19 February 1982.
Aumont, Florence. Interview with author. Foyer Gaston Monmousseau, Bobigny, 7 January 1985.
Mercier, Christine, Mathilde Lacroix, Jean Cortot. Interview with author. Foyer Gaston Monmousseau, Bobigny, 7 January 1985.

Selected Secondary Sources

Ackerman, Evelyn. *Village on the Seine.* Ithaca, 1978.

Agulhon, Maurice. "L'opinion politique dans une commune de banlieue sous la Troisième République. Bobigny de 1850 à 1914." In *Etudes sur la banlieue de Paris,* ed. Pierre George, pp. 29–56. Paris, 1950.

———. *Une Ville ouvrière au temps du socialisme utopique.* Paris, 1970.

———, ed. *Histoire de la France urbaine.* Vol. 4. Paris, 1983.

Allardyce, Gilbert. "The Political Transition of Jacques Doriot." *Journal of Contemporary History* 1 (1966): 56–74.

Amdur, Kathryn. *Syndicalist Legacy.* Urbana, 1986.

Aminzade, Ron. *Class, Politics, and Early Industrial Capitalism.* Albany, 1981.

Anderson, Michael. *Family Structure in Nineteenth-Century Lancashire.* Cambridge, 1971.

———. "Household Structure and the Industrial Revolution." In *Household and Family in Past Time,* ed. Peter Laslett. Cambridge, 1972.

Archer, Georges. *De Terentiacum à Drancy.* Montpellier, 1964.

Ariès, Philippe. *Histoire des populations françaises.* Paris, 1948.

Armengaud, André. *La Population française au XXe siècle.* Paris, 1973.

Arnal, Oscar. "A Missionary 'Main tendue' toward the French Communists: The 'Témoignages' of the Worker-Priests, 1943–1954." *French Historical Studies* 13, no. 4 (Fall 1984): 529–56.

Auffray, Danièle, ed. *La grève et la ville.* Paris, 1979.

Avakoumovitch, Ivan. "Le PCF vu par le commandement des troupes d'occupation allemandes." *Le Mouvement social* 113 (October –December 1980): 91–101.

Bailhache, Jean. *Monographie d'une famille d'ouvriers parisiens.* Paris, 1905.

Baker, Donald. "The Socialists and the Workers of Paris." *International Review of Social History* 24, no. 1 (1979): 1–33.

Barbier, Paul. *La Question des lotissements défectueux.* Levallois-Perret, 1931.

Barde, Pierre. *Les Communes et la question de l'habitation.* Paris, 1932.

Bastié, Jean. *L'Atlas de la région parisienne.* Paris, 1967.

———. *La Croissance de la banlieue parisienne.* Paris, 1964.

———. *Géographie du grand Paris.* Paris, 1984.

Bayard, Jean-Pierre. *Le Compagnonnage en France.* Paris, 1978.

Beau de Lomenie, Emanuel. *Les Responsabilités des dynasties bourgeoises.* 3 vols. Paris, 1943–1954.

Becker, Jean-Jacques. *Les Français dans la grande guerre.* Paris, 1980.

———. *1914: comment les Français sont entrés dans la guerre.* Paris, 1977.

Becker, Jean-Jacques, and Annie Kriegel. *La Guerre et le mouvement ouvrier français.* Paris, 1964.

Bell, Donald Howard. *Sesto San Giovanni.* New Brunswick, 1986.

Benard, Charles. *Le Logement de la famille.* Paris, 1928.

Bénoist, d'Etiveaud, Pierre. *Le Régime juridique des lotissements.* Paris, 1939.

Bergeron, Louis. *L'Industrialisation de la France au XIXe siècle.* Paris, 1979.

Berlanstein, Lenard. *The Working People of Paris.* Baltimore, 1984.

Bertillon, Jacques. *Essai de statistique comparée du surpeuplement des habitations à Paris et dans les capitales européennes.* Paris, 1894.

———. *De la fréquence des principales causes de décès à Paris.* Paris, 1906.
———. *De la fréquence des principales maladies à Paris pendant la période 1865–1891.* Paris, 1894.
Bertrand, Charles. *Revolutionary Situations in Europe, 1917–1922.* Montreal, 1977.
Bettelheim, Charles. *Bilan de l'économie française, 1919–1946.* Paris, 1947.
Blackmer, Donald, and Sidney Tarrow, eds. *Communism in Italy and France.* Princeton, 1975.
Blanc, Edouard. *Le Ceinture rouge.* Paris, 1927.
Bodiguel, Jean-Luc. *La Réduction du temps de travail.* Paris, 1969.
Bonnefond, M. "Les colonies de bicoques de la région parisienne." *La Vie urbaine* 25, 26 (1925): 525–62.
Bontemps, Jean-Marie, and Jacques Jolinon. "La municipalité de Montreuil-sous-Bois, 1900–1939." Mémoire de maîtrise, Université de Paris–1, 1971.
Borge, Jacques, and Nicolas Viasnoff. *Archives de Paris.* Paris, 1981.
Bott, Elizabeth. *Family and Social Network.* London, 1957.
Bouffet, René. *Un Problème d'urbanisme: l'aménagement des lotissements défectueux.* Paris, 1930.
Bremond, Arnold. *Une Explication du monde ouvrier.* Alençon, 1927.
Bouvier-Ajam, Maurice, and Gilbert Mury. *Les Classes sociales en France.* Vol. 2. Paris, 1963.
Brogan, Denis. *The Development of Modern France, 1870–1939.* 2 vols. Gloucester, Mass., 1970.
Browaeys, Xavier, and Paul Chatelain. *Les France du travail.* Paris, 1984.
Brower, Daniel. *The New Jacobins.* Ithaca, 1968.
Brunet, Jean-Paul. "Constitution d'un espace urbain: Paris et sa banlieue de la fin du XIXe siècle à 1940." *Annales—Economies, Sociétés, Civilisations* 40, no. 3 (May–June 1985): 641–59.
———. *Un Demi-siècle d'action municipale à Saint-Denis la rouge.* Paris, 1982.
———. "L'industrialisation de la région de Saint-Denis." *Acta Geographica* 4 (October 1970): 233–60.
———. *Saint-Denis, la ville rouge.* Paris, 1980.
Buell, Raymond Leslie. *Contemporary French Politics.* New York, 1920.
Bunle, Henri. "L'agglomération parisienne et ses migrations alternantes en 1936." *Bulletin de la Statistique générale de la France* 28, no. 1 (October–December 1938): 95–156.
Butler, Rémy, and Patrice Noisette. *Le logement social en France, 1815–1981: de la cité ouvrière au grand ensemble.* Paris, 1982.
Callow, Alexander, ed. *The City Boss in America: An Interpretative Reader.* Oxford, 1976.
Campbell, Peter. *French Electoral Systems and Elections, 1789–1957.* New York, 1958.
Caplat, Guy. *Le Problème des lotissements.* Dijon, 1951.
Castells, Manuel. *City, Class, and Power.* London, 1978.
———. *The City and the Grassroots.* Berkeley, 1983.
———. *The Urban Question.* Cambridge, 1979.

Cazenavette, J. *Extension des villes et lotissements*. Paris, 1936.

Chambaz, Bernard. "L'implantation du parti communiste français à Ivry." In *Sur l'implantation du parti communiste français dans l'entre-deux-guerres*, ed. Jacques Girault. Paris, 1977.

Chambelland, Colette, and Jean Maitron, eds. *Syndicalisme révolutionnaire et communisme: les archives de Pierre Monatte, 1914–1924*. Paris, 1968.

Charles, Jean, ed. *Le Congrès de Tours. Texte intégral*. Paris, 1980.

Cheronnet, Louis. *Paris extra muros*. Paris, 1929.

Chevalier, Louis. "La formation de la population parisienne au 19e siècle." *Cahiers de l'Institut national des études démographiques* 10 (1950).

———. *Laboring Classes and Dangerous Classes*. Princeton, 1973.

Chombart de Lauwe, Pierre. *Paris et l'agglomération parisienne*. Paris, 1952.

Clapham, J. H. *The Economic Development of France and Germany*. Cambridge, 1951.

Clark, T. J. *The Painting of Modern Life: Paris in the Art of Manet and His Followers*. New York, 1985.

Claudin, Fernando. *The Communist Movement: From Comintern to Cominform*. New York, 1975.

Clozier, René. "Essai sur la banlieue." *La Pensée* 2, no. 4 (July–September 1945): 49–57.

———. *La Gare du Nord*. Paris, 1940.

Collin, Charles. *Silhouettes de lotissements*. Paris, 1931.

Collinet, Michel. *Essai sur la condition ouvrière*. Paris, 1951.

Combe, Pierre. *Les Lotissements*. Lyon, 1933.

Conseil général de la Seine, *Etat des communes de la Seine à la fin du 19e siècle: Bobigny*. Paris, 1899.

———. *Procès-verbaux*. Paris, 1900–1939.

Cornau, Claude, ed. *L'Attraction de Paris sur sa banlieue*. Paris, 1965.

Courtois, Stéphane. *Le PCF dans la guerre*. Paris, 1980.

Crew, David. *Town in the Ruhr*. New York, 1979.

Crichton, Ruth. *Commuter's Village*. Dawlish, 1964.

Cronin, James. "Rethinking the Legacy of Labor, 1890–1925." In *Work, Community, and Power*, ed. James Cronin and Carmen Sirianni, pp. 20–48. Philadelphia, 1983.

Cronin, James, and Carmen Sirianni, eds. *Work, Community, and Power*. Philadelphia, 1983.

Cross, Gary. *Immigrant Workers in Industrial France*. Philadelphia, 1983.

———. "The Quest for Leisure: Reassessing the Eight-Hour Day in France." *Journal of Social History* 18, no. 2 (Winter 1984): 195–216.

———. "Les Trois Huits: Labor Movements, International Reform, and the Origins of the Eight-Hour Day, 1914–1924." *French Historical Studies* 14, no. 2 (Fall 1985): 240–68.

Crubellier, Maurice. *L'Enfance et la jeunesse dans la société française, 1800–1950*. Paris, 1979.

Daumas, Maurcie, and Jacques Payen, eds. *Evolution de la géographie industrielle de Paris et sa proche banlieue au XIXe siècle*. Paris, 1976.

Dawley, Alan. *Class and Community.* Cambridge, Mass., 1976.

DeAngelis, Richard. *Blue-Collar Workers and Politics: A French Paradox.* London, 1982.

Decaux, Alain. *Histoire des Françaises.* Vol. 2. Paris, 1972.

Degras, Jane, ed. *The Communist International, 1919–1943.* London, 1971.

Dehau, Henri, and René Ledroux-Lebard. *La Lutte antituberculeuse en France.* Paris, 1906.

de Jouvenel, Robert. *La République des camarades.* Paris, 1934.

Delon, Pierre. *Les Employés. Un siècle de lutte.* Paris, 1969.

Demangeon, Albert. *Paris, la ville et sa banlieue.* Paris, 1936.

Denis, Jean-Emile. *Puteaux. Chroniques du temps des puits.* Puteaux, 1969.

Depretto, Jean, and Sylvie Schweitzer. *Le Communisme à l'usine.* Lille, 1984.

de Rousiers, Paul. *Les Grandes Industries modernes.* Vol. 2: *La Métallurgie.* Paris, 1972.

Desanti, Dominique. *L'Internationale communiste.* Paris, 1970.

Destray-Caroux, Jacques. *Un Couple ouvrier traditionnel.* Paris, 1974.

de Vincennes, Jean. *Le Bon Dieu dans le bled.* Paris, 1929.

d'Hugues, Philippe, and Michel Peslier. "Les professions en France." *Insititut national des études démographiques* 51 (1969): 75–103.

Dobriner, William. *Class in Suburbia.* Englewood Cliffs, 1963.

Donaldson, Scott. *The Suburban Myth.* New York, 1969.

d'Ormesson, Wladimir. *Le Problème des lotissements.* Paris, 1928.

Douglass, Harlan Paul. *The Suburban Trend.* New York, 1925.

Duclos, Jacques. *Mémoires.* Vol. 1: 1896–1934. Paris, 1968.

Dumazedier, Joffre. *Vers une civilisation du loisir.* Paris, 1962.

DuMesnil, Octave, and Charles Mangenot. *Enquête sur les logements, professions, salaries, et budgets.* Paris, 1899.

Dupé, Pierre, and Pierre Thivollier. *Ferment chrétien dans une terre sans Dieu.* Paris, 1948.

Dupuy, Fernand. *Etre maire communiste.* Paris, 1975.

Duverger, Maurice, ed. *Partis politiques et classes sociales.* Paris, 1955.

Dyer, Colin. *Population and Society in Twentieth-Century France.* Paris, 1978.

Dyos, H. J. *The Study of Urban History.* London, 1961.

———. *Victorian Suburb.* Leicester, 1961.

Elwitt, Sanford. *The Making of the Third Republic.* Baton Rouge, 1975.

———. "Social Reform and Social Order in Late Nineteenth-Century France: The Musée Social and its Friends." *French Historical Studies* 11, no. 3 (Spring 1980): 431–51.

———. *The Third Republic Defended.* Baton Rouge, 1986.

Evenson, Norma. *Paris: A Century of Change, 1878–1978.* New Haven, 1979.

Ferré, Louise Marie. *Les Classes sociales dans la France contemporaine.* Paris, 1936.

Ferret, Jules. *Bobigny—ses maraîchers, ses nouveaux-venus, les Parisiens.* Paris, 1910.

Fischer, Claude. *To Dwell Among Friends.* Chicago, 1982.

———, ed. *Networks and Places.* New York, 1977.

Fishman, Robert. *Bourgeois Utopias.* New York, 1987.

Fontaine, Anne, and Françoise Gauthier, *Antony. Du petit village à la grande cité de banlieue.* Antony, 1980.

Fontaine, Arthur. *French Industry during the War.* New Haven, 1926.

Fourastié, Jean, and Françoise Fourastié. "Le genre de vie." In *Histoire économique de la France entre les deux guerres,* ed. Albert Sauvy, vol. 3, pp. 435–53. Paris, 1972.

Fourcaut, Annie. "La banlieue rouge." Doctorat du troisième cycle, Université de Paris–1, 1983.

——. "Bobigny, banlieue rouge." *Communisme* 3 (1983): 5–28.

Fourcaut, Annie, and Jacques Girault. "Les conseillers municipaux d'une commune ouvrière et communiste." *Cahiers d'histoire de l'Institut Maurice Thorez* 10, no. 19 (1976): 61–73.

François, Etienne, ed. *Immigration et société urbaine en Europe occidentale, XVIe–XXe siècles.* Paris, 1985.

Frey, Michel. "Du mariage et concubinage dans les classes populaires à Paris (1846–1847)." *Annales—Economies, Sociétés, Civilisations* 33, no. 4 (July–August 1978): 803–29.

Fridenson, Patrick. *Histoire des usines Renault.* Paris, 1972.

——, ed. *1914–1918: l'autre front.* Paris, 1977.

Friedmann, Georges. *Villes et campagnes.* Paris, 1953.

Gaillard, Jeanne. *Paris, la ville, 1852–1870.* Paris, 1976.

Gans, Herbert. *The Levittowners.* New York, 1967.

——. *The Urban Villagers.* Glencoe, N.Y., 1962.

Garchery, Jean. "Programme municipal préparé pour le congrès de Lyon." *Cahiers d'histoire de l'Institut Maurice Thorez* 36, no. 2 (1980).

Gaucher, Roland. *Histoire secrète du parti communiste français.* Paris, 1974.

Gennari, Genviève. *Le Dossier de la femme.* Paris, 1965.

Genovese, Eugene, and Elizabeth Fox. "The Political Crisis of Social History." *Journal of Social History* 10, no. 2 (Winter 1976): 205–20.

George, Pierre, ed. *Etudes sur la banlieue de Paris.* Paris, 1950.

George, Pierre, and Pierre Randet. *La Région parisienne.* Paris, 1959.

Gille, Bertrand. *Histoire de la métallurgie.* Paris, 1966.

Gillis, John R. *Youth and History.* New York, 1974.

Girard, Louis. *La Nouvelle Histoire de Paris: Paris, la Deuxième République et le Second Empire.* Paris, 1981.

Girault, Jacques, ed. *Sur l'implantation du parti communiste français dans l'entre-deux-guerres.* Paris, 1977.

Goguel, François. *Géographie des élections françaises sous la Troisième et la Quatrième République.* Paris, 1968.

——. *La Politique des partis sous la Troisième République.* Paris, 1958.

Goldberg, Harvey. *The Life of Jean Jaurès.* Madison, 1962.

Gordon, Bertram. *Collaboration in France during the Second World War.* Ithaca, 1980.

Granotier, Bernard. *La Planète des bidonvilles: perspectives de l'explosion urbaine dans le tiers monde.* Paris, 1980.

Gras, N. S. B. "The Development of a Metropolitan Economy in Europe and America." *American Historical Review* 27, no. 4 (1922): 695–708.

Grenier, Fernand. *Ce Bonheur-là.* Paris, 1974.

Gruber, Helmut, ed. *International Communism in the Era of Lenin.* New York, 1972.

Guerrand, Roger. *Le Logement populaire en France.* Paris, 1979.

———. *Les Origines du logement social en France.* Paris, 1967.

Haeger, John, and Michael Weber, eds. *The Bosses.* St. Louis, 1979.

Haines, Michael. *Fertility and Occupation: Population Patterns in Industrialization.* New York, 1979.

Halbwachs, Maurice. *Les Expropriations et le prix des terrains à Paris.* Paris, 1901.

Halévy, Daniel. *La Fin des notables.* Paris, 1930.

Hallays, André. *Autour de Paris.* Paris, 1910.

Hamilton, Richard F. *Affluence and the French Worker in the Fourth Republic.* Princeton, 1967.

Hammarstrand, Nils. "The Housing Problem in Paris." *Journal of the American Institute of Architects* (February 1920).

Hanagan, Michael. *The Logic of Solidarity.* Urbana, 1980.

Hareven, Tamara K., ed. *Family and Kin in Urban Society.* New York, 1977.

Hareven, Tamara K., and Robert Wheaton, eds. *Family and Sexuality in French History.* Philadelphia, 1980.

Harris, C. D. "Suburbs." *American Journal of Sociology* 49 (July 1943): 1-13.

Harvey, David. *Consciousness and the Urban Experience.* Baltimore, 1985.

Hatry, Gilbert. *Renault, usine de guerre.* Paris, 1978.

Hazemann, R. "Les lotissements dans la banlieue de Paris et leur répercussion sur la santé publique (à Vitry et à Ivry)." *Revue d'hygiène et médecine préventive* (1928).

Hirsch, Anita. "Le logement." In *Histoire économique de la France entre les deux guerres,* ed. Albert Sauvy, vol. 3, pp. 76–110. Paris, 1972.

Hobsbawn, Eric. *Industry and Empire.* New York, 1968.

Holt, Richard. *Sport and Society in Modern France.* Hamdcn, Conn., 1981.

Howorth, Jolyon. *Edouard Vaillant.* Paris, 1982.

Huber, Michel. *La Population de la France.* Paris, 1937.

Humbert-Droz, Jenny. *Une Pensée, une conscience, un combat: la carrière politique de Jules Humbert-Droz.* Neuchâtel, 1976.

Humbert-Droz, Jules. *L'Œil de Moscou sur Paris.* Paris, 1964.

———. *Les Partis communistes des pays latins et l'Internationale communiste dans les années 1923–1927.* Boston, 1981.

Hutton, Patrick. *The Cult of the Revolutionary Tradition: The Blanquists in French Politics, 1864–1893.* Berkeley, 1981.

Ichok, Grégoire. *La Mortalité à Paris et dans le département de la Seine.* Paris, 1937.

Jackson, Kenneth. *Crabgrass Frontier.* New York, 1985.

Jacquemet, Gérard. *Belleville au XIXe siècle.* Paris, 1984.

———. "Belleville aux XIXe et XXe siècles." *Annales—Economies, Sociétés, Civilisations* 30, no. 4 (July–August 1975): 819–43.

Jacques, Léon. *Les Partis politiques sous la Troisième République.* Paris, 1913.

jederman. *La «Bolchévisation» du parti communiste français.* Paris, 1971.

Johnson, Douglas. *France and the Dreyfus Affair*. London, 1966.

Jolly, Jean. *Dictionnaire des parlementaires français*. Vols. 3, 6, 7, 8. Paris, 1960–1977.

Jones, Gareth Stedman. *Languages of Class*. Cambridge, 1983.

———. *Outcast London*. London, 1971.

Judt, Tony. "The Clown in Regal Purple." *History Workshop* 7 (1979): 66–94.

———. "Une historiographie pas comme les autres: the French Communists and their history." *European Studies Review* 12, no. 4 (1982): 445–78.

———. *Marxism and the French Left*. Oxford, 1986.

Kaplan, Temma, "Female Consciousness and Collective Action: The Case of Barcelona, 1910–1918." *Signs* 7, no. 3 (Spring 1984): 545–66.

Katz, Michael. *The People of Hamilton, Canada West*. Cambridge, Mass., 1975.

Keller, Suzanne. *The Urban Neighborhood*. New York, 1968.

Kemp, Tom. *The French Economy, 1913–1939*. London, 1972.

Kerr, Clark, and Abraham Siegel. "The Interindustry Propensity to Strike." In *Industrial Conflict*, ed. Arnold Kornhauser, pp. 189–212. New York, 1954.

Kriegel, Annie. *La Croissance de la Confédération générale du travail, 1918–1921*. Paris, 1966.

———. *The French Communists: Portrait of a People*. Chicago, 1972.

———. *Aux origines du communisme français*. 2 vols. Paris, 1969.

Labi, Maurice. *La Grande Division des travailleurs*. Paris, 1964.

Lagarrigue, L. *Cent ans de transports en commun dans la région parisienne*. Paris, 1956.

Lagneau, Gustave. *Rapport sur les maladies épidémiques observées en 1890 dans le département de la Seine*. Paris, 1891.

Lambeau, Lucien. *Ville de Paris. Monographies. Les logements à bon marché. Recueil annoté des discussions, délibérations et rapports du conseil municipal de Paris*. Paris, 1897.

Landes, David. *The Unbound Prometheus*. Cambridge, 1972.

Landouzy, Louis. "La mortalité parisienne par tuberculose il y a vingt ans." In *Congrès international de la tuberculose*. Vol. 2, pp. 696–706. Paris, 1906.

Lavallée, Albert. *Le Régime administratif du département de la Seine et de la ville de Paris*. Paris, 1901.

Lavedan, Pierre. *Géographie des villes*. Paris, 1938.

———. *Histoire de l'urbanisme à Paris*. Paris, 1975.

Lees, Lynn Hollen. *Exiles of Erin. Irish Migrants in Victorian London*. Manchester, 1979.

Lefebvre, Henri. *Le Droit à la ville*. Paris, 1972.

———. *De l'état*. Paris, 1977.

———. *La Révolution urbaine*. Paris, 1970.

LeFranc, Georges. *Les Gauches en France, 1789–1972*. Paris, 1973.

———. *Histoire du front populaire*. Paris, 1965.

———. *Le Mouvement socialiste sous la Troisième République*. Paris, 1963.

———. *Le Mouvement syndical sous la Troisième République*. Paris, 1967.

Lequin, Yves. "Ouvriers dans la ville (XIXe et XXe siècles)." *Le Mouvement social* 118 (January–March 1982): 3–7.

———. *Les Ouvriers de la région lyonnaise, 1848–1914.* Lyon, 1977.

———. "La rationalisation du capitalisme français: A-t-elle eu lieu dans les années vingt?" *Cahiers d'histoire de l'Institut Maurice Thorez* 16 (1976).

Leroux, Charles. "Enquête sur la descendance de 442 familles ouvrières tuberculeuses." *Revue de médecine* 32 (1912).

Leroy-Beaulieu, Paul. *La Question ouvrière au XIXe siècle.* Paris, 1899.

Lesselier, Claudie. "Employées de grands magasins à Paris avant 1914." *Le Mouvement social* 105 (1978): 109–26.

Leyret, Henri. *En plein faubourg.* Paris, 1895.

Lipset, Seymour Martin, and Reinhard Bendix. *Social Mobility in Industrial Society.* Berkeley, 1967.

Lhande, Pierre. *Le Christ dans la banlieue.* Paris, 1927.

———. *Le Dieu qui bouge.* Paris, 1930.

Lorwin, Val. *The French Labor Movement.* Cambridge, Mass., 1966.

———. "Working-Class Politics and Economic Development in Western Europe." *American Historical Review* 63, no. 2 (January 1958): 338–51.

Lynd, Robert, and Helen Lynd. *Middletown.* New York, 1929.

McBride, Theresa. "A Woman's World: Department Stores and the Evolution of Women's Employment, 1870–1920." *French Historical Studies* 10, no. 4 (1978): 664–83.

———. *The Domestic Revolution. The Modernization of Household Service in England and France, 1820–1920.* London, 1976.

McKay, John. *Tramways and Trolleys. The Rise of Urban Mass Transit in Europe.* Princeton, 1976.

McMillan, James F. *Housewife or Harlot: The Place of Women in French Society, 1870–1940.* New York, 1981.

McQuillen, M. J. "The Development of Municipal Socialism in France, 1880–1914." Ph.D. diss., University of Virginia, 1973.

Magri, Susanna. *Politique du logement et besoins en main-d'œuvre.* Paris, 1972.

Maier, Charles. *Recasting Bourgeois Europe.* Princeton, 1975.

Maitron, Jean, ed. *Dictionnaire biographique du mouvement ouvrier français, 1914–1939.* Vols. 18, 22. Paris, 1982–84.

Mandelbaum, Seymour. *Boss Tweed's New York.* New York, 1965.

Mangin, J. F. "Les tranformations de structure d'une commune en banlieue: Bobigny, 1871–1970." Mémoire de maîtrise, Université de Paris–1, 1971–1972.

Marrus, Michael. "Social Drinking in the Belle Epoque." *Journal of Social History* 7, no. 2 (Winter 1974): 115–42.

Masson, Abbé. *Bobigny-lez-Paris.* Paris, 1887.

Mastrangelo, Domenico. "Bologna, 1889–1914." Ph.D. diss., University of Wisconsin, Madison, 1977.

Mayer, Arno. "The Lower Middle Class as a Historical Problem." *Journal of Modern History* 47, no. 3 (1975): 409–36.

Merlin, Pierre. *Les Transports parisiens. Etude de géographie économique et sociale.* Paris, 1967.

Merriman, John. *French Cities in the Nineteenth Century.* New York, 1981.

——. *The Red City.* Oxford, 1985.
Metton, Alain. *Le Commerce et la ville en banlieue parisienne.* Paris, 1980.
Meyer, Alain, and Christine Moissinac. *Représenatations sociales et littéraires: centre et périphérie, Paris 1908–1939.* Paris, 1979.
Michaud, René. *J'avais vingt ans.* Paris, 1967.
Milch, Jerome. "The PCF and Local Government." In *Communism in Italy and France*, ed. Donald Blackmer and Sidney Tarrow. Princeton, 1975.
Mimin, Pierre. *Le Socialisme municipal.* Paris, 1911.
Minar, David, and Scott Greer. *The Concept of Community.* Chicago, 1969.
Minvielle, Geo, *L'imbroglio du problème des lotissements.* Paris, 1934.
——. *La réglementation légale des lotissements-jardins.* Paris, 1936.
——. *Traité pratique des lotissements.* Paris, 1936.
Moch, Leslie Page. *Paths to the City.* Beverly Hills, 1983.
Mollat, Michel, ed. *Histoire de l'Ile-de-France et de Paris.* Toulouse, 1971.
Monjauvis, Lucien. *Jean-Pierre Timbaud.* Paris, 1971.
Morgand, Léon. *La Loi municipale.* Paris, 1923.
Morris, R. N., and John Hogey. *The Sociology of Housing.* London, 1965.
Moss, Bernard. *The Origins of the French Labor Movement: The Socialism of Skilled Workers.* Berkeley, 1976.
Munro, William. *The Government of European Cities.* New York, 1927.
Nettl, Peter, "The German Social Democratic Party 1890–1914 as a Political Model." *Past and Present* 30 (April 1965): 65–95.
Noiriel, Gérard. *Les Ouvriers dans la société française.* Paris, 1986.
Nord, Philip. *Paris Shopkeepers and the Politics of Resentment.* Princeton, 1986.
Nordmann, Jean-Thomas. *Histoire des radicaux, 1820–1973.* Paris, 1974.
Papayanis, Nicholas. "Alphonse Merrheim and Revolutionary Syndicalism." Ph.D. diss., University of Wisconsin, Madison, 1969.
Parti communiste. "Le parti communiste et le parlementarisme." In *Thèses, manifestes et résolutions adoptés par les Ier, IIe, IIIe et IVe congrès de l'Internationale communiste.* Paris, 1919–1926.
Parti communiste français (PCF). *Compte rendu du congrès national du parti communiste français.* Villeurbanne, 1936.
Paxton, Robert. *Vichy France.* New York, 1972.
Perlman, Janice. *The Myth of Marginality.* Berkeley, 1976.
Perrot, Michelle. "Histoire de la condition féminine et histoire de l'électricité." *Electricité dans l'histoire, problèmes et méthodes.* Actes du colloque de l'Association pour l'histoire de l'électricité en France. Paris, 1985.
——. *Les Ouvriers en grève.* Paris, 1974.
Peru, Jean-Jacques. "Du village à la cité ouvrière, Drancy, 1896–1936." Mémoire de maîtrise, Université de Paris–1, 1977–1978.
Phlipponneau, Michel. *La Vie rurale de la banlieue parisienne.* Paris, 1956.
Pierrard, Pierre. *L'Eglise et les ouvriers en France.* Paris, 1984.
Pinkney, David. *Napoleon III and the Rebuilding of Paris.* Princeton, 1958.
——. "Migrations to Paris during the Second Empire." *Journal of Modern History* 25, no. 1 (1953): 1–12.
Pisani-Ferry, F. *Monsieur l'instituteur.* Paris, 1981.

Plancke, René-Charles. *La Vie rurale en Seine-et-Marne de 1853 à 1953.* Paris, 1984.

Platone, François. "L'implantation municipale du parti communiste français dans la Seine et sa conception de l'administration communale." Mémoire de maîtrise, Fondation nationale des sciences politiques, 1967.

Poisson, Georges. *Evocation du grand Paris.* Vol. 3. *La Banlieue nord-est.* Paris, 1961.

Polti, Maurice. *Etude théorique et pratique sur les lotissements.* Paris, 1926.

Pourteau, Roger. *Pantin. Deux mille ans d'histoire.* Paris, 1982.

Price, Roger. *The Modernization of Rural France.* New York, 1984.

————. *A Social History of Nineteenth-Century France.* London, 1987.

Pronier, Raymond. *Les Municipalités communistes, bilan de trente années de gestion.* Paris, 1983.

Prost, Antoine. *Les Anciens Combattants et la société française 1914–1939.* 3 vols. Paris, 1977.

————. *Histoire de l'enseignement en France, 1800–1967.* 2d ed. Paris, 1977.

Pryce-Jones, David. *Paris in the Third Reich.* New York, 1981.

Rabut, Odile. "Les étrangers en France." *Population,* special issue ed. Roland Pressat (June 1974).

Raiga, Eugène, and Maurice Félix. *Le Régime administratif et financier du département de la Seine et de la ville de Paris.* 2 vols. Paris, 1935.

Raison-Jourde, Françoise. *La Colonie auvergnate de Paris au XIXe siècle.* Paris, 1976.

Raphael-Leygues, Jacques. *Les Mutins de la mer Noire.* Paris, 1981.

Rearick, Charles. *Pleasures of the Belle Epoque: Entertainment and Festivity in Turn-of-the-Century France.* New Haven, 1985.

Rébérioux, Madeleine. *La République radicale? 1989–1914.* Paris, 1975.

Réclus, Maurice. *L'Avènement de la Troisième République, 1871–1875.* Paris, 1900.

Righter, Rosemary, and Peter Wilsher. *The Exploding Cities.* London, 1975.

Robert, Jean. *Les Tramways parisiens.* Paris, 1959.

Robert, Jean-Louis. *La Scission syndicale de 1921.* Paris, 1980.

Roberts, Bryan. *Cities of Peasants.* London, 1978.

Roberts, Robert. *The Classic Slum.* Manchester, 1971.

Robrieux, Philippe. *Histoire intérieure du parti communiste.* Paris, 1980–1983.

Rodier, Catherine, and Fathi Bentabet. "L'immigration algérienne et l'hôpital franco-musulman, dans la région parisienne entre les deux guerres (1915–1947)." Mémoire de maîtrise, Université de Paris–1, 1980–1981.

Roncayolo, Maurice, ed. *Histoire de la France urbaine.* Vol. 5. Paris, 1985.

Ronsin, Francis. *La Grève des ventres.* Paris, 1980.

Rosmer, Alfred. *Le Mouvement ouvrier pendant la guerre.* 2 vols. Paris, 1936–1956.

Roth, Guenther. *The Social Democrats in Imperial Germany.* London, 1963.

Rouilly, Paul. *Les Lotissements: droits et obligations des acquéreurs et des vendeurs.* Paris, 1925.

Sauvy, Albert, ed. *Histoire économique de la France entre les deux guerres.* 3 vols. Paris, 1972.

Schweitzer, Sylvie. *Des engrenages à la chaîne.* Lyon, 1982.

Scott, Joan. *The Glassworkers of Carmaux.* Cambridge, Mass., 1974.

———. "Mayors versus Police Chiefs: Socialist Municipalities Confront the French State." In *French Cities in the Nineteenth Century,* ed. John Merriman. New York, 1981.

Scott, Joan, and Louise Tilly. *Women, Work, and Family.* New York, 1978.

Seidman, Michael. "The Birth of the Weekend and the Revolts against Work: The Workers of the Paris Region during the Popular Front." *French Historical Studies* 12, no. 2 (Fall 1982): 249–76.

Sellier, Henri. *Les Banlieues urbaines.* Paris, 1920.

———. *La Crise du logement et l'intervention publique.* Paris, 1921.

Sewell, William H., Jr. "Social Mobility in a Nineteenth-Century European City." In *Industrialization and Urbanization,* ed. Theodore Rabb and Robert Rotberg. Princeton, 1981.

Shorter, Edward. *The Making of the Modern Family.* New York, 1975.

Shapiro, Anne-Louise. *Housing the Poor of Paris.* Madison, 1984.

Shorter, Edward, and Charles Tilly. *Strikes in France.* Cambridge, Mass., 1974.

Silver, Catherine Bodard, ed. *Frédéric Le Play: On Family, Work, and Social Change.* Chicago, 1982.

Smith, Bonnie. *Confessions of a Concierge.* New Haven, 1985.

Sordes, René. *Histoire de Suresnes.* Suresnes, 1965.

Sorlin, Pierre. *La Société française.* 2 vols. Paris, 1969.

Spengler, Joseph. *France Faces Depopulation.* Durham, N.C., 1938.

———, ed. *Urban Bosses, Machines, and Progressive Reformers.* Malabar, Fla., 1984.

Stearns, Peter. *Lives of Labor: Work in a Maturing Industrial Society.* New York, 1975.

———. "Modernization and Social History." *Journal of Social History* 14, no. 2 (Winter 1980): 189–210.

Stovall, Tyler. "Sous les toits de Paris: The Working Class and the Paris Housing Crisis, 1914–1924." *Proceedings of the Annual Meeting of the Western Society for French History* 14 (1987): 265–72.

———. "The Urbanization of Bobigny." Ph.D. diss., University of Wisconsin, Madison, 1984.

Sullerot, Evelyne. "Conditions de la femme." In *Histoire économique de la France entre les deux guerres,* ed. Albert Sauvy, vol. 3, pp. 418–34. Paris, 1972.

Sutcliffe, Anthony. *The Autumn of Central Paris.* Montreal, 1971.

Sweets, John. *Choices in Vichy France.* Oxford, 1986.

Tartakowsky, Danielle. "Ecoles et éditions communistes, 1921–1933." Doctorat du troisième cycle, Université de Paris–8, 1977.

Taylor, Graham. *Satellite Cities.* New York, 1915.

Thernstrom, Stephen. *The Other Bostonians.* Cambridge, Mass., 1973.

Thernstrom, Stephen, and Richard Sennett, eds. *Nineteenth-Century Cities.* New Haven, 1969.

Thiers, Adolphe. *Notes et souvenirs, 1870–1873.* Paris, 1903.

Thomas, Louis. *Le Grand Paris.* Paris, 1941.

Tiersky, Ronald. *French Communism, 1920–1972.* New York, 1974.

Tilly, Charles, and Richard Louise. *The Rebellious Century*. Cambridge, 1975.

Tönnies, Ferdinand. *Community and Society*. New York, 1957.

Touraine, Alain. *L'Evolution du travail ouvrier aux usines Renault*. Paris, 1955.

Trempé, Rolande. *Les Mineurs de Carmaux*. 2 vols. Paris, 1971.

Tressell, Robert. *The Ragged-Trousered Philanthropists*. London, 1971.

Turner, F. M. L. *The Rise of Suburbia*. Leicester, 1982.

Valdour, Jacques. *Ateliers et taudis de la banlieue de Paris*. Paris, 1923.

———. *Le Désordre ouvrier*. Paris, 1937.

———. *Ouvriers parisiens d'après-guerre*. Paris, 1921.

———. *De la Popinqu'à Menilmuch'*. Paris, 1924.

Veber, Adrien. *Le Socialisme municipale*. Paris, 1908.

Videcoq, Charles. *Les Aspects permanents de la crise du logement dans la région parisienne*. Paris, 1932.

Vielledent, Henri. *Souvenirs d'un travailleur manuel syndicaliste*. Paris, 1978.

Waksman, Selman. *The Conquest of Tuberculosis*. Berkeley, 1964.

Walkowitz, Daniel. *Worker City, Company Town*. Urbana, 1978.

Warner, Sam Bass. *Streetcar Suburbs*. Cambridge, 1978.

Weber, Adna. *The Growth of Cities in the Nineteenth Century*. New York, 1899.

Weil, Simone. *La Condition ouvrière*. Paris, 1951.

Weissbach, Lee Shai. "Artisanal Response to Artistic Decline: The Cabinet-makers of Paris in the Era of Industrialization." *Journal of Social History* 16, no. 2 (1982): 67–82.

Werner, Françoise. "Du ménage à l'art ménager: l'évolution du travail ménager et son écho dans la presse féminine française de 1919 à 1939." *Le Mouvement social* 129 (October–December 1984): 61–87.

Whyte, William F. *Streetcorner Society*. Chicago, 1955.

Willard, Claude. *Le Mouvement socialiste en France. Les Guesdistes*. Paris, 1965.

Williams, Raymond. *The Long Revolution*. New York, 1961.

Wohl, Robert. *French Communism in the Making, 1914–1924*. Stanford, 1966.

Wrigley, E. A. *Industrial Growth and Population Change*. Cambridge, 1961.

Wylie, Lawrence. *Village in the Vaucluse*. Cambridge, 1974.

Young, Michael, and Peter Willmott. *Family and Kinship in East London*. New York, 1958.

Zdatny, Steven. "The Artisanat in France: An Economic Portrait, 1900–1956." *French Historical Studies* 13, no. 3 (Spring 1984): 415–40.

Zeldin, Theodore. *France, 1848–1945: Ambition and Love*. Oxford, 1979.

Zevaes, Alexandre. *Le Socialisme en France depuis 1871*. Paris, 1908.

Index

242 *Index*

Compositor:	A-R Editions, Inc.
Text:	10/13 Sabon
Display:	Sabon
Printer:	Braun-Brumfield, Inc.
Binder:	Braun Brumfield, Inc.